SEARCHING THROUGH

THE OLD RECORDS OF NEW FRANCE

FOR ALL OF THOSE

PRECIOUS

GENEALOGICAL DETAILS

A Translation

of

Father Cyprien Tanguay's

'A TRAVERS LES REGISTRES'

(Notes Recueillies

par

L'Abbé Cyprien Tanguay)

Attaché to the Bureau of Statistics of Canada
Doctor of Letters from Laval University
Member of the Royal Society of Canada
Member of the Historical Societies of Montréal and Missouri

Edited and Translated by
Armand H. Demers, Jr.

Colligite fragmenta...ne pereant.
[Gather together the fragments for fear that they will disappear.]

Quintin Publications - 28 Felsmere Avenue
Pawtucket, Rhode Island
02861-2903
401-723-6797
fax 401-726-0327
www.quintinpublications.com

Revised Edition - April 1999
Copyright © 1999 Armand H. Demers, Jr.

To order this book please ask for item number 098002.
ISBN: 1-58211-044-1

A complete catalog listing hundreds of titles on Canadian genealogy and history
is available free upon request or can be downloaded on our website.

A WORD FROM THE AUTHOR OF THIS TRANSLATION

From Father Tanguay's own words: *"Colligite fragmenta...ne pereant"* came an idea and then a challenge as he, the educator, had undoubtedly intended that it be. His challenge was simply to rescue as much as could possibly be rescued of the knowledge pertaining to our ancestors before that information disappeared forever - the paper on which the information was stored destroyed by the ravages of time.

That challenge still holds true for many of us but for slightly different reasons. Over the years, most of us have almost automatically come to overlook any little words of wisdom or knowledge which authors have sent our way but in Latin, or even - God forbid - in Greek, simply because so few of us are still familiar with these so-called *dead* languages. Today, since so many of us have lost the ability to read French, we might also be unable to benefit from some of Father Tanguay's words because so many of us would be unable to add any of his precious little tidbits of information to our own genealogies if they applied because we couldn't read them even if they did !

Quintin Publications has therefore embarked on a journey of having French genealogical and timely historical materials translated, principally for the benefit of those of us who cannot – for whatever reasons – translate those works. What better place to start than with a work by the man who certainly deserves to be called the Father of our Canadian Genealogy especially since his *"Dictionnaire Généalogique des Familles Canadiennes Depuis la Fondation de la Colonie Jusqu'a Nos Jours"* was first viewed as Canada's *Golden Book of Genealogy,* its own *Livre d'Or.* His *"A Travers les Registres"* is an excellent starting point since it is one of his lesser-known works yet is loaded with thousands of those precious little bits of genealogical and timely historical information.

A few notes regarding my approach to this work:

a)   *Everything within brackets is an editorial comment.* They are used very liberally throughout for several reasons: (1) to define or show their translated forms; (2) to assist in better understanding the times – its practices or mores; (3) to account for periods of time during which Reverend Tanguay might not have made any notations, keeping in mind that his work should also be viewed as an historical outline of the times; (4) to add or update information or to complete a thought; and also (5) to further reinforce points with related quotations from other historical or genealogical works.

b) Quotation marks were retained or used whenever I felt that they would help to retain the flavor of the times or to further establish the authenticity of various passages.

c) In determining whether I should use either the English or the French spelling for the names of places, I simply considered the context and used whatever seemed appropriate.

d) When there were no clear English equivalents for various French words, I used the French. For easily translatable French words such as *paroisse* for parish, *missionnaire* for missionary, *commandeur* for commander, *ambassadeur* for ambassador, *gouverneur* for governor and *Registre* for Register, I simply chose the form which best fit the situation since both forms are clearly recognizable. Words which are the same in both languages were obviously not a problem but some of French origin – *seigneur* or *sieur and others* – remained that way.

e) Italics have been used as sparingly as possible to avoid a cluttered look on the printed page.

f) Titles and localities were retained in their original French as much as possible.

i) Accents were also retained as much as possible.

g) Questions raised in some of the more controversial areas were meant to inform and to generate further questions since Reverend Tanguay's challenge has also become my very own.

h) References are shown as he showed them. Missing references were missing in his book.

i) Graphics have also been added for general interest.

We might not all be able to gather *specific* information about our respective families in this book but we can certainly all learn something of the times and practices in New France from 1500-1800.

Dedication

This work is dedicated to my parents, Armand and Doris Demers, without whose love of and thoroughly ingrained devotion to their

and my cultural background I might never have become interested in this type of project.

My thanks for their assistance to Dr. Marcel Trudel, Canadian author and historian; to Arthur Delorey, Robert Pelland and so many other members of the American-French Genealogical Society in Woonsocket, Rhode Island; to Father Maurice Hazebrouck; to the folks out in Salt Lake City; to my publisher, Robert Quintin; and to any others whom I might have inadvertently overlooked.

As always, my special thanks to my wife, Rita, whose love and understanding of my need for my own space continues to amaze me.

WHAT'S THIS BOOK ALL ABOUT ?

It is *the* translation of Reverend Cyprien Tanguay's *"A TRAVERS LES REGISTRES"* and principally a collection of genealogical and historical details compiled by this same Fr. Tanguay who so patiently worked through almost all of the existing Canadian *Registres* to come up with his superlative effort, his nation's own *Livre d'Or*, his *"Dictionnaire Généalogique des Familles Canadiennes Depuis la Fondation de la Colonie Jusqu'a nos Jours"*, to gather together all of the genealogical material that he could before that same material was lost forever to wars, fires, lack of care, and the ravages of time. Many of the details surrounding some of the individuals are furnished here and, collectively, only here. The book is about the times and the people who lived in New France in the 17th and 18th centuries. It tells of plots against leaders ... of Amantacha, the *'son of the king of Canada'* ... of specific dates, names and places of thousands of births, marriages, illnesses and deaths ... of the brutal attacks both against and by the Amerindians ... of quaint old church practices ... of the parents of 27 children ... of a man who chose to live by himself for almost 40 years on a secluded island in search of his salvation ... of an oftentimes bloodthirsty populace cheering their public executioners on ... of Jesuit attempts to protect their Amerindian brothers from the same greed which our society seems to thrive on today ... of the mighty Dubocq who single-handedly sent 8 warriors to their happy hunting grounds and then *'finished off'* his deed in that *special* way ... of Canada's first known artist ... of the power of an unpaid dowry ... of the mysterious shipboard demise of a returning ex-wife ... of the man who surely must have been wearing red when he wandered off into the forest forever ... of the tragic deaths of many unknowns ... of the blessings of the church bells ... of the possible reason for the strange odors in your great-great grandparents' church ... of the fevers and spreading illnesses ... of a society's doctors who couldn't even set broken bones ... of the need to rebury so many of the dead ... of the brutal cold which "froze one's words and then thawed them out in the following Spring" ... of society's way of dealing with its criminals ... of a nation held together by its parish priests ... of tokens used as a medium of exchange ... of .10 cent per cord wood ... of scalp whoops ... of *'à-la-Gaumine'* marriages ... of the family with 3-twins ... of the *eau-de-vie* ... of the value of cod, corn and furs ... of M. DeChatte's lead coffin ... of Mrs. DeFrontenac's reason for literally returning her husband's heart to its' sender ... of instances of *superfétation* ... of Madeleine de Verchère's bravery ... of the woman who tragically drowned with 6 of her children ... of the brutal executions of prisoners who stood while *nuds en chemise* ... of a hanging in effigy... of 12-year olders marrying legally... of the tragic reason for the death of Louis Hébert ... of the desperate Huguenot ... of children and wives forced to assist at the executions of their fathers and husbands ... and on and on and on. You might find a few of these details in some form or other in Fr. Tanguay's *"Dictionnaire"* or elsewhere but until now you certainly could not find them all in any one single place ! So, even if you are not able to locate specific information pertaining to your own family lineage, you *will* enjoy:

" SEARCHING THROUGH THE OLD RECORDS OF NEW FRANCE FOR ALL OF THOSE *PRECIOUS* GENEALOGICAL DETAILS !"

FATHER TANGUAY'S INTRODUCTION

The History of New France is known to us although not necessarily in great detail. The works of our historians have shown us the contributions made by the discoverers of Canada, the laying of the groundwork for New France, the trials and tribulations encountered by our ancestors, the happy moments and the sad moments of those same ancestors. That work need not be redone - it will last.

Yet, must we conclude that any further investigation into our History is unnecessary? Certainly not. The broader lines have been drawn yet so many details remain to be clarified! So many conclusions drawn on incomplete information remain to be corrected! So much remains to be explained about our very origins!

A modest contributor in the ranks of our historians, I've often had some new insight almost literally burst forth from my historical notes which had - until then - remained obscure or incomplete. And the *registres* which I examined throughout New France gave me a wealth of information which I delighted in gathering.

Here are seven or eight examples from among the many which I had the opportunity to gather from throughout the *registres* - from *"A Travers les Registres"*.

1.   We've often wondered if the census taken in 1666 - the first in the land - was taken at the beginning or at the end of the year and if, as a result, it did or did not include families which had arrived in the Summer of 1666. The *registres* enabled me to prove that it only included the families which had arrived before the Summer.

2.   In 1687, the victims of an Iroquois massacre along the banks of Lac Saint-Louis were buried in that same area. All of the information regarding those poor unfortunates - their names, their ages, etc. - was recorded in the Lachine *registre* for that same year although we searched in vain almost everywhere else for any scrap of information.

3.   I also found the last of the pages telling of the bloody massacre at Lachine in 1689. The *curé* at Saints-Anges in Lachine had caringly gathered up the remains of many of the victims so that they might receive their religious burial accompanied by the appropriate prayers.

4. The authenticity of some unedited and very interesting letters regarding the *supplice du feu* [punishment by fire] of 4 Iroquois braves who had been condemned back in 1695 was proven by the *registres* at Ville-Marie.

5. I was able to prove that the name of Kondiaronk-le-Rat - a name given to an Indian chief whom our historians had extolled and made famous - was not his real name. His burial record - certainly a legal document - referred to him as Gaspard Soiaga-dit-le-Rat.

6. From that same source, I was also able to trace the background of the mighty Dubocq whom Charlevoix referred to (Book XVI, p. 199), and who was taken prisoner near Orange in 1697 by the *Mahingans* and the *Agniers*; and in the collection of letters mentioned above, I was able to pull together the details of the blood-curdling events leading to his being saved.

7. The *registres* for the year 1700 enabled me to determine the approximate date - within months - of the death of Jolliet, the discoverer of the Mississippi.

8. In addition to those references - so important to our history - those same *registres* also furnished us with the origin of some names as well as the precise geographical locations of certain places which had been mentioned in our historical records; for example, Pointe-à-Lacaille, we now know is Saint-Thomas de Montmagny; Cap Lauzon is Deschambault; Cap-à-l'Arbre is Saint-Jean-Deschaillons.

That proof, I'm certain, will help to build up the interest of the readers who have been awaiting the publication of the book which I now present to them.

I firmly believe that the examples which I've included will make it easier for my readers to better understand what I was trying to accomplish with my work , to grasp its details and to more easily place my work within the context of the history of our beloved nation.

Cyprien Tanguay, priest

Searching Through the Old Records of New France
for all of those
Precious
Genealogical Details

1543

THE ARRIVAL OF A SHIP IN THE EARLY 1500S - JACQUES CARTIER'S TIME

[Very little documentation of any consequence had been written on early 16th century attempts at colonizing New France and even less had survived when Reverend Tanguay wrote his book. He therefore had very little from which to draw.]

1. **Jean de Nantes who arrived with M. de Roberval was convicted of theft and clamped in irons.**

   [M. de Roberval was with Jacques Cartier in 1541 when they attempted to establish a colony in Canada as a basis for the conquest of the Saguenay Territory – the Gulf of St-Lawrence area.]

2. M. de Roberval had Michel Gaillon executed on the scaffold after he had been convicted of theft. This was the first such execution in New France.

NOTE: These two executions – the one clamped in irons and the other executed on the scaffold – served to highlight the historical fact regarding the poor character of some of the settlers which *Vice-roi* de Roberval had brought with him to begin the settlement of this vast nation. Actually, his three big ships held several noblemen, a company of soldiers and sailors, and **many** very common people - some from prison.
[Historian Gustave Lanctot notes that France's King Francis I[st] had authorized Roberval "to recruit as many prisoners awaiting execution or serving terms as he might desire.", (Lanctot, '*A History of Canada*', 1963, Clarke, Irwin & Co., V1, p. 68)].

M.. Ferland [priest and historian] wrote: "to maintain order during winter-time surrounded by these undisciplined individuals, it was necessary that we resort to the whip, prison cells and the gallows. Fortunately for France and for Canada, these attempts at colonization failed."

[Lanctot also notes that the King had ordered everyone back from Canada by early 1543 since "the first Canadian colony had lived and died." Raymond Douville and Jacques-Donat Casanova note that their retreat back to Europe "was the signal for the neglect of New France by those in authority....for 60 years".('*Daily Life in Early Canada*', Macmillan Co,1968, p. 6).]

Father Ferland continued: "If they [the early attempts at colonisation] had succeeded, we would have continued with the same system and God knows what a dismal society would have resulted." We learned from the experience. Three quarters of a century later, when we wished to establish a firm foundation at the foot of Québec, we understood that it was necessary above all to appeal to a sober, frugal, and religious population who desired an orderly society and the work ethic. No one can ignore the meticulous care by which the Canadian people's ancestors were [finally] selected.

THE DEATH OF COMMANDANT CHATTES

[Commandant Aymar deChattes was the Vice-Admiral entrusted by France's King Henry IV with the establishment of a permanent colony in Canada in the early 1600s. He was the one who obtained the services of Samuel de Champlain, later to be known as the 'Father of New France'.]

Reverend Tanguay was permitted to reproduce a letter from an antique dealer in Rouen [Normandy, France] which [letter] gave the details about the coffin containing the remains of M. de Chattes:

Antiquities Museum of Rouen
Rouen   21 September 1871

"My Dear Colleague,

I had spoken to you about the coffin of M. de Chattes, Governor of Dieppe [France] and Viceroy of Canada, under King Henry IV. I , today, have the pleasure of sending you a drawing of that coffin as it was in 1827. I hope that the design will interest you and your numerous friends in New France.

Farewell, my dear Father. Believe in all of my love for you."

'Father Cochart'

Reverend Father C. Tanguay - Québec, Canada

THE LEAD COFFIN OF AYMAR DeCHATTES

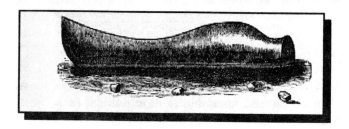

Commander of the Order of Malta
Governor of Dieppe [in France from 1582-1603], Viceroy of Canada
Buried in the Minimes [a religious order] Chapel in 1603
In 1827, his remains were transferred to St-Remi's Church in Dieppe
and reburied in the Governors' Vault

ANNUAL FLUCTUATIONS IN THE WHITE
(NON-SLAVE) POPULATION [1]

[As you read through the first part of this translation, keep in mind that a ship's arrival in New France during the 17th Century was **always** an occasion for some excitement. The only tangible link between a very small French population and the mother country, it was often the first connection to the outside world for the colony's population for at least 6 months due to climactic conditions. The ships brought in a (very) few settlers, artisans, clerics and soldiers, in addition to the much-needed tools and supplies, letters and other written items which the population sorely lacked.]

ARRIVED IN 1608	DEPARTED IN 1608	MARRIED IN 1608	BORN IN 1608	DIED IN 1608	QUÉBEC IN THE WINTER 1608	HURONS IN THE WINTER 1608	MAXIMUM IN QUÉBEC 1608
31	3 a.	...	...	3 b.	25	...	31 c.

[1]

We reflected the changes in the white population annually until 1631. From 1632 on, we've shown it *every ten years* – in tabular form – by adding the increase in that decade to the beginning totals compiled since the establishment of Québec.

a. Three prisoners who were implicated in the Duval plot [to assassinate] Champlain ['the Father of New France'] were sent back to France.   *(Champlain, 1613, p. 155)*

[The actual number of individuals who 'DEPARTED IN 1608' is to be questioned. Around 1600, Vice-Admiral Aymar DeChattes had associated himself with a responsible merchant, Pontgravé, who was still in the colony at the time of the Duval plot. Historian James Douglas specifically mentions that "Pontgravé followed with the [three] prisoners to France as there was no prison in Québec" ("*Old France in the New World*", Burrows Brothers, 1905, pp. 72-88). Since Pontgravé was clearly not a prisoner, he would not have been included as one of Tanguay's three who 'DEPARTED IN 1608' (above) although he had obviously also left with them. Francis Parkman also notes that Duval's "three accomplices were carried by Pontgravé to France" ("*France and England in North America*", Library of America, 1983, p. 247) and so at least 4 individuals would have had to depart.]

b. One of the implicated prisoners was Jean Duval who had been sentenced to death by M. de Champlain for conspiring against him; the other 2 deaths were Antoine Natel, *serrurier*[locksmith], and an un-named *matelot*[sailor], who had both died in November.   *Champlain, 1613, pp. 154-166)*

[Duval, also a *serrurier*, and four others "hatched a plot to murder Champlain and sell the [Québec] settlement and all of its contents to the Basques (from the French and Spanish Pyrenees) in Tadoussac. One of the conspirators was 'stricken with remorse' and revealed the plan, and Champlain had them all arrested and brought before a court of master mariners." (G. Lanctot, "*A History of Canada*", Clarke, Irwin & Co., 1963, V 1, p. 103). Douglas in his "*Old France in the New World*" (pp. 87-88) and Parkman in his "*France and England in North America*" (p. 246) both note that Antoine Natel *was* one of the conspirators although Champlain (and Tanguay) apparently did not agree.]

c. These population figures are from M. de Champlain's notes, 1613 Ed., p166.

ARRIVED IN 1609	DEPARTED IN 1609	MARRIED IN 1609	BORN IN 1609	DIED IN 1609	QUÉBEC IN THE WINTER 1609	HURONS IN THE WINTER 1609	MAXIMUM IN QUÉBEC 1609
...	...	...	...	17a.	8 b.	...	25

a. From February to mid-April, 10 Frenchmen died of scurvy and 5 of dysentery. Shortly thereafter, *chirurgien* [surgeon] Bonnerme and an Indian who had wintered with them also died.   *(Champlain, 1613, p. 170)*

b. Of the 25 winter residents in 1608 "there remained but 8."

(Champlain, 1613, p. 205)

ARRIVED IN 1610	DEPARTED IN 1610	MARRIED IN 1610	BORN IN 1610	DIED IN 1610	QUÉBEC IN THE WINTER 1610	HURONS IN THE WINTER 1610	MAXIMUM IN QUÉBEC 1610
11 a.	1 b.	...	...	...	17	1 c.	19

a. Champlain brought 10 *artisans* [craftsmen] and *manoeuvriers* [skilled tacticians] over from France (*Champlain, Part I, p. 116*) thereby increasing Québec's 1610 maximum population to 19.

b. Champlain returned to France leaving DuPrac in charge of 16 men.
    (*Champlain, 1613, pp. 225, 226 and 241*)

c. Champlain's assistant, Étienne Brulé, went up to Huron country. (*Champlain, I, p. 163*). By 1618, he was serving as an interpreter.
    (*Champlain, 1615-1618, Édit. Laverdière, p. 133*)

ARRIVED IN 1611	DEPARTED IN 1611	MARRIED IN 1611	BORN IN 1611	DIED IN 1611	QUÉBEC IN THE WINTER 1611	HURONS IN THE WINTER 1611	MAXIMUM IN QUÉBEC 1611
...	[1 a.]	...	...	1 b.	16	1 c.	17 d.

a. On August 4th, Champlain returned to France on Captain Tibaut's ship.
    (*Champlain, Part I, 1611, p. 265*)

b. A young man by the name of Louis drowned in Sault St-Louis.
    (*Champlain, Part I, p. 171*)

c. On June 17th, a young Frenchman left for Huron country from Sault St-Louis.
    (*Champlain, Part I, p. 180*)

d. Champlain recorded these population changes when he returned to Québec in the Spring of 1611.
    (*Champlain, 1613, p. 241*)

ARRIVED IN 1612	DEPARTED IN 1612	MARRIED IN 1612	BORN IN 1612	DIED IN 1612	QUÉBEC IN THE WINTER 1612	HURONS IN THE WINTER 1612	MAXIMUM in QUÉBEC 1612
...	...	...	...	...	16	...	16

There were no population changes in 1612. Champlain went to France in the Fall of 1611 and did not return until some time in 1613.

ARRIVED IN 1613	DEPARTED IN 1613	MARRIED IN 1613	BORN IN 1613	DIED IN 1613	QUÉBEC IN THE WINTER 1613	HURONS IN THE WINTER 1613	MAXIMUM IN QUÉBEC 1613
31 a.	[1 b.]	...	...	...	47	...	47

a.   Champlain arrived in Québec with the Sieur de l'Ange and 30 men – 6 in each of 5 ships furnished by the Mercantile Society – which increased Québec's the population to 47.

(Champlain, 1613, pp. 288-289 AND Part I, p. 235)

Marsolet [Nicholas], a 12 year old native of Rouën [Normandy, France], came with Champlain to learn the Algonquin and Montagnaise languages.
[Marsolet eventually served as interpreter/mediator for the French and – after 1629 – for the English.]

b.   Champlain went back to France and did not return until the Spring of 1615.

ARRIVED IN 1614	DEPARTED IN 1614	MARRIED IN 1614	BORN IN 1614	DIED IN 1614	QUÉBEC IN THE WINTER 1614	HURONS IN THE WINTER 1614	MAXIMUM IN QUÉBEC 1614
...	...	...	...	...	47	...	47 a.

a.   Same population as in 1613.

ARRIVED IN 1615	DEPARTED IN 1615	MARRIED IN 1615	BORN IN 1615	DIED IN 1615	QUÉBEC IN THE WINTER 1615	HURONS IN THE WINTER 1615	MAXIMUM IN QUÉBEC 1615
5 a.	19	...	...	...	32	19 b.	52

a.   Four Récollet religious[2] arrived with Champlain causing the population to increase to 52.

(Champlain, 1615-1618, pp. 7, 9 and 248)

b.   In August, Champlain met 13 or 14 Frenchmen and 2 Récollet priests [wintering] in Huron country. They had left before him from *Rivière-des-Prairies.*

(Champlain, Part I, p. 248)

2

Fathers Denis Jamay, Dolbeau and Le Caron and Brother Pacifique Duplessis.

[No explanation is given for the difference between the tabular total of 19 'HURONS IN THE WINTER 1615' and this detail for 15 or 16 individuals.]

ARRIVED IN 1616	DEPARTED IN 1616	MARRIED IN 1616	BORN IN 1616	DIED IN 1616	QUÉBEC IN THE WINTER 1616	HURONS IN THE WINTER 1616	MAXIMUM IN QUÉBEC 1616
33 a.	3 b.	...	...	2 c.	60 d.	...	64

a.   The number of immigrants from France was estimated at 33 which included Marguerite Vienne and her husband, Michel Colin. In his *"Histoire du Canada"*, Sagard referred to Michel Colin as having been "the first in the nation to receive the honor of being accorded the full burial rites of the holy Roman Church by Father Dolbeau."

Although Michel Colin had arrived at the same time as his wife, Marguerite Vienne, she died several weeks later. She holds the distinction of having been the first European woman to arrive in New France.

(Sagard, p. 31, 1636 Edition)

b.   Fathers Le Caron [Joseph] and Denis Jamet returned to France with Champlain.

(Sagard, p. 31)

c.   Colin [Michel] and his wife both died in the year of their arrival.

(Sagard, p. 31)

d.   Only 60 people spent the winter with the Hurons.

(Sagard, p. 40)

ARRIVED IN 1617	DEPARTED IN 1617	MARRIED IN 1617	BORN IN 1617	DIED IN 1617	QUÉBEC IN THE WINTER 1617	HURONS IN THE WINTER 1617	MAXIMUM IN QUÉBEC 1617
7 a.	1 b.	...	...	2 c.	64	...	67

a.   The Hébert family arrived from France – Hébert, his wife, 2 daughters [Guillemette and Anne] and young son [Guillaume], (Sagard, p. 41) along with 2 Récollet priests (Champlain, Part II, p.23), Fathers LeCaron [Joseph] and Paul Huet. (Leclercq, "Établissement de la Foi", V I, pp. 104-5, 1691 ed.)
[Louis Hébert is recognized as Canada's first colonist or settler.]

b.   Father Dolbeau [Jean] returned to France.

(Sagard, p. 52)

c.   In mid-April, two Frenchmen [a sailor, Charles Pillet, and a locksmith] were killed by the Montagnais Indians around Île-d'Orleans.

(Champlain, 1627 edition AND Sagard, pp. 42 & 235)

ARRIVED IN 1618	DEPARTED IN 1618	MARRIED IN 1618	BORN IN 1618	DIED IN 1618	QUÉBEC IN THE WINTER 1618	HURONS IN THE WINTER 1618	MAXIMUM IN QUÉBEC 1618
6 a.	3 b.	1 c.	...	1 d.	66	...	70.

a.   The 6 immigrants were: Father Dolbeau; Brother Modeste Guines *(Sagard, p. 40)*; Eustache Boullé; the Sieur de la Mothe; Loquin [Jacques], a clerk *(Champlain, 1615-18, pp. 120, 122 and 138)*; and Sieur Nicolet [Jean] *(Relations, 1643, p. 34)*. The population was now 70.

b.   Father Huet [Paul] and Brother Pacifique Duplessis returned to France with Champlain *(Champlain, 1615-1618, p.157)*, and another Récollet.

(Mercure Français, 1618, p. 296)

[No explanation is given for the difference between the tabular total of the 3 who did 'DEPART IN 1618' and this detail for 4.]

c.   Étienne Jonquest married Anne Hébert.

(Sagard, p. 41)

d.   The death of a Scottish Huguenot [17th Century French Protestant] in despair: "Although a Huguenot, this poor man wished to have Father Paul at his bedside at the time of his death *and not sooner,* as if God had spoken to him and allowed him to choose the time for his conversion and had entrusted Dame Hébert, who would never miss out on a charitable deed concerning the conversion and salvation of a lost soul; she did her duty and begged the priest to go to him, which he immediately did, but Father Paul thought that he would be speaking to him of his salvation and of bringing him back to the bosom of the Church as a true convert to God, but he answered him with a hopeless and often repetitious voice: 'Father, it is too late...it is too late', and he was not able to get him to say *anything* else for the three-quarters of an hour that he stayed with him, and he died just so hopeless of the mercy of God."

(Sagard, pp. 47-48)

ARRIVED IN 1619	DEPARTED IN 1619	MARRIED IN 1619	BORN IN 1619	DIED IN 1619	QUÉBEC IN THE WINTER 1619	HURONS IN THE WINTER 1619	MAXIMUM IN QUÉBEC 1619
13 a.	...	...	1 b.	3 c.	77	...	80 d.

a. The arrival of Guillaume Poulain, Brother Pacifique *(Sagard, p. 49)*, Captain Dupont *(Champlain, I, p. 226 AND Part II, p.6)*; 2 families *(Id. pp. 23-31)*, 3 servants and 2 workers.

(Leclercq, I, p. 152)

b. Étienne Jonquest's child was born.

(Champlain)

c. The deaths of Brother Pacifique Duplessis *(Sagard, p. 55)*; Mme. [Anne Hébert] Jonquest and her [newborn] child.

(Champlain, II, p.3)

d. Thirteen new arrivals and one birth raised the 1619 population to 80 people.

ARRIVED IN 1620	DEPARTED IN 1620	MARRIED IN 1620	BORN IN 1620	DIED IN 1620	QUÉBEC IN THE WINTER 1620	HURONS IN THE WINTER 1620	MAXIMUM IN QUÉBEC 1620
6 a.	22 b.	...	...	1 c.	60	...	83 d.

a. The population was brought to 83 when Mme. de Champlain [Hélène Boullé]; Eustache Boullé; Guers[3] [Baptiste]; Fathers LeBailly and Jamay, and Brother Bonaventure arrived.

(Champlain, II, pp. 2-10 AND Sagard, pp. 58,59 and 64)

b. Dupont and Roumier *(Champlain, II, p. 6)* returned to France with several workers.

(Leclercq, I, p. 165)

c. A man was killed by a falling tree.

(Champlain, II, p. 6)

d. This count was given by Champlain.

(Ibid.)

3

Messenger for Monsigneur de Montmorency, the Viceroy.

(Sagard, p. 58)

ARRIVED IN 1621	DEPARTED IN 1621	*MARRIED IN 1621*	BORN IN 1621	DIED IN 1621	QUÉBEC IN THE WINTER 1621	HURONS IN THE WINTER 1621	MAXIMUM IN QUÉBEC 1621
24 a.	5 b.	1 c.	1 d.	1 e.	79	...	85

a. Roumier returned from France with 5 merchants from *l'ancienne société* and 18 agricultural or industrial workers from *la nouvelle société*.

(Champlain, II, pp. 17, 21 and 30)

[The *sociétés* were associations of merchants and manufacturers set up for mutual protection and for regulation of prices. Their motives and methods differed. The French commercial *Compagnie de Canada* OR *de la Nouvelle France* OR *de Condé* OR *de Champlain* OR *de Rouën* OR *de St. Malo* – *l'ancienne société* – was the direct creation of the government, but lacked the spirit of free trade and believed that public funds should not be drawn on to set up the colonies. They wished to limit colonization to those who dealt *directly* with Indians for the ever-so-important furs and pelts. The private *Compagnie des Cent-Associés* – *la nouvelle société* – believed in free trade and in colonizing provided that the company would own whatever was traded for.]

b. Father Lebailly [Georges] (*Sagard, p. 72* AND *Leclercq, I, p. 177*) and two families returned to France.

(Champlain, II, p. 31)

c. The marriage of Guillaume Couillard and Guillemette Hébert.

(Québec Registers, 1621)

d. The Abraham Martin family had a new baby.

(Idem)

e. The death of a [the Martin's] newborn child.

(Idem)

The number of winter residents in Québec was now 79.

ARRIVED IN 1622	DEPARTED IN 1622	MARRIED IN 1622	BORN IN 1622	DIED IN 1622	QUÉBEC IN THE WINTER 1622	HURONS IN THE WINTER 1622	MAXIMUM IN QUÉBEC 1622
6 a.	19 b.	...	...	...	50	*16 c.*	85 d.

a.&d The 6 individuals who arrived and were added to the previous year's total of 79 winter residents were: Dupont [also known as Pontgravé or Sieur de Gravé]; Fathers Galleran [Guillaume] and Piat [Irenée]; and Brother Charles (Champlain, II, pp. 48-52 AND Sagard, pp. 91-101); Sieur Soutien, a clerk from New France who returned home from France on the 8th of June *(Champlain, II, p. 34)*; and Le Sire. [a clerk].

(Id., p. 46)

b.   According to Champlain (II, p. 49) , the number of departures rose to 19 in light of the number of people wintering in Québec being down to 50.

c.   Duvernay and 15 men[4] left to winter with the Hurons.

(Champlain, II, p. 56)

ARRIVED IN 1623	DEPARTED IN 1623	MARRIED IN 1623	BORN IN 1623	DIED IN 1623	QUÉBEC IN THE WINTER 1623	HURONS IN THE WINTER 1623	MAXIMUM IN QUÉBEC 1623
2 a.	1 b.	...	...	1 c.	50	16 d.	52

a.   Father Viel [Nicolas] and Brother Sagard [Gabriel] arrived from France.

(Champlain, II, p. 54 AND Sagard, pp. 112-159)

b.   Dupont returned to France.

(Id., II, p. 62)

c.   A young man, Jean Lebocq, was crushed to death when a stack of wood fell on him on the 8th of May.

(Id. II, p. 53)

d.   Duvernay and the Frenchmen who had wintered with the Hurons arrived in Québec on the 23rd of July. *(Champlain, II, p. 56)*. On the following 11th of August, Fathers Viel [Nicolas] and LeCaron [Joseph] and Brother Sagard [Gabriel] and eleven Frenchmen left for Huron country. Two other Frenchmen left for Upper Algonquin territory.
(Champlain, II, p. 60 AND Sagard, "Grand Voyage", p. 266 AND Leclercq, Vol II, p. 248)

ARRIVED IN 1624	DEPARTED IN 1624	MARRIED IN 1624	BORN IN 1624	DIED IN 1624	QUÉBEC IN THE WINTER 1624	HURONS IN THE WINTER 1624	MAXIMUM IN QUÉBEC 1624
6 a.	4 b.	...	1 c.	1 d.	52 e.	10 f.	57 g.

a.   Duvernay, Father LeCaron [Joseph], Brother Sagard [Gabriel] and three Frenchmen returned from Huron country.

(Champlain, II, p. 72 AND Sagard, "Grand Voyage", p. 365)

b.   The departure of Mme. Champlain [Hélène Boullé], Eustache Boullé *(Champlain, II, p. 76)*, Father Piat [Irenée], and Brother Sagard [Gabriel].

(Sagard, p. 841)

4

Champlain didn't specifically mention this total. It was calculated from the figures which he gave to the residents.

c.   The birth of Marguerite Martin, Abraham's daughter.

(Québec Register, 1624)

d.   A Frenchman [Guillaume Chaudron] died in Huron territory.

(Champlain, II, p. 72)

e.   After Champlain left for France, the population of Québec as of the 15th of August 1624 was up slightly to 52.

(Id., II, p. 76)

f.   Father Viel [Nicolas] and nine Frenchmen wintered with the Hurons.

(Id., pp. 72-73)

g.   Six arrivals and one birth added to the preceding year's totals made for a maximum population of 57 souls for the year.

ARRIVED IN 1625	DEPARTED IN 1625	MARRIED IN 1625	BORN IN 1625	DIED IN 1625	QUÉBEC IN THE WINTER 1625	HURONS IN THE WINTER 1625	MAXIMUM IN QUÉBEC 1625
6 a.	1 b.	...	1 c.	2 d.	56	...	59

a.   The arrival of Fathers Charles Lallemant, de Brébeuf [Jean] and Massé [Enemond] and Brothers Gilbert (Burot) and François (Charton) – all Jesuits – and of Father Joseph de la Roche Daillon, a Récollet priest.

(Champlain, II, pp. 78, 84 and 114)

b.   Father Joseph LeCaron, a *Récollet* priest, returned to France.

(Sagard, p. 871)

c.   The birth of Louise Couillard, Guillaume's newest daughter.

(Québec Register, 1625)

d.   The deaths of Father Viel [Nicolas] as recorded in the Récollet Priests' Death Records *(Relations, 1634, p. 92)*, and of a young [anonymous] French boy [Huron name was Auhaitsique].

(Sagard, "Grand Voyage", p. 350)

ARRIVED IN 1626	DEPARTED IN 1626	MARRIED IN 1626	BORN IN 1626	DIED IN 1626	QUÉBEC IN THE WINTER 1626	HURONS IN THE WINTER 1626	MAXIMUM IN QUÉBEC 1626
27 a.	2 b.	...	1 c.	1 d.	71 e.	10	84

a. The arrival of Boullé [Eustache], Destouches, Fathers Noyrot [Philibert] and DeNoüe [Anne] and 20 workers [to help to build a Jesuit mission] *(Champlain, II, pp. 85, 114)*; and of Father LeCaron [Joseph] and Brothers Gervais Mohier and Jean Gaufestre, Récollets.

(Sagard, pp. 697 & 871)

b. Sieur Dupont and Father Noyrot [Philibert] departed.

c. The birth of Marguerite Couillard, Guillaume's daughter.

(Québec Register)

d. A worker for the Jesuits died from yellow fever.

(Champlain, II, p. 117)

e. Jesuit Fathers de la Noüe [Anne] and de Brébeuf [Jean], and Récollet Father de la Roche Daillon, as well as several other Frenchmen all went up to Huron country in July. Now, only 71 winter-residents remained in Québec.

(Champlain, II. p. 115 AND Sagard, pp. 875, 879)

ARRIVED IN 1627	DEPARTED IN 1627	MARRIED IN 1627	BORN IN 1627	DIED IN 1627	QUÉBEC IN THE WINTER 1627	HURONS IN THE WINTER 1627	MAXIMUM IN QUÉBEC 1627
2 a.	15 b.	...	1 c.	4 d.	55 e.	...	71

a. Dupont and his grandson, Desmarets, arrived from France.

(Champlain, II, pp. 126-127 AND Sagard, p. 482)

a. The workers for the Jesuit fathers – among others – *(Champlain, II, p. 131)*, and Father Lallemand [Charles] *(Leclercq, I, p. 373)* left for France.

c. The birth of Hélène Martin, the daughter of Abraham.

(Québec Register, 1627)

d. Louis Hébert died from a fall on the 25th of January 1627.

(Champlain, II, p. 117 AND Sagard, pp. 589-591)
[He fell from a scaffolding and then died from lack of care in the hard winter weather.]

Pierre Magnan was also killed by the Iroquois *(Champlain, II, p. 127)*, and two other men [Henri Choppard and a Dumoulin] were killed by Indians near Québec
(Champlain, II, p. 134)

Leclercq said that these last two had been "killed by the Mohican, Aticouche".
(V.I, pp. 377+)

e.   After a few ships left for France, the September 1627 population of Québec was 55.
(Champlain, II, p. 131)

In 1867, I was commissioned by the Canadian government to study the French records to see if I could unearth some new historical information on New France.

During my stay in Rouën [Normandy, France], I first visited the library of the Archdiocese of Rouën in the hope of unearthing some new historical information. Monsignor the Archbishop had been the first one to exercise any ecclesiastical jurisdiction in New France by empowering Jesuit priests. I was very fortunate to locate the following article: "*Un petit roi du Canada*", from which I have extracted:
> "In 1627, on the Day of the Immaculate Conception [December 8], Monsignor François de Harlay, Archbishop of Rouën [Normandy, France], conferred the sacrament of baptism on the son of 'un petit roi du Canada.'"
> *(Dom Pommeraie, "History of the Archbishops of Rouën", p. 661)*

Upon my return to Canada, I compared the extract with a story by Sagard which read as follows:
> "Among the Hurons whom he (Father Nicholas Viel)[5] was most attached to, was a man who brought his son [Amantacha] to us to be instructed in our monastery-school and to whom Father Joseph LeCaron had given the warmest possible welcome, as if for a young soul enrolling under the banner of God."
> *(Sagard, p. 876)*

[Someone "enrolling under the banner of God" would ordinarily be someone who was committing himself to the life of a Jesuit.]

---

[5]

Father Nicholas Viel, a Récollet, had drowned in 1625 in the rapids to the north of the *Île-de-Montréal*. The site of that tragic occurrence has retained the name '*Sault-au-Récollet* [Récollet Rapids].

"Supervised and accompanied by Sieur de Caen who left him [Amantacha] for some time at his father's home in Rouën [Normandy, France], the youngster was brought to the Jesuits in Paris and placed under the care of M. le Duc de Vantadour who, with some difficulty [language], asked him just who had instructed him since there was no one who knew his language except for a layman who only saw him once in a great while. [Sagard felt that the layman was Nicolas Marsolet.] Then they ceremoniously baptized him in the Cathedral of Rouën. He was named Louis de Sainte Foi by M. le Duc de Longueville, his godfather, and Mme. de Villars, his godmother, in the presence of a great number of people who had hastened to him out of a sense of curiosity since several sailors had reported him to be '*the son of the king of Canada*' ".

(Sagard, pp. 878-879)

[Crosses similar to this one being raised by Cartier at Gaspé were commonly raised in the French forts and seigneurial areas. The barely-legible message on this one was 'Vive le Roy de France' - ('Long Live the King of France') and showed the respect which the colonists held for their form of government. Any reference to a 'king of Canada' or to a supposed 'son of a king of Canada' was certain to generate a great deal of interest !]

[Marcel Trudel noted that when Amantacha later fell into the hands of the English soldiers led by the Kirks, they also viewed him as the son of the king of Canada and treated him like a young dauphin [prince], at least until a poor, half-naked Huron proclaimed himself to be Amantacha's father as he begged them for food. At that point, most of the lavish clothing-gifts were withdrawn and he returned home. Amantacha eventually disappeared and is thought to have been killed by the Iroquois.]

ARRIVED IN 1628	DEPARTED IN 1628	MARRIED IN 1628	BORN IN 1628	DIED IN 1628	QUÉBEC IN THE WINTER 1628	HURONS IN THE WINTER 1628	MAXIMUM IN QUÉBEC 1628
...	...	...	...	...	55	21 a.	55

a.   Twenty-one Frenchmen wintered with the Hurons.

(Champlain, II, pp. 152, 208 & 210)

There was a young Greek in Québec at this time.

(Id., II, p. 152)

[Trudel notes that this same young Greek was an interpreter for the French who later altered his appearance to dress as an Indian and serve as a spy.]

A large number of families and workers were on route to Québec on Sieur Roquemont's ships; however, they never arrived since they were captured by Kirk's fleet and returned to France.

(Id., II, pp. 161-185)

Foucher, Commandant in charge of security at Cap-Tourmente[6], was surprised by the British and left for Gaspé with Eustache Boullé, M. de Champlain's brother-in-law.

(Sagard, p. 917)

This was the year of a serious famine in Québec.

ARRIVED IN 1629		DEPARTED IN 1629		MARRIED IN 1629	BORN IN 1629	DIED IN 1629	QUÉBEC IN THE WINTER 1629		HURON IN THE WINTER 1629		MAXIMUM IN QUÉBEC 1629	
Fr	En	Fr	En				Fr	En	Fr	En	Fr	En
...	600	74 a.	510 b.	1 c.	1 d.	1 e.	22	90	...	...	76 f	600
600		584					112		....		676	

6

That location is found on Jean Bourbon's 1641 map under the name of 'vieille habitation' [old settlement].

Eustache Boullé, born on the 19th of November 1600, had arrived from France in 1618. He was Samuel de Champlain's Lieutenant. He crossed over to Italy after the surrender of Québec and became a religious in the 'Minimes' Order [established by St- François-de-Paul]. Mme. De Champlain, who loved him tenderly, provided him with 1000 francs a year for each of ten years.

(State Paper Office, Volume V, Article 26)

a.	After the surrender of Québec, Champlain and some other Frenchmen returned to France with all of the religious priests and brothers.

(Champlain, II, p. 226)

b.	The English fleet consisted of 600 men in 5 large ships, each with a crew of 120. At the time of surrender, 120 men disembarked but only 90 (which included 1 minister) stayed behind to occupy the site. *(Champlain, pp. 222-288).* The remaining 510 returned to England.

c.	Guillaume Hubou married Louis Hébert's widow.

(Québec Register, 1629)

d.	The birth of Louis Couillard, the son of Guillaume.

(Idem)

e.	Jacques Michel died of apoplexy and was buried in Tadoussac.

(Champlain, II, pp. 256-262)
[Apoplexy is a sudden paralysis with total or partial loss of consciousness or sensation usually as a result of a hemorrhage causing pressure on the brain.]

f.	The 21 Frenchmen in Huron country returned to Québec increasing the French population to 76.

(Idem., II, p. 210)

According to Champlain the population of Québec at the time of its surrender was about 100 - 76 in Québec proper and the others in Tadoussac and elsewhere.[7]

(Idem., II, p. 217)

---

[7]
That population of about 100 souls consisted of:

Jesuits	4	Récollets	4
Men	29	Laborers	18
Women+Girls	5 (in 4 families)	Women	3
Children	7 (in 4 families)	Children	8
		Officers+Volunteers	22
	45 Settlers +	Mercantile Society Total of	55 = the 100 souls

FAMILIES AND SETTLERS RESIDING IN QUÉBEC
AFTER THE SURRENDER OF 1629

1.   Guillaume Hubou and his [new] wife, Marie Rollet [Louis Hébert's widow]; Guillaume Hébert, son of the late Louis Hébert.

2.   Guillaume Couillard and his wife, Guillemette   [one of Louis Hébert's two daughters] and their children: Louise, 4 years old; Marguerite, 3 years old; and Louis, 2 months old.

3.   Abraham Martin and his wife, Marguerite Langlois, and their children: Anne, 25 years old; Marguerite, 5 years old; and Hélène, 2 years old.

4.   Pivert[8] [Nicolas] and his wife, Marguerite Lesage[9], a niece and a young man.

5.   Adrien Duchesne, chirurgien. [surgeon]
                                            (Rélations of 1632, p. 8; and of 1634, p. 7)

6.   D'Amiens LeBailly, Louis Kirk's ship's steward; Étienne Brûlé from Champigny, interpreter for the Hurons; Nicholas Marsolet from Rouën [Normandy, France], interpreter for the Montagnais Indians; and Pierre Royer, a wheelwright from Paris. (Champlain, II, p. 220); LeBocq, carpenter; Froidemouche; Gros Jean [Big John] from Dieppe [France], interpreter for the Algonquins.
                                            (Champlain, II, pp. 236-245)

---

[8]

This family resided at Cap-Tourmente and went to Québec after Champlain left in 1629.
                                            (Champlain, II, p. 154)

[9]

Marguerite Lesage died in Québec and was buried on the 29th of November 1643.
                                            (Québec Register)

THE ENGLISH GOVERNORS' RULE IN QUÉBEC

Louis Kirk

(Champlain, II, p. 220)

ARRIVE IN 1630		DEPART IN 1630		WED IN 1630	BORN IN 1630	DIED IN 1630	QUÉBEC IN THE WINTER 1630		HURON IN THE WINTER 1630		MAXIMUM IN QUÉBEC 1630	
Fr	En	Fr	En	....	....	14 b.	Fr	En	Fr	En	Fr	En
...	...	2 a.	....				24	76	...	...	26c	90
...		2				14 b.	100		....		116	

a. A carpenter and a French laborer were brought from Québec to London on English ships.

(Champlain, II, p. 288)

b. Fourteen Englishmen died from exposure and starvation.

c. The population of 26 Frenchmen was further reduced by the carpenter and the laborer who did 'DEPART IN 1630'.

ARRIVE IN 1631		DEPART IN 1631		WED IN 1631	BORN IN 1631	DIED IN 1631	QUÉBEC IN THE WINTER 1631		HURON IN THE WINTER 1631		MAXIMUM IN QUÉBEC 1631	
Fr	En	Fr	En	....	1 a.	....	Fr	En	Fr	En	Fr	En
...	...	....	....				25	76	...	...	25	76
...		....			1 a.	....	101		....		101	

a. Élizabeth, Guillaume Couillard's new baby daughter, was baptized by an Englishman, most likely the minister who stayed behind as part of the occupation force after the surrender of Québec in 1629.   While the Kirks remained as 'masters' of Québec, there were no French priests there. Indeed, the Mass celebrated by Father Lejeune in 1632 in the home of Guillaume Couillard was the first to have been celebrated in New France by the French in three years.

(Jesuits' Relations)

[The "*Jesuit Relations*" were the 1611 to 1768 reports of the Jesuits' lives in North America which (reports) were made to their superiors in Québec or to the Provincial of the order in France. As used in Canada, however, "*Jesuit Relations*" refers to those same reports for the period from 1632 to 1673 and consists of 41 small volumes.]

NEW FRANCE'S NON-SLAVE POPULATION

(From the accounts of Champlain, Sagard, Leclercq and from the various Registres 1608-31)

YEAR	# ARRIVE	# DEPART	# MARRY	# BORN	# DIED	WINTER QUÉBEC	WINTER HURONS	MAX QUÉBEC
1608	31	3	....	....	3	25	....	31
1609	....	....	....	....	17	8	....	25
1610	11	1	....	....	....	17	1	19
1611	1	1	....	....	1	16	1	17
1612	....	....	....	....	....	16	....	16
1613	31	1	....	....	....	47	....	47
1614	....	....	....	....	....	47	....	47
1615	5	19	....	....	....	32	19	52
1616	33	3	....	....	2	60	....	64
1617	7	1	....	....	2	64	....	67
1618	6	3	1	....	1	66	....	70
1619	13	....	....	1	3	77	....	80
1620	6	22	....	....	1	60	....	83
1621	24	5	1	1	1	79	....	8
1622	6	19	....	....	....	50	16	85
1623	2	1	....	....	1	50	16	52
1624	6	4	....	1	1	52	10	57
1625	6	1	....	1	2	56	....	59
1626	27	2	....	1	1	71	10	84
1627	2	15	....	1	4	55	....	71
1628	....	....	....	....	....	55	21	55
1629	600	560 F 50 E 510	1	1	1	116 F 26 E 90	....	676 F 76 E 600
1630	....	2	....	....	14	100 F 24 E 76	....	116 F 26 E 90
1631	....	....	....	1	....	101 F 25 E 76	....	101 F 25 E 76

[The English had conquered Québec and were taking particular pains to strengthen their hold on Acadia. Negotiations for the return of Canada to France resumed in January of 1631 and the fate of the nation now lay in the hands of the politicians.]

1631

June 12
A letter from His Majesty, Charles I, King of England, to Sir Isaac Wake, Ambassador to France giving the real reason for the surrender of Québec and of Acadia to France, June 12, 1631...

CHARLES I

"To our Faithful and Beloved, Greetings:

Based on your dispatches to the Viscount Dorchester since your arrival in this Court, it is quite obvious that it took quite some time for you to be presented to the King and his Prime Ministers, although you were treated with respect once you finally did meet with them. We were quite surprised that you had not been admitted earlier because of your persistence and especially because Angier had himself petitioned for that audience. You seem to have handled the situation quite well once you did meet with them, however. Apparently, the entire matter was then brought up for discussion and the King himself voiced his desire and willingness to maintain friendly relations with you. As to the welcome on the part of some of the King's Ministers and to the somewhat strained relations which others have noticed relative to Cardinal Richelieu, you were wise to have dealt with matters as you did. You should continue to work with the King's representatives as you see fit since you have again shown your skill in this arena. We have no need to give you any new orders regarding those whom you must deal with in this Court; continue to do things as you have already begun to do in accordance with the responsibilities of your position.

This dispatch is to advise you of your main objective which is to put an end to all of the differences between the two kingdoms and to work towards a more cooperative relationship than has existed during recent years. There is nothing new to this assignment; it merely consists of renewing old alliances and looking at what – if anything – has resulted from promises made in the past.

Your prior negotiations were geared to that same aim and the 1st article of the treaty concluded just 2 years ago after an unfortunate breach was a result of those same talks. On our part, we made a serious attempt to follow all of the terms of the treaty, even if those terms were not clearly spelled out. The major difference now is that any action merely requested at the time is now absolutely essential.

According to the terms of the 3rd article of the treaty, we have allowed a change in the household of our worthy spouse by increasing the number of clergy linked to her person and we have made various restitution of ships with their valuable cargoes, without either having stolen nor kept anything of similar nature for ourselves, although payment for goods was, in fact, called for according to our rights of arrest or of reprisal.
> [The 'worthy spouse' alluded to here is King Charles' wife, Queen Henrietta Maria – originally from France – whose preliminary marriage negotiations allowed her 28 religious attendants for her worship.]

Although we feel that we've lived according to the terms of the treaty, that spirit of cooperation has not been reciprocated as one might reasonably expect from such a two-fold relationship. For instance, the previously-mentioned 3rd article expressly requires the ratification of all the articles and stipulations of our marriage contract and excludes only the characteristics of the home of our dear spouse [the Queen], which was itself the object of a specific clause in that treaty. It also requires that both the amount and the time of payment of the dowry be clearly stipulated in these matrimonial articles. Based on those agreements, promises to pay were often made to us, especially by M de Chasteauneuf who is now the *Garde-des-Sceaux* [Keeper of the Seals], when he was here as *Ambassadeur*, but nevertheless, half [of the Queen's dowry] has yet to be paid.
> [The French gave the bride a dowry of as much as 1,600,000 crowns, only half-paid at this time and badly needed due to severe cash problems at home.]

In addition, at least three costly pieces of property belonging to our subjects were taken and kept without any legitimate reason nor even shadow of a reason, and are still being held despite repeated requests for restitution. They have also taken some cloth and fabrics manufactured in our own kingdom from us – a direct violation of the terms of the treaty. Payment of the balance of the dowry has often been promised to us or to our representatives both by the King's Ministers and by the French *Ambassadeur* who resides near us. We cannot grant any further delays of this payment and have – as a result – attached it to any other conditions which we might have made for a full settlement between us.

Although the French *Ambassadeur* still promises to pay, he wishes nevertheless that the various conditions be handled separately, although he has stated that his nation would honor any new terms geared to the payment of this pre-existing debt. We understand the importance of not interrupting the present negotiations and since we have always made it a point of honor to be able to be held to our word and to do things in a timely fashion, we must approach our agreements somewhat prudently. Everything should be dealt with at the same time. Considering the importance of the matters which we are asked to deal with here, we cannot agree to separate them such that the one could be either rejected (or performed) without the other.

What we see as a condition for your payment to us of the balance due on the dowry, is the return of Québec, the Canadian city taken by a company of our English subjects as we had ordered during the last war, and the evacuation of Port-Royal, near New England, where we settled a company of our Scottish subjects at that same time; this latter action was a result of an order given by my father, the King, whom we remember so fondly.

> [King Charles, then at issue with his Parliament and in desperate need of money, instructed his ambassador that when he received the balance due on the dowry and not before, he [was] to give up both Québec and Port Royal to the French.]

It is true that one of the cities [Québec] was taken before and the other [the Scottish colony in Port Royal] was set up after the peace treaty; and for that reason (and in order to accommodate all of the differences) we formally agree that the one, that is Québec, be yielded back, and those of our subjects who have settled in the other withdraw, thereby leaving them both in the same state that they were in before the signing of the treaty. Note that we do not agree to this out of ignorance as to just what we are legally required to do according to the terms of this last treaty's 7th article relating to restitutions but which really only dealt with ships with distinctive markings in foreign waters at the time of the treaty. Rather, we do this because of our affection for and a desire to please our brother, the King of France, in all which might be requested of us in a friendly and reasonable fashion, and with a desire to please Him even if the restitutions have perhaps not been justly and lawfully requested.

And we can readily and with good reason list what we ask for:
1.   payment of the balance of the dowry ...
2.   the return of certain property taken and kept without the slightest reason ...
3.   the restoration of the goods which were seized in this Kingdom from our subjects – contrary to the treaties.

All of this is right and just, yet we have asked ourselves about the other instances of property in Canada and other places and several other ships in that nation which have not yet been returned to us, yet which our *haute cour d'admirauté* [High Admiralty

Court] has, for judiciously valid reasons, condemned to confiscation, which will not be accorded except as a matter of courtesy and in the interest of a cordial understanding. Now that the entire matter has been laid out, I defer to the letters exchanged between the *Ambassadeur de France* and our Lords *Commissaires*, who were responsible for those matters, for the details. Also to Philippe Burlamachy [Charles' trusted financial adviser] who will work with you and who has some of the required reports as well as the powers to assign which he will give you.

The reports pertain to the buildings, the merchandise and other things, and are necessary to furnish you with all of the details of that which has to do with a mutual restitution; and on that account, we leave you the freedom to grant, more or less according to what you deem appropriate for the conclusion of a satisfactory agreement.

The powers to assign are to facilitate our receiving the balance of the dowry which is due us either in money or in some good and valid assignment of something which will satisfy the debt. On your part, you should return Québec and evacuate Port-Royal, which is why Philippe Burlamachy will give you some of these formal instruments under my hand and seal. Our pleasure is that you would remit them to the King or to a specific member of his Council whom he will name once Burlamachy shall have received the money or the above-referenced assignations and once satisfaction will have been given you for the other above-specified details; but in case of refusal or of delay relative to payment or to the delivery or assignment of goods, for which Burlamachy is held responsible to us, you should then look to those powers and return them to him, because in that case, he will have nothing further to do and should return home.

> [Francis Parkman notes: "...the letter was accompanied by solemn instruments under our hand and seal to make good the transfer on fulfilment of the condition...for a sum equal to about $240,00.00." ('*France and England in North America* ', Library of America, 1983, p. 323.]

As to the balance of the dowry, one thing remains to be regulated and it is the deduction which we make of the amounts which we have otherwise allocated to those members of our dear spouse's household who have returned to France, an adjustment which we readily agree to. Another point remains to be resolved as to the obligation imposed on our subjects to leave Canada and other places; it is that all of the acts initiated in France against all of those who are engaged in this undertaking be repealed, especially those against the three Kirk brothers, as we have at other times asked for the Baron de la Tour and his son, with whom William Alexander had traded, which was judged reasonable by the Ministers of this King, and on which we must again insist.

There is one document relating to the freedom of commerce which was negotiated and formulated in writing by our *Commissaires* and the *Garde des Sceaux* of this Kingdom while he was ambassadeur extraordinaire here, and as *Ambassadeur de France* residing today in our Court, he asks that the regulation be ratified and approved. We voluntarily agree to it, principally because it gives some life and meaning to treaties already concluded between the two crowns; and as much for this particular matter – and to that end, we direct that you be furnished with a copy of that regulation – as for the other matters of which you are actually charged, we give ample commission under our great seal and in the format currently used in such a case.

"Given under our seal in our Greenwich Château on the 12th of June in the 7th year of our reign."

"To our faithful and beloved Sir Isaac Wake, *chevalier*, our Ambassador to the King of France.   On behalf of the King, 12 June 1631."

> [Negotiations for the return of Canada had resumed in January of 1631 and England had finally agreed to hand over Québec but had refused to surrender Port Royal unless they received the balance still due on Queen Henrietta's dowry. Delays followed but after Richelieu ordered a fleet to put to sea to force the British Crown to reach a decision, Charles I did – on March 23, 1632 – sign the Treaty of St-Germain-en-Laye and so Québec, Port Royal as well as all vessels and merchandise seized during the war were returned. The Treaty proved keenly disappointing to Charles for he had to pay 14,330 sterling pounds (abt. $63,668.00 @ $4.45 per pound sterling) in compensation for ships and merchandise seized but had received only 400,000 in French *livres* (abt. $80,000.00 @ .20 per *livre*) towards the balance due on the dowry.

[Please note that the author of this translation readily admits to having taken particular liberty with the translation of this letter in order to retain the interest of its readers. The course of History shall not have been affected by that license, however, since nothing of any historical significance has been changed.]

1635

December 25th

> The burial of Samuel de Champlain in his newly founded Québec. He was born in 1567 in Brouage, Xaintonge, the son of Antoine de Champlain, capitaine de vaisseau [ship's captain], and of Marguerite Leroy.
>
> *(Québec Register)*
>
> In the course of the year, several Frenchmen died of scurvy at Trois-Rivières. They were: Jean Guillot, Pierre Drouet, Isaac Lecomte, Guillaume Mec, Michel Souet and Michel Cousy.

M. DuPlessis-Bouchard's valet, a man called Lefebvre, was drowned, and a man named Antoine was killed by a [falling] tree.

(Trois-Rivières Register)

A young Huron woman named Geneviève (Ondakion), born in 1638, daughter of the first Huron family to be married as Christians, became a *Hospitalière-de-la-Miséricorde-de-Jésus* in Québec.

[These were religious nuns who looked after a hospital, the Hôtel-Dieu in Québec.]

1640

June 1st

Although the marriage, baptismal and burial Registers for Québec were destroyed in a fire which destroyed the *Notre-Dame-de-Recouvrance* Church, we have been able to preserve a copy of the first volume of those precious genealogical records thanks to Father Lejeune's painstaking work. In 1636, that same Father Lejeune also started the Trois-Rivières Registers which were the oldest original Registers in Canada.

MOVEMENT OF THE CATHOLIC POPULATION OF THE PROVINCE OF QUÉBEC 1631 to 1640

	MARRIAGES	BIRTHS	DEATHS	OTHERS
1631	....	1	....	1
1632	....	....	....	....
1633	....	1	....	1
1634	2	1	1	....
1635	3	4	13	....
1636	1	6	17	....
1637	6	8	8	....
1638	3	9	2	7
1639	5	15	9	6
1640	3	21	2	19
TOTALS	23	66	52	34
1608-1640	26	73	92	....

1641

May 26th

The burial of Adrien Dabancour dit Lacaille, the father-in-law of Jean Nicolet. He and his companion, Étienne Sévestre, had drowned on the 2nd of May in 1640 while hunting on the Îles-de-Bellechasse opposite Berthier. On the 20th of May in 1641, Jean Nicolet found his father-in-law's remains[10] and brought them to Québec where they were solemnly buried in the Québec cemetery.

(Notre-Dame de Québec Registers)

1642

From a note in the old Québec Registers...

"On October 29th, we conducted memorial services for M. Nicollet and three men who had worked for M. de Chavigny. They had all drowned in a sloop while going from Québec to Sillery. Their remains were never found."

[François de Chavigny was born in 1619 and married Éléonore de Grandmaison in about 1640 and also received the fief (land held from a lord in return for service) of Deschambault in 1640. He died back in France in 1651.]

1643

June 9th

The Iroquois massacred Guillaume Boissier, Bernard Berté and Pierre Lafond dit Laforest, AKA *'l'Auvergnat'.*

(Montréal Register)

[*L'Auvergnat* could have been referred to here as a surname or as a nickname. Since there is an obvious distinction between the two in the English language, it is better to show it here simply as an AKA (Also Known As) name.]

November 29th

The burial of Marguerite Lesage, the wife of Nicholas Pivert.

(Québec Register)

The Pivert family lived in Québec after Champlain's departure in 1629 although Pivert, his wife, a niece and a young man had resided in Cap-Tourmente in 1628.

(Champlain, II, p. 154)

10

The location of Lacaille's remains was named after him – Lacaille's Point – but is now known as Saint-Thomas-de- Montmagny.

(Tanguay)

1644

March 30th

The brutal killing of Jean Matte-Massé and Pierre Bigot by the Iroquois. Guillaume Lebeau was burned at the stake by those same Indians at just about that same time.

(Montréal Register)

November 3rd

The first marriage of a Frenchman to an Indian woman to be blessed by the Church was celebrated in Québec. The husband was Martin Prévost and his wife was Marie-Olivier (Manitouabéwich) [a Huron Indian with Sylvestre as her family-name]. He became a widower in 1665 [the 10th of September] and married Marie Dabancour, the widow of Godfroy Guillot and sister of Mme. Jean Nicolet on the 8th of November of that same year.

(Québec Register)

1645

September

Father Lallemant started a record which we called the "*Journal des Jésuites*". [This "*Journal des Jésuites*" was the running story of daily life at Québec as kept by the Jesuit <u>superiors</u> from 1645 to 1668. Do not confuse it with the "*Jesuit Relations*" which were the 1611 to 1768 reports of the Jesuits' lives in North America which (reports) were made to their superiors in Québec or to the Provincial of the Order in France. As used in Canada, however, "*Jesuit Relations*" refers to those same reports for the period from 1632 to 1673 and consists of 41 small volumes.]

November 21st

The marriage of Jean Guyon-Dubuisson to Élizabeth Couillard, grand-daughter of Louis Hébert. This same Élizabeth was baptized in Québec in 1631.[11] On page 44 of the "*Journal des Jésuites*", it is noted that the newlyweds were serenaded by 2 violins at their wedding festivities – a first!

---

[11]

Élizabeth, Guillaume Couillard's new baby daughter, was baptized by an Englishman, most likely the minister who stayed behind as part of the occupation force after the surrender of Québec in 1629. While the Kirks remained as 'masters' of Québec, there were no French priests there. Indeed, the Mass celebrated by Father Lejeune in 1632 in the home of Guillaume Couillard was the first to have been celebrated in New France by the French in three years.

In 1645, a loaf of bread cost 15 *sols* [about 15¢]; a cord of wood 10 *sols* [about 10¢].

[a) Canada used the regular 1 and 2 *sol* coins of France until 1763. One *sol* (sou) was equal to 12 *deniers* [about 1 ¢]; 20 *sols* equaled 1 *livre* [about 20 ¢]; 1 *écu* (crown) was equal to 5 *livres* [about $1.00] in 1715; to 6 *livres* in 1718; to 9 *livres* in 1724; back to 5 *livres* in 1737; and 6 *livres* from 1740 onward to 1794. Later, local Canadian monies were minted and finally a decimal system was begun in the 1850s.

b) It's almost impossible to give the present-day value for the *livre*, a *theoretical* Canadian *denomination*, although the purchasing power of 1 *livre* in French money (France) might approximate $12.00 in Canadian funds. Even that conversion is be used with caution, however. A *theoretical denomination* simply means that the denomination was created for accounting-purposes only as there were *never* any *livre* coins issued in Canada.]

1646

February 7th

    The burial of Father Anne du Noüe.

(Trois-Rivières Register)

    The announcement of his death.

(Journal des Jésuites, pp. 33-34)

May 12th

    The death and burial (in the Sillery Chapel) of Father Massé, the 1st missionary in Canada.

(Journal des Jésuites, p. 44)

October 12th

> A marriage contract was drawn up between Nicholas Macard and Marguerite Couillard, the widow of Jean Nicolet and daughter of Guillaume Couillard. Friends and witnesses were: MM. DeMontmagny, *Gouverneur;* René and Louis Maheu, cousins of the bride. The actual ceremony was celebrated on the 16th of November in the Church of Québec.
>
> *(Québec Register)*

October 18th

> The murder of Father Jogues (*Répertoire, p. 34 AND Journal des Jésuites, p. 86),* and of his companion, Jean Lalande from Dieppe [France].
>
> *(Relations des Jésuites, 1647-3)*

November 6th

> Nine men drowned when their barge going from Québec to Trois-Rivières ran aground at Cap-à-l'Arbre[12]. *(Québec Register AND Journal des Jésuites, p.72).* Those unfortunate victims' names were listed in the Québec Register as: Jean Fleury from Sedan [France], *matelot* [sailor]; Jean Basque, *charpentier de navire* [ship's carpenter] and *matelot;* Jacques Figeux from Dieppe [France], *matelot;* Jean Fougereau, *matelot;* Jean Mechin from LaRochelle, *ouvrier* [laborer] and *matelot;* Jacques Arenaine from Tours [France], *soldat* [soldier]; Guillaume Lasue [also] from Tours; Jacques Clèque dit Lafontaine [also] from Tours, *soldat;* and Gaspard Gouault, *apothicaire* [druggist] from Poitiers [France], who was due to go to Huron country with the Jesuit priests.
>
> *(Québec Register)*

1647

February

> Barbe, a young Huron woman, left the Ursuline convent in Québec after having studied with them for four years. She was apparently very strongly sought after by a Frenchman named Chastillon[13] who begged the nuns to detain her until his vessel arrived. He assured them of his [honorable marital] intentions by giving them a money-order for 300 *livres* [about $60.00], 100 specifically for Barbe's benefit in the event that he broke his promise. She loved an Indian man, however, and wanted also to obey the wishes of her parents, so she chose not to have anything to do with Chastillon.
>
> *(Journal des Jésuites, p. 77)*

12

The exact location known by this name is none other than the promontory upon which St-Jean Deschaillons Church is built. This Cap-à-l'Arbre is now known as St-Jean Deschaillons.

13

This young Frenchman was Jean Mignot dit Chaillon, 20 years of age, who married Louise Cloutier, widow of François Marguerie, interpreter at Trois-Rivières in Québec on the 10th of November in 1648 .

March 4th

Julien Petau married Marie Pelletier from the *Bourg* [market-town] *de Marennes* in Saintonge.[14]

May 6th

François Raison from LaRochelle, hired out to the fort as *ouvrier* [laborer], drowned while canoeing with the town's *boulanger* [baker] on the Rivière-St-Charles near Notre-Dame-des-Anges. His body was not found until the 27th of May in the same area and almost exactly where he would ordinarily have disembarked. He was buried on that same day by Father Barthélemy Vimont behind the garden in the church's small cemetery.

(Québec Register)

June 25th

The first horse to be brought to the nation was given to the Governor [Charles Huault de Montmagny] by the residents of Québec.

(Journal des Jésuites, p. 90)

August 21st

Jean St-Léger, a native of Normandy [in France], drowned near M. Couillard's mill after his canoe capsized.

(Québec Register)

14

It is worthy of note that after we had published the first ban before the above-mentioned marriage, it was rumored that Mlle. Marie Pelletier had been married in France and that her husband was still alive and living in or around La Rochelle. We were obliged to look into the matter and to contact those who might have known the said Marie Pelletier and/or of the alleged marriage in France. It was found by the testimony of the witnesses that after having been widowed by a César Gouin, Marie was courted by a certain coachman in LaRochelle and married him; but that the said coachman was in fact married to another woman by which he had had ten children: that being discovered by the said Pelletier, she left the coachman and took the marriage to be invalid, and for that reason left the country. A document dated 18 February 1647 regarding the above is on file with the Clerk of Courts in Québec and I, Barthelemy Vimont, have retained a copy before marrying the said Pelletier to the said Julien Petau, and have filed that said copy with my papers.   (Signed,)   B. Vimont
(Québec Register)

MONTMORENCY FALLS

October 2nd

Antoine Pelletier, a native of Perche, fell out of his canoe and drowned near his home at Sault Montmorency. He had only been married for 1½ months. His widow, Françoise Morin, married Étienne Dumay (Demers) on the following 28th of January.

(Québec Register)

[Étienne and Françoise are the 7th great-grandparents of the Editor-Translator]

October 4th

The burial of Gabriel Trut, *homme de confiance* [confidant] to M. Cauchon, at Château-Richer. He had died at the Hôpital of Québec of a wound received in a skirmish with the Iroquois.

(Québec Register)

1648

May 23rd

We buried François Marguerie, the brother-in-law of Jacques Herte, who had drowned near Trois-Rivières where he worked as an *interprète* [interpreter]. His body had been found near Québec.

(Québec Register)

The body of Jean Amyot, who had drowned along with Marguerie, was recovered near the *Restitution-de-St-Joseph* in Sillery. They were both buried in Québec, on June 10th 1648.

(Québec Register)

[Historian James Douglas referred to the *Restitution-de-St-Joseph* as "the site of the first (very unsucessful) Mission which attempted to wean the Indian from his roving life and to teach him good and patient work habits" ("*Old France in the New World*", Burrows Brothers, 1905, pp. 253-254) .]

June 6th

The burial of a young man, Nicolas Garnier, who had drowned during the winter at Trois-Rivières and was found at Pointe-Lévis.

(Québec Register)

July 4th

The burial of a man named Lachaussée, who had been killed by the Iroquois.

(Trois-Rivières Register)

August 2nd

Mathurin Bonenfant, 25, was killed by the Iroquois.

(Montréal Register)

August 14th

A surgeon named Bélanger arrived in Québec bearing official letters from the King regarding a change of Governor [to Louis d'Ailleboust de Coulonge et d'Argentenay].

(Journal des Jésuites, p. 114)

1649

January 19th

The first execution[15] in Québec by the *bourreau* [executioner] was of a 15-16 year old girl who had been convicted of theft.

(Journal des Jésuites, p. 120 AND Québec Register)

1650

June 21st

Mme. la Gouvernante (d'Aillebout) and Mme. de Monceaux buried a Huron named Kandahietsi[16] right after he had been executed.

June 22nd

Captain Jammes' ship arrived from France. A matelot [sailor] from the crew brought news of the loss of the ship *Le St-Sauveur* which had left Québec for France in October of 1648. In March of 1649, the ship had set sail for a return trip to Canada but was lost at sea near Lisbon.

(Journal des Jésuites, p. 141)

---

15   In 1543 M. de Roberval had had a Michel Gaillon – also convicted of theft – executed on the scaffold. Also, M. de Champlain had had the same penalty served on Jean Duval who had plotted against him.

16   Deemed 'worthy' of death, the Huron was baptized on June 20th and named Louis – all of this before he even knew whether he would live or die. The following day, he was led *au carqan* [e.g. to an iron collar which was attached to a pole] by the executioner and a sergeant and left to be disposed of by some Hurons and Algonquins. A Huron called Henheonsa struck him twice on the skull with his hatchet and killed him at once. He was then buried by the Governess and by Mme. de Monceaux..

(Journal des Jésuites, pp. 140-141)

August 20th

A party of Iroquois killed Robert LeCoq, a Jesuit Brother *donné*, and injured several other Frenchmen near Trois-Rivières.

(Journal des Jésuites, p. 142)

[The *donnés* were a class of lay auxiliaries founded especially to help in the work of construction in New France. They were people who wished to serve God in some capacity yet they hesitated to take irrevocable religious vows and were bound to the society by a civil contract to work for life and without remuneration although the Society agreed to take care of their material needs. Mostly unskilled volunteers, many of them were craftsmen of considerable skill. By enrolling men dedicated to a religious ideal, it was possible also to get rid of the 'vicious' and 'licentious' workmen - imported labor referred to as *engagés* - who by their example were continually embarrassing to the missionaries. There were never sufficient *donnés* to preclude the hiring of some *engagés*, however.]

September 19th

The burial of Girard Laval, approximately 25, from Rouën [Normandy, France], *commis* [steward] on board the ship *La Dunia* commanded by Captain Terrien, after he had drowned on that same day in Québec.

(Québec Register)

MOVEMENT OF THE CATHOLIC POPULATION OF THE PROVINCE OF QUÉBEC 1641 TO 1650

	MARRIAGES	BIRTHS	DEATHS	OTHERS
1641	3	16	8	8
1642	3	9	6	3
1643	1	15	5	10
1644	4	10	9	1
1645	4	10	1	9
1646	4	16	15	1
1647	15	19	11	8
1648	12	31	24	7
1649	10	43	21	22
1650	9	43	10	33
TOTALS ➡	65	212	110	102
1608-1650	91	285	202	83

1651

February 13th

The Ursuline Sisters retired into their cloister.

(Journal des Jésuites, p. 148)

THE URSULINE CONVENT

April 19th

We baptized the first Canadian twins, Marguerite and Élizabeth, the daughters of Massé Gravel in Québec.

NOTE: Both of the twins married: Marguerite, in 1667, to Noël Racine, and Élizabeth, in 1669, to Matthieu Côté, and they now count thousands of grand-children.

(Tanguay)

May 6th

A party of Iroquois killed a man named *Grand-Jean* [17], cut his head off and kidnapped his wife, Cathérine.
[Cathérine was cruelly burned to death after having been tortured.]

On that same occasion, the Iroquois scalped Jean Chicot, a 21-year old man, and left him for dead..

(Journal des Jésuites, p. 153)

[Gustave Lanctot notes that Chicot survived his ordeal.]

17

His real name is Jean Boudart, married to a Cathérine Messier. At the burial services for them both, they were described as having had a morally or spiritually uplifting life.

(Montréal Register)

Léonard Lukos was also killed by the Hurons[18]. He had married a Barbe Poisson on the 12th of October 1648.

(Montréal Register)

August 13th

Jean Hébert was killed by the Iroquois.

(Montréal Register)

[René Jetté notes that he was buried on the 14th.]

August 25th

"We – in Québec – were informed that Denis Archambault had been killed by a cannon which blew up in his face after he had fired it at a party of 60 Iroquois for the third time."

(Journal des Jésuites AND Montréal Register)

November 11th

Guillaume DuPlessis-Bochard, Governor of Trois-Rivières, was on the barge, *La Ste-Anne* when it ran aground on some rocks and filled with water while only 1 league [about 2.5 miles] away from Cap-à-l'Arbre[19].

(Journal des Jésuites, p.164 AND Trois-Rivières Register)

On the same date, three or M. Giffard's French serviteurs [servants] drowned when they went beaver-fur trading at night on Île-d'Orléans.

(Journal des Jésuites, p. 164)

[a. Robert Giffard successfully took over the colonizing activities when Louis Hébert died. He is regarded as being much more successful than Hébert although Hébert died when he was quite young. Ray Douville and J.-Donat Casanova said of Giffard: "The little group (Giffard and his compatriots) formed the true foundation-stone of a new people" ('*La Vie Quotidienne en Nouvelle France*', George Allen & Unwin,1967, p.18).
b. Trading for furs was tightly controlled. Those wishing to do any such trading on their own - as was done here - would have had to do it secretively and at a real risk.]

We meet up with the name 'Cap-à-l'Arbre' several times in the *"Journal des Jésuites"*.

SEE: September 1646, p. 65; 19 May 1650, p. 138 ;1 December 1651, p. 164; 16 October, p. 221; 25 June 1661, p. 299.

18

Father Verreau recalled his marriage date as the 12th of October 1642.

19

A note at the bottom of page 65e of the *"Journal des Jésuites"* fixed that locale at Platon which – in Champlain's time – was called Pointe Ste-Croix, yet another note in 1729 fixed it at St-Jean Deschaillons. Also, Cap-à-l'Arbre is now known as St-Jean Deschaillons.

1652

Guillaume Couillard and his wife Guillemette Hébert ceded a portion of their property to the *fabrique de Notre-Dame de Québec*, and in 1656 *l'ancienne compagnie* granted the rest of the land [needed] for the construction of Notre-Dame Church.

(Registre des actes de foi et hommage, 1673, Volume I, Part II, p. 643)

[a) In a seigneury, we would normally find some land called the *terre de la Fabrique*, not far from the manor, which the seigneur reserved for a church and a presbytery [home for a clergy], and for the support of the curé.

b) The *fabrique* itself was the church council which administered the material affairs of the parish. It was composed of the *curé* [parish priest] and a number of representatives – *marguillers* (churchwardens) – elected by the parishioners. Unfortunately, very few of the parishes were organized enough to have these representative councils. The role of the *fabrique* was essentially economic and used revenues from voluntary contributions and pew rentals to manage the upkeep of the church, the rectory and the cemetery. On occasion, it was even involved in hiring teachers or in providing funds for building a new school.

c) The *ancienne compagnie*, or the *Compagnie de Canada* OR *de la Nouvelle France*, was the direct creation of the government but lacked the spirit of free trade and believed that public funds should not be drawn on to set up the colonies. They wished to limit colonization to those who dealt directly with Indians for the ever-so-important furs and pelts.]

March 1st

According to *"Les Actes de foi et hommage"*, (p. 386 in the copy in the Archives of the Department of Agriculture in Ottawa), Sieur de Chavigny de Berchereau had returned to France to retire. M. [Jean] de Lauzon, the then Governor, had conveyed the fief d'Eschambault to Eléonore de Grandmaison, the wife of the said Sieur Chavigny de Berchereau[20].

During the year, the following individuals were buried after being killed by the Iroquois. Their names were listed in the Montréal Register:
...on the 26th of May, Antoine Bau,
...on the 16th of September, Andre David dit Mingré,
...on the 14th of October, Étienne Tibaut dit LaLochetière.

---

[20]

M. de Berchereau had returned to France because of ill health and died there in 1651; and Eleanor Grandmaison was married for the third time in August 1652 to a Jacques Gourdeau.

(Québec Register)

Two Iroquois, Agontarisati and Taak'enrat had been given over to the Algonquins as compensation for the deaths of an Algonquin and a Huron, (Journal des Jésuites, p. 173). They were sentenced to the *supplice-du-feu* [punishment by fire] but had the good fortune to be baptized by Father Menard the night before they died. The record of their Baptism is in the Trois-Rivières Register, dated 3 July 1652, and reads as follows:

"Anno Dmni 1652, 3 julii ego Renatus Menard sacerdos Societatis Jesu baptisavi sine ceremoniis in sacello nostro captivos duos hostes Agontarisati et Taak'enrat. Prior Franciscus vocatus est, posterior Petrus. Uterque sequenti die igne vitam finiit."

["On the 3rd of July in the year of our Lord, 1652, I, Raymond Menard, priest in the Society of Jesus, baptized two enemies without ceremony in our chapel: Agontarisati and Taak'enrat. The first was named Francis and the other, Peter. On the following day, they died by fire."]

(Journal des Jésuites, p. 173 AND Trois-Rivières Register)

August

Guillaume Guilmot, Sieur DuPlessis de Kerbodot, Governor of Trois-Rivières, was killed by the Iroquois on Lac St-Pierre.

(Journal des Jésuites, p. 174)

1653

May 8th

Pascal Pasquier who worked for M. Claude Charon, was executed for having shot his employer in the throat on the 29th of April in his home on Île-d'Orléans.

(Journal des Jésuites, p. 179 AND Québec Register)

July 20th

The burial of Michel Noël who had been killed by the Iroquois.

(Montréal Register)

1654

April 10th

A 28-year-old man named André Julien dit Vantabon, who worked for Louis Gagné, was crushed to death by a falling tree.

(Québec Register)

June 30th

André Bazin, who worked for M. LeTardif, drowned.

(Idem)

October 10th

A man named Yves Bastar was killed by the Iroquois.

(Montréal Register)

November 10th

Guillaume Boest died after having been shot twice by the Iroquois.

(Québec Registers)

November 23rd

Three Frenchmen were killed by the Iroquois... Jean Languedoc, Louis Lebécheur and Mathieu Labat.

(Trois-Rivières Registers)

November 26th

Michel Morin also died after being shot twice in the head on the 10th of November.

(Québec Register)

November 30th

Pierre DeLaunay was another victim of the Iroquois.

(Idem)

1655

L'ancienne compagnie ceded 2 parcels of land to the fabrique-de-Notre-Dame-de-Québec: the first, located on the Côte-de-la-Montagne, was to serve as a cemetery; and the second, encompassing 8 *arpents* [about 1536 feet square] at Cap-aux-Diamants.

[a] The *ancienne compagnie*, or the *Compagnie de Canada* or *de la Nouvelle France*, was the direct creation of the government but lacked the spirit of free trade and believed that public funds should not be drawn upon to set up the colonies. They wished to limit

colonization to those who dealt directly with Indians for the ever-so-important furs.

b) The *fabrique* itself was the church council which administered the material affairs of the parish. It was composed of the *curé* [parish priest] and a number of representatives – *marguillers* (churchwardens) – elected by the parishioners. Unfortunately, very few of the parishes were organized enough to have these representative councils. The role of the *fabrique* was essentially economic and used revenues from voluntary contributions and pew rentals to manage the upkeep of the church, the rectory and the cemetery. On occasion, it was even involved in hiring teachers or in providing funds for building a new school.

c) A *côte* is a line of settlement along the St. Lawrence River, a tributary or a road.]

Nicholas Dupont was the *marguiller-en-charge* of the Fabrique in Québec during 1655.

(Registre des actes de foi et hommage, Volume I, Part II, pp. 646, 1674)

[The *marguiller-en-charge* or churchwarden was currently responsible for the secular affairs of the parish. It was a position which was sought after by all and which "became a form of consecration for those who had not yet made their fortunes". (Louise Dechêne, "*Habitants and Merchants- 17th Century Montréal*", McGill, 1992, p. 264).]

February 8th

A man named Simon Richaume was crushed by a falling tree.

(Montréal Register)

March 30th

Pierre Juneau was killed by the Iroquois.   *(Québec Register)*

April 12th

Marguerite Sédilot who had first married Jean Aubuchon on the 19th of September 1654 at Trois-Rivières and had then had it declared invalid because of her age, now had her marriage reinstated. She was born on April 4th in 1643 and was, therefore, only 11½ years of age at the time of her marriage.

(Montréal Register)

[Marcel Trudel noted that in order "to enter into a contract of marriage, the groom had to be at least 14... and the bride, at least 12. Both required parental consent, the boy until age 30, and the girl (even if a widow), until the age of 25." ("*Introduction to New France*", Quintin Publications, 1997, p. 255) .]

April 27th

Pierre Chapiteau was killed by the Iroquois.   *(Trois-Rivières Register)*

May 31st

Jean DuLigneron was killed by the Iroquois.   *(Montréal Register)*

June 9th

Marc, one of the *Hospitalières de Québec* servants, was drowned and then buried in Québec.   *(Québec Register)*

July 8th

Jacques Macardé, Demoiselle de Repentigny's *serviteur* [servant], was buried after he died at the Hôpital of Québec.

(Québec Register)

September 18th

Nicholas Pinel dit LaFrance died at the Hôtel-Dieu of Québec, Québec's hospital for the sick, after having been wounded by an arquebus discharged by an Iroquois Indian.

(Idem)

[An arquebus was an old form of firearm first appearing in the 15th century following the invention of gunpowder. It varied in size from a cannon to a musket and was carried by soldiers and supported on a rest. The musket replaced it in the 17th century.]

1656

February 17th

Jacques, *domestique* [domestic servant] for the Ursuline Sisters, died after being stricken by apoplexy.

(Idem)

[Apoplexy is a sudden paralysis with total or partial loss of consciousness or sensation usually as a result of a hemorrhage causing pressure on the brain.]

June 25th

Christophe Roger drowned and was buried in Montréal.

(Montréal Register)

July 12th

Christophe Lacroix was buried in Trois-Rivières after being killed by a Huron Indian.

(Trois-Rivières Register)

July 15th

M. Jacques Maheu's *domestique* named Jacques drowned today.

(Québec Register)

August 28th

Gabriel Rouleau watched as two of his children burned to death as his home burned down.

(Idem)

September 2nd

Father Léonard Gareau, a Jesuit, was buried in Montréal after being mortally wounded by the Iroquois on the 30th of August.

(Montréal Register)

1657

February 28th

The drowning of Charlotte Barbier, the 5-year-old daughter of Gilbert Barbier dit LeMinime.

(Idem)

May 14th

Nicolas Hébert, the nine-year-old son of François Hébert, died after eating a poisonous herb.

(Québec Register)

May 27th

Pierre Duval, 22, married for only ten months, drowned along with Jacques Montfort when their canoe capsized as they tried to board a ship commanded by Captain Marot.

(Journal des Jésuites, p. 113 AND Québec Register)

June 24th

Sieur François Peuvret de Margontier, the son of Jacques Peuvret, *conseiller du Roi*[royal advisor], and *lieutenant criminel* for Perche, drowned at *Cap-à-l'Ange* where he had gone swimming.

(Journal des Jésuites, p. 216 AND Québec Register)

[The *lieutenant criminel* was a judge <u>usually</u> appointed by the King for a Court of royal jurisdiction where all cases except those which were subject to seigneurial justice (minor civil cases, guardianship issues, and property inventories) were heard.]

August 28th

A solemn service was held for the repose of the soul of Jean Danou, a native of Clermont in Anjou [in France], who had drowned at Sault St-Louis while returning from a trip to Onontaïe on which he had served as a guide for Father Duperon. His remains were recovered on *Île-Perrot* and were buried on the 15th of September.

(Montréal Register)

October 25th

The burial of three men who were killed by the Iroquois: Nicolas Godé, 74; Jean Saint-Pair, his son-in-law, 39 and a Royal Notary; and his servant, Jacques Noël, 32.

(Idem)

1658

February 8th

The burial of Gilles Trotier, *interprète* [interpreter]. He left all of his worldly possessions to the Church.

(Idem)

August 4th

M. Paul Chomedey from Maisonneuve was the godfather of a 10-month-old Indian girl whom he had named Marie and adopted as his own.

(Idem)

August 30th

Eloi Jarry dit LaHaye had his daughter Marguerite baptized at a ceremony at which Marguerite Bourgeois served as godmother. Eloi was later kidnapped and killed by the Iroquois.

(Idem)

October 6th

Jean Barry and René Chemin, both employees of M. Eustache Lambert, *marchand* [shopkeeper] in Québec, were drowned at *Cap-Rouge*.

(Québec Register)

December 8th

Monsignor Laval was consecrated as Bishop of Petrée in the St-Germain-des-Prés Church. In memory of his consecration, Mgr. Laval chose the Immaculate Conception as the patron for his Cathedral with St-Louis as its Second Patron.

(Archdiocesan Register)

1659

February 1st

The burial of Pierre Lefebvre, *boulanger* [baker], 24 years of age, who left all of his books to the Church.

(Montréal Register)

May 11th

The burial of François Heude, *matelot* [sailor], and Jean Péleau, *boulanger* [baker], who both drowned at Cap-aux-Diamants.

(Québec Register)

July 20th

Jean Ferré, M. Couillard's servant, drowned while swimming in Rivière-St-Charles.

(Idem)

October 26th

We buried Sylvestre Vacher dit St-Julien who had been killed by the Iroquois near Lac-aux-Loutres.

(Montréal Register)

November 24th

Chevalier Jacques Testard, Sieur de la Forest, married Marie Pournain, 28, the widow of Guillaume de la Bardelière, in Montréal. He died in June 1663 and his widow married Jacques de la Marque in 1668.

(Idem)

[At the end of the 17th century, when the King of France no longer allowed Canadians to become nobles, only one important honor remained, *l'Ordre-Royal-et-Militaire-de-Saint-Louis*. That military order was divided into 8 Grand-Croix, 24 commanders and an unlimited number of *chevaliers* and was the only military order in which New France had the honor of taking part. To obtain the decoration, one had to be an officer in the regular forces which immediately eliminated the entire parish militia system and other ranks. Also, one could only serve the King of France in order to qualify.

The first person to receive the decoration in Canada was Callières, the Governor of Montréal, who received it in 1694, and the first Canadian chevalier was Pierre le Moyne d'Iberville who attained that distinction in 1699. From 1693-1760, *only about 145 men* were so decorated in Canada whereas France decorated 12,180 of its citizens from 1814-1830 alone. After the Conquest, only about a dozen of these *Chevaliers-de-Saint-Louis* remained in Canada and about 6 of those eventually took an oath of alliegance to the King of England, thereby severing their alliegance to Canada and France.

The glory and prestige of the decoration still remains in Canada because of its rarity whereas comparatively little value remains to the holders of the French decoration.]

1660

April 19th

Blaise Juillet dit Avignon and Mathurin Soulard, both companions of Dollard Desormeaux, drowned near Île-St-Paul in Montréal while trying to escape from a party of Iroquois Indians. Blaise was the father of four children.

(Idem)

April 20th

Nicolas Duval, *serviteur du fort* [laborer in the fort], was buried in Montréal after having been killed by the Iroquois on the 19th of the month. He was also one of Dollard Desormeaux's companions on the Long-Sault expedition.

(Idem)

May 15th

The burial of Noël Legal who was only 20 when he drowned in Montréal. He had worked as a servant for the Jesuits.

(Idem)

July 20th

Chartier, *chirurgien* [surgeon], drowned when he went swimming in Montréal.

(Idem)

August 1st

Pierre Bringodin was buried after having been killed by the Iroquois on July 31st. His wife, Marguerite Maillet, drowned on the following day while on her way to Québec from Beauport.

(Québec Register)

August 22nd

Mgr. Laval, the Bishop of Petrée, baptized Angélique, the daughter of Pierre Raguideau dit St-Germain, while he was in Montréal. Lambert Closse, *major* [military rank] in Montréal, was her godfather and Demoiselle Jeanne Mance, *administratrice de l'hôpital* [hospital administratrix], was her godmother.

(Montréal Register)

August 30th

An official ruling from the *officialité* [ecclesiastical court] of Monseigneur de Petrée declared invalid the August 12th 1657 marriage (in Québec)[21] of Pierre Gadois and Marie Pontenier. The said Marie Pontenier married Pierre Martin[22] on the following 3rd of November in Montréal.

MOVEMENT OF THE CATHOLIC POPULATION OF THE PROVINCE OF QUÉBEC 1651 TO 1660

	MARRIAGES	BIRTHS	DEATHS	OTHERS
1651	10	34	16	18
1652	17	46	8	38
1653	16	51	15	36
1654	35	64	24	40

21

From the Archdiocesan Register of Québec.

22

From the Montréal Register.

	MARRIAGES	BIRTHS	DEATHS	OTHERS
1655	22	81	19	62
1656	26	84	22	64
1657	22	83	32	51
1658	35	90	18	72
1659	36	91	31	60
1660	24	113	47	66
TOTALS ➡	243	737	230	507
1608-1660	334	1022	432	590

[Tanguay's 'DEATHS' detail adds up to 232 but his 'TOTAL' is shown as 230.]

1661

March 24th

Urbain Tessier, a 37-year-old father, was abducted by the Iroquois. As of the date of the entry in this *Registre*, we still did not know if he was dead or alive. On the 18th of June of this same year, Michel Messier[23], 21, the husband of Anne Lemoyne, was also abducted by the Iroquois and as of the date of his daughter Jeanne's baptism [18th of June, 1661], we also did not know whether he was dead or alive.

(Montréal Register)

[According to Tanguay's "*Dictionnaire Généalogique*", Urbain Tessier died in Montréal on March 21[st,] 1689 and Michel Messier died in Varennes on November 3rd, 1725.]

March 28th

We buried Vincent Boutereau, 34; Sébastien DuPuy, 27; and Olivier Martin, also 27, after they were all killed by the Iroquois.

April 9th

Charles Sevestre, 16-year-old son of M. Charles Sevestre, drowned in Montréal.

(Idem)

23

These 2 brave citizens [Urbain Tessier and Michel Messier] could easily have returned to the bosoms of their families since they both had numerous descendants.

(Per Tanguay, see the *Genealogical Dictionary*, pp. 427 & 561)

June 24th

The bodies of Jean de Lauzon, *sénéchal du pays* [court officer for the region]; Nicolas Couillard dit Belleroche, 20, son of M. Guillaume Couillard, one of the first residents in this country; and Ignace Sevestre dit Desrochers, 24, were buried together in the same church after they had all been killed by the Iroquois on the 22nd of the month. On the same day, in the same year, and at the same hour, 4 others who had been with those three were also buried together. They were: Elie Jacquet dit Champagne, Mme. de Repentigny's *serviteur* [servant]; Jacques Perroche; and Toussaint and François, M. Couillard's *serviteurs*.

(Notre-Dame de Québec Register AND Journal des Jésuites, p. 298)

July 20th

Lightning struck a woman named Jaquete on the head and killed her as well as a cow which had been standing next to her. She had been the wife of Leguay[24].

(Journal des Jésuites, p. 300)

August 24th

Elie Hanctin dit Lanqueleur, 30, a *cultivateur* [farmer] in Trois-Rivières, was killed by the Iroquois while working in his fields. He had been married since 1657.

(Trois-Rivières Register)

August 30th

Martin Duval, the husband of Antoinette Durand, was killed by the Iroquois.

(Montréal Register)

24

According to the Notre-Dame de Québec Register, Jacquette Vivran, wife of Jean Normand, was killed by lightening on the 19th, and was buried on the 20th. *'LeGuay'* was undoubtedly Jean Normand's surname [or nickname].

(Journal des Jésuites, p. 300).

NOTE:: In the 'Notre-Dame de Québec' Register, on 12 September 1650, we find a record of the marriage of Jean Normand, son of François and Jeanne Boissel, a native of Igré , near Bellesme, in Perche; and Jacquette Riverin, daughter of Grégoire Riverin and of Claudine Ajonne, from True in Poitou. The marriage contract which was approved the day before is in the Clerk of Court Audouard's Office in Québec. The surname *'LeGuay'*, mentioned in the *Journal des Jésuites*, probably comes from the location of his birth, d'Igré, or *LeGuay* in its corrupted form.

(Tanguay)

1662

February 6th

The burial of Sieur Lambert Closse[25], *major* [military rank] in Montréal. He and 12 other Frenchmen perished in a battle with the Iroquois.

(Idem)

May 4th

Jeanne Françoise Poisson, born in 1647, and the daughter of Jean Poisson, seigneur de Gentilly, and of Jacqueline Chamboy, pronounced her vows of *religieuse hospitalière* as [Sister] *Sainte-Gertrude-de-la-Présentation-de-Notre-Dame* in the presence of Mgr. L'Évêque de Petrée. This was the first such religious profession received by Mgr. de Petrée.

1663

In the absence of Governor [Pierre] Dubois d'Avangour, Jacques Descailhaut, Sieur de la Tesserie, exercised his duties as Lieutenant-Governor.

(Conseil Supérieur Register)

June 2nd

Jacques Gourdeau, 41 years of age, Sieur de Beaulieu, the husband of Eléonore de Grandmaison, was buried in Québec after perishing in a May 29th fire which destroyed his home on Île-d'Orléans. His *engagé* [hired helper], Nicolas Duval, suffered the same fate.

(Québec Register)

September 24th

The ship the *Jardin d'Hollande* arrived today. It was commanded by Captain Guyon who was also responsible for several prisoners on board who had been accused of having assassinated the *commandant du Fort de Plaisance*, his brother, the missionary, and several other people.

(Conseil Souverain Register)

During 1663, the royal ships transported a certain number of families as well as some poor young men and women. The Governor and Bishop of Petrée were authorized by the *Conseil Souverain* to provide for their needs as it was deemed necessary.

(Conseil Souverain Register, 10 October 1663)

25

Lambert Closse had married Élizabeth Moyen in 1657.

[The *conseil souverain* was instituted in 1663 to take the place of an executive council and a court of appeal. It became the *conseil superieur early in* the 18th Century. Originally composed of the Governor and Bishop and 5 other members appointed by them, it later consisted of 16 members (with the Intendant serving as president) appointed by the King and a number of Councillor-Assessors, who were young gentlemen destined to be involved in the judicial system. The *conseil* really had jurisdiction only in Canada but it took the place of a provincial *'Parlement'* or high judicial court, and as such reviewed and recorded all of the King's decrees before they were considered law.]

October 10th

Étienne Renault was the *écrivain* [he maintained the log] on the ship *Aigle d'Or* which was at anchor in Québec.

(Conseil Souverain Register)

October 24th

Jacques Fournier, Sieur de la Ville who had married Marguerite Crevier, the daughter of Christophe Crevier in Trois-Rivières in 1657 [the 14th of May], only to have it annulled, now married Hélène Dufiguier in Québec.

(Québec Register)

[Reverend Tanguay wrote that Marguerite Crevier was born in 1645 – nothing more specific. René Jetté noted that she was born around 1643 or 1645. Although her actual age at the time of her marriage might have seemed suspect because of this confusion as to just when she was born, Robert-Lionel Seguin tells us that the marriage was actually annulled because it was proven that it had never been consummated! Louise Dechêne notes that any such non-consummated marriages would be annulled after public proceedings that <u>no one</u> found embarrassing.

Despite the question of consummation, the confusion surrounding her age continued – the 1667 census showed her to be 24 and therefore born in 1643 and the 1683 census showed her to be 38 and therefore born in 1645. Marcel Trudel has perhaps explained this lack of consistency simply by noting that once one had attained the age of majority and the age for marrying or proclaiming of religious vows in the 17th century, very little importance was attached to precise ages.

Incidentally, both Marguerite Crevier and her husband remarried and had many children.]

According to the Conseil Souverain Register for the 3rd of November 1663, it appeared that the annulment was due to an *empêchement dirimant*.
[In the eyes of the Roman Catholic Church, an *empêchement dirimant* was any of several obstacles which automatically rendered a marriage null and void. It simply made one incapable of contracting a valid marriage. The obstacles included: being too young (in the 1600 and 1700s – 14 for men and 12 for women); being impotent and therefore not able to consummate the marriage; already being married; both parties

not being baptised in the Roman Catholic faith; being in a religious order; being bound by a vow of chastity in a religious group; killing one's own or a particular person's spouse specifically to be able to marry that particular person; marrying someone who was too closely-related by blood; marrying someone who was insane at the time of marriage; in some instances, marrying someone who was legally related by reason of adoption; marrying someone who was too-closely-related to one's deceased wife; being abducted if the abduction was meant to force marriage; and marrying someone such as the mother, sister or daughter of one's deceased fianceé. Although this last obstacle might seem somewhat strange today, it was apparently meant to deal with questions of propriety or appearance.

In addition, marriage during certain periods such as during Lent, the 40 day period of fasting immediately preceeding Easter, made a marriage unlawful although not nul and void. If one married on such a proscribed date, than they might be unable to have a banquet or a marriage cortège which was the traditional ceremonial escorting of the bride and groom to the church for their wedding. Again, one could have obtained dispensation from just about anything but only by paying a sum which would vary according to the impediment to be overcome.]

October 30th

Pierre Duquet, *notaire royal* [royal notary], purchased Guillaume Audouard's notarial records.

(Conseil Souverain Register)

[Guillaume Audouard began his career at Trois-Rivières in 1648 and was, in fact, the first official notary of New France. His predecessors had performed notarial duties but more because they had to although they had not necessarily been authorized or trained to. Audouard began collecting the scattered documents of those predecessors to make them a part of his Registry which he then sold in its entirety to Pierre Duquet who was then but 20 years of age and freshly out of college. In the process he, Duquet, Canada's first native-born notary, also succeeded Audouard as notaire royal [royal notary]. Although he was a very industrious youth, Pierre apparently did not give the required attention to his notarial acts and so many errors and omissions can be found in those acts.]

December 22nd

A young widow, Marie Charlotte de Poitiers[26], requested permission to have her marriage contract dated the 2nd of May 1660 inserted in the records. Until that time, she had been uncertain as to whether or not her husband, Joseph Hébert, the grandson of Louis Hébert, was dead or alive. At the end of October,

---

26

Daughter of Pierre de Poitiers, Sieur du Buisson, *capitaine d'Infanterie* [infantry Captain], and Hélène de Belleau, from Sevestre d'Amiens in Picardie.

1662, several prisoners of the Iroquois had returned from Iroquois country and had vouched for his death[27].   *(Idem)*

[Louis Hébert died in 1627 and left 3 children. His only son, Guillaume, was married in 1634 and died in 1639, also leaving only one son, Joseph, whose fate was attested to above. *His* only son, also Joseph, died as a youngster before 1666 and was the last of Louis Hébert's direct male descendants.]

1664

January 6th

Jean Gitton, *marchand* [merchant], put in a claim for September 1663 damages due to late delivery by the 28-man ship *Le Taureau* which he had chartered to freight to this country.   *(Idem)*

February 8th [a Friday]

M. Henry de Bernières, while performing some of the functions of parish priest in Notre-Dame-de-Québec church, drew to the attention of the Conseil that despite having already received and published the banns of marriage for the first time for Pierre Martin, he was of the opinion that the said Martin was having epileptic seizures and that he felt that he should advise the appropriate officials before continuing. He felt that they should look into the problem to determine if it was perhaps wiser to return people with similar problems to France because of the great dangers from the waters and snows and fires which they all continually faced in this new nation. Also, any such illnesses could not be handled by the hospitals and so it was very difficult to protect these people in the new nation. Although this particular case was not an *empêchement écclesiastique* [for a specific religious reason], he had delayed further publication of the banns until the Conseil could take action on his concerns. Martin had spent some time with Jean and François Pelletier, and François had stated that Martin had – even on the night before – had another epileptic seizure, and that it was - to his knowledge - the fifth time. Martin in turn had stated that he had

---

27

The '*Relations des Jésuites*' made mention of the brutal killing of Joseph Hébert in these terms: "As for M. Hébert who had been shot in the shoulder and arms, he was given to the Onneïout Iroquois and was stabbed by some of the local drunks."
(Accounts of the Jésuites, Volume III, 1661, p. 35)

On the 11th of January in 1667, Marie Charlotte de Poitiers married Simon Lefebvre in Québec. The Coutancineau, Voyer, Gingras and Hardy families from Pointe-aux-Trembles can be included among their ancestors.
(Genealogical Dictionary, Volume 1, p. 365)

no such knowledge of that event and could remember nothing [not an unusual reaction for epileptics] of those supposed-occurrences.

In response to the above, the Conseil Souverain permitted the said Pierre Martin[28] to marry in this country if that was what he wished to do, but ordered that he and his wife would be obliged to return to France for the above-stated reasons if he were to have another seizure.

(Idem)

February 10th

Jean Levasseur, *huissier* [bailiff or process-server], posted a decree made by His Majesty at the main entrance of the Notre-Dame de Québec Church. The decree, dated the previous 18th of September, announced that His Majesty had authorized and set up a local Conseil Souverain and nominated specially-selected individuals to serve as *conseillers* [counselors], *procureur général* [attorney-general] and *greffier* [clerk of the court].

(Idem)

In that same month, an Indian called Robert Haché[29] had met a young woman and had violated her while he was very drunk. The young woman was Marthe Hubert, the wife of Lafontaine and a resident on *Île-d'Orléans*. Shortly after being taken prisoner, Robert Haché succeeded in escaping from prison. In the meantime, the procureur du Roi [royal counselor] summoned: Noël Tek8erimat, chief of the Algonquins in Québec; Kaetmagnechis, commonly known as Boyer, chief of Tadoussac; Mangouche, chief of the Nepissinien Indians; Gahyk8an, chief of the Iroquets [a tribal nation in the heart of Canada] ; Nauch8ape8ith dit le Saumonnier, chief of the (tribal name not readable, per Fr. Tanguay); and Jean Baptiste Pipouikih, an Abnakiois captain, to meet before the *Conseil Souverain* to answer for the said Robert Haché and to be formally advised that the penalty for the crime of rape was hanging and strangling. The

---

28

NOTE: Pierre Martin married Joachine Lafleur on the 11th of February 1664. They raised 6 children in Canada.

29

As far back as in 1645, he had passed himself off as servant for life for the Jesuit Fathers but his poor conduct had forced the Fathers – in 1659 – to evict him from their house.

(Journal des Jésuites, p. 265)

procureur [solicitor] – in turn – wished to learn about the ways of those friendly Indians who ignored their laws and penalties for criminals. Nicolas Marsolet, *interprète*[interpreter-spokesman], conveyed that information to the Indians in the presence of Father Druillette, a Jesuit; the Indian chiefs, speaking through Noël Tek8erimat, interpreted by Marsolet, answered in turn "that for many successive years they had always maintained good relations with the French, and if their young had not behaved well in certain instances and they had had reason to complain, than the French youngsters had not been any less exempt; that until now they had not been given to understand that rape was punishable by death, although certainly murder was; and so the action of the said Robert Haché, although clearly not proper, should not be considered at its worst here since it was a first offense, nor should it be allowed to harm such an old friendship; but for the future, they would voluntarily agree [to abide by the laws], and for that purpose, they would now require that the matter be drafted in writing, so that it remain for future generations to see".

After deliberating, the Conseil deferred the punishment which the said Robert Haché deserved for his crime, except for some civil compensation for Marthe Hubert. To prevent similar problems in the future, [the Conseil] ordered, with the assent of the chiefs, that the Indians would henceforth be subject to the penalties called for by French laws and ordinances for murder and rape.

(Conseil Souverain Register, Edicts and Ordinances, Volume II, p. 16)

[The exact spelling of <u>Indian</u> <u>names</u> is almost impossible to determine since they were often distorted both by the French and by the English who usually phonetically transcribed the names. One especially peculiar sound was the sound of an 8 or '*huit*', a whistling sound in French. The 8's have been retained in many of the old names.]

March 29th

Mgr. Laval issued an ordinance requiring that fathers and mothers <u>not delay</u> with baptizing their children after their births.

(Archdiocesan Register of Québec)

NOTE: This ordinance was renewed [and considerably strengthened] on the 5th of February 1677.

May 26th

The ship *Le Noir* commanded by Sieur Pierre Fillye arrived from Holland with 300 men sent by His Majesty. According to the Conseil Supérieur's Ordinance, they were to be allocated in the following manner: 150 men to Québec and vicinity; 75 men to Trois-Rivières; 25 men to Cap-de-la-Madeleine; and 50 men to Montréal.

(Conseil Supérieur Register)

June 13th

His Majesty the King of France sent 2 vessels commanded by Captains Gargot and Guillon from the port of La Rochelle with about 300 people aboard to colonize New France. Of that total, 75 were left on Île-de-Terreneuve in Plaisance and as many as 60 died while en route. Another 159 disembarked in Québec – that included 21 people from 6 families; and 38 girls moved into the Québec, Trois-Rivières and Montréal areas. All but three of them were married during that same year and one of those was captured by the Iroquois at Île-d'Orléans and held captive. Among the hundred others, about 20 men were ready to do some kind of work whereas the others were too sick or so weak that they were not even able to stand; the remainder were young clerks, students or others who had – for the most part – never worked. Thirty-eight were hospitalized and 12 died; the others were distributed among families in the Québec and neighboring areas, 10 in Trois-Rivières and 6 in Montréal.

(Excerpt from a letter dated the 13th of June 1664 from the Conseil Souverain)

August 27th

The marriage of Jean Poitras, who became the father of 27 children!

(Québec Register)

[Tanguay's "*Dictionnaire Généalogique*" lists 2 wives/mothers for his 27 children. Marie-Xainte Vivier who bore 17 children over a 26-year period and Marie-Anne De La Voye who bore another 10 over a 15-year period. Jean died – a very happy man – when he was about 74 years of age.]

August 28th

The burial of Pierre Raguideau dit St-Germain who had been *sergent royal* [royal solicitor] of the *Sénéchaussée* [jurisdiction] of Montréal, *notaire royal* [royal notary], and a victim of Iroquois cruelty.

(Montréal Register)

In 1664, the garrison at the fort in Québec was under the command of Captain Louis Peronne, Sieur de Mazé, and [counselor] in the *Conseil Souverain*.

(Conseil Souverain Register)

1665

January 14th

Nicolas Marsolet[30] from St-Agnan had purchased the home of Guillaume Bonhomme, and then sold it to the Conseil Souverain for 230 *livres* [about $46.00] to house the *exécuteur des hautes oeuvres* [public executioner].

(Conseil Souverain Register)

April 29th

A young *militaire* [serviceman] named Laurent Philippe dit Lafontaine, the son of a *notaire* [notary] of the town of Blois, had made numerous trips as a year-round *courrier* [courier] for the Governors and officers of Canada for about 4 years and now asked the Conseil Souverain for a salary.

(Idem)

August 6th

The burial of [Pierre] Couc dit Lafleur, 41, one of M. de Froment's soldiers, who had married Marie Mite8ameg8k8e in 1657 in Trois-Rivières. He had been shot accidentally by one of his companions. "Occisus glande catapultae[31] fortuito â socio." [32]

(Trois-Rivières Register)

[a] "Killed with a lead projectile catapulted by an ally."

b) For more on the problems encountered when spelling or pronouncing Indian names, please see my comments after the February 10th of 1664 entry.]

30

Marsolet, a native of Rouën [Normandy, France], came to Québec with Champlain in 1613. He was only 12 years old and before long became familiar with the Montagnaise and Algonquin languages. He was the interpreter for the French for a long time. In 1629, when Québec was captured by Kirk, he surrendered to the English. He later stated that the English had forced him to stay with them. He obtained several rights to property and settled on one of them – Marsolet Meadows (les Prairies Marsolet) – where he raised his large family.

31

Glans-dis was a lead bullet.

32

Catapultae was a catapult or military device for throwing stones, spears, arrows, bullets of some kind, etc. .

November 25th

Pierre Pichet or Picher, 29, a native of St-Georges parish in the diocese of Poitiers, married Cathérine Durand, 26, in Québec. She was a native of St-Eustache in Paris.

(Québec Register)

NOTE:: At the time of the marriage, we find the following petition dated the 11th of September in 1673 in the Register of the Conseil Souverain:

"The petition of Pierre Picher confirming that he had been in this country since 1642, [and that] Louis Picher, his brother, had sent him a *lettre missive* [a letter, usually sworn to before a sovereign. by which someone could take some sort of action] in which he announced that Pierre's wife, Marie Lefebvre, was dead: because of that notice, Pierre had married his fiancée, Cathérine Durand [on this date in 1665]. Three children were born of this marriage: Jean-Baptiste, 7 years of age; Adrien, 4 years of age; and Marie-Madeleine, 3 years of age. The petitioner did not receive any further news from his family nor from those of the said 'deceased' Lefebvre until 1671, when a man coming from France told him that his ex-wife was still alive, and what had been told to him [earlier] was simply not true. He immediately met to discuss the situation with the Bishop of Petrée who was preparing for a return trip to France. The Bishop promised him that he would check on it and would advise him of his findings. [Tanguay is not entirely clear here as to just which course of action was to be taken by the Bishop or by Picher since we suddenly find Picher himself preparing to go to France to do the searching for his ex-wife]. After securing a leave of absence, Picher left for France, where he found Marie Lefebvre still living, and then knew that he had been deceived by the lettre missive. Pierre was very fond of his three children and of his second wife, Catherine Durand, whom he had quite innocently deceived.

He set out to bring Marie Lefebvre with him to Canada as the Bishop had advised. Unfortunately [for her but certainly not for him], Marie died [and was buried at sea] on the return-trip on the ship *La Nouvelle France* commanded by Captain Poullet. Pierre and Catherine then met with the Bishop shortly after he had returned home but they were now faced with the reality of no longer being legally married since Marie had still been alive at the time of his marriage to Catherine. In addition [to having had 2 wives for a while], of course, their children's legal status was also in doubt since they were no longer legally able to inherit from their parents without an appeal. So they sought to have their marriage of the 25th of November rehabilitated before Fillion, a notary. This would also have allowed the children as well as any further offspring to be legally able to inherit from their parents. So, the original contract of marriage between Picher and Durand on a copy carefully checked and signed by a notary, Vachon; a statement made on the 22nd of April in 1673 by Louis Picher, who was responsible for the care of Mgr. le Duc Davynion's clothing, before Sainfray and LeSemelier, notaries at the *Chatelet de Paris* [a small court in Paris]; testimony made by Sieur Dudouyt and dated today, stating that he had renewed the marriage of the said Pierre Picher and Catherine Durand in the eyes of the Church, on the 9th of the current month; a verbal opinion from the *procureur général*'s [attorney-general's] replacement – all things were considered. The Conseil – acting in lieu of the letters from the Chancellory – legitimized the issued children of Picher and Catherine Durand and declared them competent to succeed them, did order and does order that the contract of marriage between the said Picher and the said Durand was now a legitimate and valid one.

And is held that the *grand-vicaire* [the Bishop's representative] of the Sieur Bishop of Petrée, *vicaire apostolique* [the intermediary between the French King and Canada] in this nation, shall be advised by the said substitute to await the decisions of the Conseil before rehabilitating any people in similar situations by the use of the sacrament of marriage."

(SIGNED.)

Frontenac

1665-66

The first head count or census in New France was made in 1666. The specific time of the Census was not given and it seemed impossible to ascertain if it only included the population of 1665 without including the colonists who had arrived during the Summer of 1666. Had it been done in the Spring or in the Fall of 1666? Only by studying the Parish Registers were we able to ascertain whether it had been done in February and March 1666 and as a result could not include the names of those who had arrived during the following Summer. To ensure myself of that fact, after having compiled the names of several children whose ages were under 6 months, I set up the following table up by the birth dates of those same children.

In the census, I found that:

Marie-Madeleine, daughter of Philippe Matou, was 6 months old.
(the Registre showed the 5th of July 1665 as her birth date.)
Ignace, son of Sébast Liénard, 6 months old, born on the 16th of April 1665
Madeleine, daughter of Et. Sedilot, 6 months old, born on the 12th of June 1665
Élizabeth, daughter of Jean Lehoux, 3 months old, born on the 12th of October 1665
Nicolas, son of G. Bonhomme, 3 months old, born on the 25th of October 1665
Marie Barbe, daughter of Joach. Girard, 15 days old, born on the 27th of January 1666
François, son of René Emond, 12 days old, born on the 30th of January 1666
Marguerite, daughter of Pierre Tremblay, 3 months old, born on the 4th of October 1665
Marie-Anne, daughter of Jean Caron, born on the 11th of November 1665
Marie-Madeleine, daughter of Paul Chalifour, born on the 25th of March 1665
Marie-Charlotte, daughter of Louis Artus, 6 months old, born on the May 15th 1665.

Then, I verified that the children who were born after March 1666 had not been entered in the Census. Among others - all born in 1666 -,

Cathérine, the daughter of Gabriel Celle-Duclos, had been born on May 2nd,
Françoise, the daughter of Pierre Chamarre, had been born on August 3rd,
Cathérine, the daughter of André Charly, had been born on June 3rd,
and Pierre, the son of Guill. Constantin, had been born on April 21^{s}

...proof certain that the census had been taken before April 1666 and only reflected the 1665 population.

1666

There were still only 7 parishes or missions in all of New France which maintained Registers for the vital information of its people:

1. Québec whose Registers opened in 1621.
2. Trois-Rivières whose Registers opened in 1635.
3. Sillery whose Registers opened in 1636.
4. Montréal whose Registers opened in 1642.
5. Ste-Anne-de-Beaupré whose Registers opened in 1657.
6. Château Richer whose Registers were opened in 1661.
7. Ste-Famille-de-l'Île-d'Orléans whose Register opened in 1666.

January 14th

François Lemaistre-Lamorille, 35, was buried in Trois-Rivières. He had married a Judith Rigaud in 1654. The record of his burial is reduced to the following words: "miserabiliter trucidatus est sine vela voce interiit."

(Trois-Rivières Register)

["He was cruelly massacred and passed away without the slightest sound."]

May 31st

We found the body of François Dumontier after an accident on the road to St-Michel[33]. He was immediately buried in Québec.

(Québec Register)

33

The concession 'dite St-Michel' was located to the north of the Rivière-St-Charles.
[Defining a *concession* might be in order here. One of the essential duties of a seigneur was the granting of land. He was obliged to grant sufficient land to every settler whom he recruited or who presented himself. This grant, or *concession*, was first attested to by a *billet* (certificate) *de concession* and once the settler had proved that he was serious about taking up residence, a *contrat de concession* was signed. If the seigneur was negligent in his duty to grant land, the Intendant (Chief Administrative Officer) could replace him or even add this land to the King's domain . This happened in 18 seigneuries in 1741 alone! (Marcel Trudel, "*Introduction to New France*",1997, Quintin Publications, p. 175.)]

1666-1667

Almost all of the marriages celebrated in Montréal during the years 1666 and 1667 had MM. Paul DeMaisonneuve and Dupuy, *major* [military rank], as well as a large number of relatives and friends as witnesses. This is one way of showing the spirit of comradeship which existed among the families during that period.

February 4th (1667)

The first ball given in Canada was held at Sieur Chartier's.

(Journal des Jésuites, p. 353)

February 14th

Nicolas Grisard, Sieur Desormeaux, *garde-magasin* [storekeeper], accused a *soldat* [soldier] of theft. The guilty party was condemned to one hour on the *cheval-de-bois* with 6-pound weights attached to each of his feet.

(Conseil Souverain Register)

[A *cheval-de-bois* was a kind of wooden horse used to punish people who were made to ride the horse for varying amounts of time with weights attached to their feet.] Another thief was also found guilty of the theft of 13 minots [about 13.65 bushels] of corn and condemned to be *battu et flétri de verges* [birched and branded] by the *éxécuteur de la haute justice* [public executioner] in both Upper and Lower Québec and to a 23 livre [abt $4.60] fine.

(Idem)

June 2nd

Two criminals, Pierre Nicolas dit Lavalée and René Jouchon, *soldats* [soldiers], were sentenced as *voleurs* [thieves] and *déserteurs* [deserters]:

1. Pierre Nicolas dit Lavalée, for a night time robbery from the Hospitalières, was sentenced to be branded in the shape of a *fleur-de-lis;* to spend 4 hours in the *carqan* [to spend that time in an iron collar attached to a pole with weights attached to his feet] and 3 years at hard labor; for having stolen a pair of wilderness snowshoes, he was sentenced to have his right ear cut off; and for desertion, he was sentenced to be hanged and to have his possessions confiscated.

2. René Jouchon, *déserteur* and *voleur*, was sentenced to stand at the foot of the gallows and to assist - with a rope around his neck - during the execution of the said Lavalée; and to be birched and branded in the shape of a *fleur-de-lis;* and to be held in prison in leg irons until it was otherwise ordered.

(Idem)

June 6th

A *soldat* [soldier] named Maugrain had been convicted of indecent assault on a young girl. He was sentenced to receive 12 lashes of a birch, in the presence of that young girl and of her mother and 2 other women; and to pay the costs for the proceeding.

(Idem)

On that same day, a man named Jean Caré was sentenced to be whipped in the Public Squares of both the Upper and Lower City and to pay a reasonable fine for having stolen 292 *livres* [about $60.00] from M. Pommier, a missionary at Île-d'Orléans.

(Idem)

A decision rendered against 12 *marchands* [shopkeepers] for having sold some *eau-de-vie* [brandy] to Indians ordered them to pay fines ranging from 50 to 200 *livres*, [abt $10.00-40.00] and one month in prison of which one hour a day for fifteen days was to be spent on the *cheval-de-bois* with a sign reading: 'for having sold some *eau-de-vie* to the Indians'.

(Idem)

[A *cheval-de-bois* was a kind of wooden horse used to punish people who were made to ride the horse for varying amounts of time with weights attached to their feet.]

June 27th

The four sons of Pierre Legardeur de Repentigny revealed in a petition that their father had come to Canada in 1636 with his family and his *papiers de noblesse* and they asked that the papers be recorded.

(Idem)

[*Papiers de noblesse* or 'Letters Patent of Nobility' are documents open to public examination and which, in this case, would seem to have granted a title.]

June 28th

A *faux monnayeur* [counterfeiter] died today on the gallows in Québec.

(Journal des Jésuites, p. 354)

July 22nd

The burial of Sieur Bondy, who drowned while drunk near *Île-d'Orléans* on the 19th of the month. He was buried like a dog near the Jesuits mill.

(Journal des Jésuites, p. 355)

[Public drunkenness was expressly forbidden and cause for losing one's right to be buried with the blessing of the Church.]

Here are the names of the ships which visited the Port of Québec in the Summer of 1667:

1. The *Oranger* on July 1st ,
2. The *Nouvelle France* on July 2nd,
3. The *Saint-Philippe* on July 29th,
4. The *Saint-Sébastien* on August 5th,
5. The *Sainte-Cathérine* on September 12th,
6. The *Prophète Élie* on September 12th,
7. The *Saint-Louis* on September 25th.

1668

October 1st

A man named Pierre Pinel, accused and convicted of raping Ursule Trut, a 10½ year old child, and Geneviève Hayot, a 10 year old child, was sentenced to have his head shaved and to be birched by *l'exécuteur de la haute justice* [public executioner] until blood was drawn, at the Public Squares and other such locations in both Upper and Lower Québec, and moreover he was condemned to hard labor for nine years. In order to accomplish that, it was ordered that irons be placed on his feet and that he be brought to jail on the first ship bound for France.

(Conseil Souverain Register)

[Due to the size of the colony, there were no facilities for long-term incarceration and so those prisoners had to be shipped back to France.]

October 29th

Martin, Sieur de St-Aignant, juge prévost [provost judge] of Beaupré and of Île-d'Orléans, exchanged a house in the town of Roche-Beaucort, diocese of Périgord, for Île-d'Orléans property measuring 2 *arpents* [about 384 feet] by 3 *perches* [about 57.5 feet] owned by Pierre Roussert dit Beaucort.

(Records of Aubert, Royal Notary)

[a) A *juge prévost* was a judge in a lower seigneurial court, i.e. a court at the lower end of the judicial system. They were called lower courts because they could not hear all cases and because the court officers were therefore only entitled to lower fees, i.e. two-thirds of the royal-court fees.

b) As was true of most French units of measurement at the time, the values of the *perche* and of the *arpent* were not consistent and would often vary from one province to another. A '*perche de Paris*' was equal to 18 feet, whereas a '*perche royale et forestière*' equaled 22 feet, and a '*perche moyenne*' equaled about 20 feet. One *arpent* was made up of 100 *perches* and therefore also varied according to the province. Standardization attempts were slow in coming especially since merchants often used stones instead of the recommended iron-weighted 'measurements of Paris'.]

November 2nd

A man by the name of Gaboury who had been duly convicted of the crime of rape which was punishable with all of the severity of law, received the following sentence: he was to have his head shaved and to be birched near the Public Square in Québec, and to serve nine years of hard labor, in addition to paying a fine of 500 *livres* [about $100.00]. Half of that fine was to be applied to the care and maintenance of the violated girl for two years as a boarder at the Ursuline Convent in Québec; and the rest was for hospital and court costs.

That same year, in the *Registre des actes de foi et hommage,* (Volume I, Part II, p. 493), we found a note regarding a place called the *Pointe-des-Roches* in Lower Québec which, in 1660, was ceded to Sieur Simon Denys "to build a tower made of stone to fortify the said location and on the tower, a windmill which shall serve for the defense of the Lower City whenever necessary, and there shall be kept in front of the tower, a place large enough to build a platform to place the battery of cannons which are now in the city's market square".

In 1663, M. de Tracy negotiated with the Iroquois to return any French citizens whom they held captive. Among those prisoners was a young girl named Jeanne Baillargeon.

NOTE: "After having massacred several families and taken several prisoners, the Iroquois pursued the Hurons up to *Île-d'Orléans,*. Among others, they kidnapped a Jeanne Baillargeon, a young girl of about 9 years of age[34] who was then brought to their territory where she lived for almost 9 years. She became so accustomed to their ways of doing things that she resigned herself to living with them for the rest of her life. When M. de Tracy forced the Indians to return all of their French captives, she ran off into the forest for fear of having to return home. Once she was satisfied that she would be safe, a nun suddenly appeared before her and threatened to punish her if she did not return with the French. Fear drove her from the forest to join the other captives who were being freed. Upon her return, M. de Tracy gave her 50 *écus* to marry her; but he wished that she first be placed with the Ursulines to rekindle her spirit of Christianity which had become very weak while she was among the Iroquois. When she saw a picture of Mère Marie de St-Joseph, she cried: "Ah! It was she who spoke to me.......and...............she wore the same habit."

(Letter from Mère de l'Incarnation to the Ursulines de Tours)

34

She had been taken away in 1655 and was only 4 years of age.

[Until 1794, an *écu* (or crown) was worth 5 *livres* o about $1.00 so the 50 *écus* given by de Tracy was worth about $10.00]

1670

A decree urged parents to marry off their children at a young age.

(Archdiocesan Register of Québec, A, p. 514)

[Marcel Trudel places the legal marriage age for a groom at 14 and a bride at 12. The King began to encourage early marriages with financial subsidies as high as "an annual pension of 300 *livres* ($60.00) to fathers having 10 children and 400 *livres* ($80.00) to fathers having 12" (*'Introduction to New France'*, Quintin Publications, 1997, p. 140) because so few immigrants wished to migrate or remain in New France. The birth rate was often the highest in the world, reaching as high as 65.2 children per 1000 residents as opposed to a high of 55 per 1000 in other areas.]

January 4th

A French woman named Renée Chauvreux, a native of Orléans, who had arrived the previous Fall, was found dead in the snow.

(Québec Register)

September 2nd

The burial of François Bedard who also drowned in Québec. He was a native of Cogne in the diocese of LaRochelle.

(Idem)

MOVEMENT OF THE CATHOLIC POPULATION OF THE PROVINCE OF QUÉBEC 1661 TO 1670

	MARRIAGES	BIRTHS	DEATHS	OTHERS
1661	31	114	50	64
1662	39	144	34	110
1663	67	143	35	108
1664	38	204	38	166
1665	74	178	54	124
1666	35	206	54	152
1667	75	227	33	194
1668	84	211	31	180
1669	125	288	61	227
1670	122	311	85	226
TOTALS ➡	690	2026	475	1551
1608-1670	1024	3048	907	2141

1671

June 22nd

Julien Dufour, 18, a native of Rouën [Normandy, France], drowned in Lower Town. He worked for M. Michel Guyon-DuRonvray, *charpentier de navires* [shipbuilder].

(Québec Register)

July 16th

Charles Menard, 35, a native of Saint-Malo, drowned opposite Québec. He was a matelot [sailor] who worked for M. de Chambly.

(Idem)

July 23rd

Étienne Tessier, 15, drowned off the Isles.

(Idem)

December 10th

Henri Piot, 18, a native of Rouën [Normandy, France], accidentally drowned in Mme. Daillebout's fountain while working for [her husband] the Governor.

(Idem)

1672

March 19th

The burial of J. Bte. Halay, the husband of Mathurine Valet, on the same day that he was found dead in the woods.

(Idem)

June 9th

Jacques Bertault and Gilette Baune, his wife, and their daughter Isabelle were convicted of having intentionally poisoned and killed Isabelle's husband, Julien Latouche, and are sentenced as follows:

"Jacques Bertault and Gilette Baune...the Bertaults were [each] to be removed from their Québec prisons by *l'exécuteur-de-la-haute-justice* [the public executioner], brought before the city's parish church, both with ropes around their necks and burning torches in their hands; he, Bertault, '*nud en chemise*', and she, Baune, also '*nue en chemise*', but from the shoulders to the waist, and there, kneeling, to beg for God's and the King's forgiveness for the crimes which they had committed: moreover Bertault was sentenced to be strangled on a *croix St-André*, which was to be placed on a scaffolding set up for that purpose in the main square of the Upper City, and then to have both arms and legs broken by sharp blows from an iron rod: also condemned Baune to be present at the execution of her husband, and to be hanged and strangled in a gallows which was also to have been built for that purpose in the said place; ordered further that after the execution of Bertault, his body was to be brought on the 'wheel' to the Public Square at Cap-aux-Diamants, to serve as an example; and, in consideration of the [youthful] age³⁵ of the said Isabelle Bertault, and in good faith, [the Conseil] sentenced [Isabelle] Bertault to pay a reasonable fine in the stated form and manner, and to assist at the execution of her father and her mother; also sentenced Bertault, Baune and Isabelle, jointly, to a fine of 60 *livres* [about $12.00] to be applied, half to the Récollets to pray for the rest of the soul of the said Julien Latouche and to pay the [court] expenses, the balance of their belongings already obtained and yet to be confiscated for the King; and

---

35

She was only 13½ years old.

obligated the Conseil to return to Nicolas and Jeanne Bertault, minor children of the said Jacques Bertault and Gillette Baune, the remaining half of the fine together with the said confiscation.   **Courcelle**

(Conseil Souverain Register)

[a] *'Nud en chemise'*, or more correctly written *'nud , en chemise'* simply meant that the prisoner was to be executed while naked except for a shirt or shift of some kind. In Gilette Baune's case, *'nue en chemise'* more correctly written *'nue , en chemise'* (*depuis les épaules jusqu'à la ceinture*), simply meant that she was also to be executed while naked except for a shift or shirt covering her shoulders to her waist.

b) A *croix St-André* was a cross shaped like an X similar to the one on which he was martyred in about 70 AD.

c) The practice of breaking the limbs on a wheel was, appropriately enough, referred to as 'breaking on the wheel' and referred to an instrument of torture where the victim's arms and legs were stretched along the spokes and his limbs broken by blows from an iron bar.

d) Although it might not seem as if he had been spared very much suffering here, the appropriate officials had apparently sought to have Bertault's right arm broken by a swift blow from an iron bar before being strangled and having his other three limbs broken after. The Conseil Souverain had decided instead that he should be strangled *before* having all four of his limbs broken by swift blows from that same bar.]

1673

March 6th

"Charles Alexis dit Dessessards, convicted of having ambushed a man named Herme, his *camarade de voyage* [travel companion], and of having stolen his clothing and furs, shall be escorted by *l'exécuteur-de-la-haute-justice* [public executioner] to the Public Square in Québec, on a Monday at three o'clock in the afternoon, and there on a gallows to be built for that purpose, will have his arms and legs broken by 4 sharp blows; he will then be strangled and placed on a wheel where his body shall remain until seven o'clock in the evening. His body will be brought to the hanging gallows to remain until it has been totally consumed. Also sentenced to pay a fine of 200 *livres* [about $40.00] to the King, to return the stolen items, and to have his remaining belongings confiscated. And until Charles Alexis was apprehended, he was to be executed in effigy at the hanging gallows, on a Monday, at the above hour."

(Idem)

October 17th

The burial at Château-Richer of Nicolas Maheu who was killed by a falling tree. A native of the diocese of Meaux, he had married a Parisian, Marie Guillaume from St-Médard, at the Ange-Gardien church in 1671.

(Château Richer Register)

October 18th

The Conseil sentenced a man named Chollet to 2 hours *de carqan* [in an iron collar attached to a pole, undoubtedly with weights attached to his feet] in Lower City carrying a placard reading: "*Serviteur domestique*[domestic servant] who, for the first time, left his master's worksite without permission."

1674

January 29th

After several *propriétaires des terres et emplacements* [property owners] had disagreements because of some differences found between their *arpenteurs'* [land-surveyors'] compasses and other land-surveying tools, the Conseil directed the surveyors to place their compasses and land-surveying instruments into the hands of Martin Boutet, *professeur des mathématiques dans la quinzaine*[within 2 weeks], so that they could be standardized by him, and ordered that no *arpenteur* [surveyor] would – in the future – be allowed to survey, unless Boutet had standardized their tools beforehand.

(Conseil Souverain Register)

August 25th

Jean Guerganivet dit l'Espérance, a resident of Champigny, sold a dwelling with 9 *arpents* of frontage by 40 of depth [300 acres] at Rivière-aux-Roches, Saints-Anges seigneurie, for 55 *livres* and 20 *sols* [about $11.20] to Jean Juchereau, Sieur de la Ferté.

(Duquet's Records)

[Based on a value of 5/6 acre per square *arpent*. As was true of most French units of measurement at the time, however, the value of the *arpent* was not at all consistent and could vary from one province to another. Standardization attempts were slow in coming especially since merchants often used stones instead of the recommended iron-weighted 'measurements of Paris'.]

1675

January 28th

The governors and seigneurs made it their duty to give Christian names to Indians and to their children over the baptismal fonts. They also tried to use the Indian chiefs or members of their tribes as godfathers and godmothers. That is why M. J.-Baptiste LeGardeur de Repentigny, the husband of Marguerite Nicolet, today had his son named François by Marie Makats8ing8ots, an Algonquin.   NOTE: Also see Blondeau in 1715.

(Repentigny Register)

[For more information regarding problems encountered when spelling or pronouncing Indian names, please see my comments after the entry of February 10th 1664.]

June 27th

Jean LePicard, a 40-year-old *soldat* [soldier], was put to death by the Iroquois. "Tormenti ritu subito perierat." was written in his burial record.

(Trois-Rivières Register)

["He perished quickly in a ritual of torment."]

August 22nd

A death sentence is pronounced on Simon Raymond dit Deslauriers of Québec with the following words:

"The *Conseil Souverain* sentences Simon Raymond dit Deslauriers to be removed from prison by *l'exécuteur-de-la-haute-justice* [public executioner] and brought to the door of the Church of the Hôtel-Dieu of Québec, *nud, en chemise* [naked except for a shirt], with a rope around his neck, and kneeling, while holding a burning torch in his hand, to beg for his God's, the King's, and Justice's forgiveness, for having gone into Sisters' cloister at the said Hôtel-Dieu and having stolen from them in their home; and, moreover, to be hanged and strangled on a gallows which shall have been set up for that purpose in the Public Square in Lower Québec."

(Conseil Souverain Register)

1676

During his Spring visit, Mgr. [Laval] the Bishop of Québec established a new parish in Lachine with Saints-Anges as the patrons. The first recorded act dates back to the 27th of February 1676.

September 3rd

Mgr. Laval purchased the property of Jean Serreau, Sieur de St-Aubain, at Baie-St-Paul for 11 *livres* [about $2.20].

(Becquet's Records)

Jean Serreau had been accused of killing a man named Jean Terme, a Swiss. The Conseil Souverain declared him not guilty of the charge.

(Conseil Souverain Register, 14 February 1667)

November 22nd

MM. Charles Aubert de LaChenaye, Pierre Denys de la Ronde, and Charles Bazire, seigneurs of Île-Percée, gave a parcel of land measuring 4 by 40 *arpents* [133 acres] located on the Rivière-St-Pierre to M. de Frontenac, *protecteur*[patron] of the Récollet fathers. They also gave him a house near the beach on *Île-Percée* near where the Récollets had already settled.

(Records of Duquet, Royal Notary)

[Based on a value of 5/6 acre per *square arpent*. As was true of most French units of measurement at the time, however, the value of the *arpent* was not at all consistent and could vary from one province to another.]

1677

February 5th

An edict from the Bishop of Québec reinforced the edict of the 29th of March 1664 which <u>obliged</u> fathers and mothers to have their children baptized <u>immediately after</u> their births.

(Archdiocesan Register of Québec)

[Notice the much stronger language in this so-called 'reinforcement' legislation ....the first edict called for the parents <u>not to delay</u> in baptizing their children after they were born whereas this edict called for them to have their children baptized <u>immediately after</u> they were born.]

June 25th

The burial of Jean LaTour, 45, *sculpteur* [sculptor], and native of Lagny in the diocese of Paris.

(Québec Register)

1678

August 3rd

Nicolas Boissonneau dit St-Onge, a *cultivateur* [farmer], from Ste-Famille-de-l'Île-d'Orléans parish, watched as three of his children perished when his home burned down.

(Ste-Famille-de-l'Île-d'Orléans Register)

November 7th

To comply with Louis XIV's Ordinance dated April 1667, the Conseil Supérieur de Québec issued a decree ordering that the Registers be kept in accordance with the Ordinance.

1679

April 2nd

The son of Bénigne Basset, 19, *notaire royal*[royal notary] in Montréal, drowned along with a man named Ptolomée, *commis* [clerk] working for M. de la Salle.

(Montréal Register)

September 23rd

Pierre Nodin, 22, of the diocese of Poitiers, drowned at Québec City.

(Québec Register)

1680

March 27th

Jacques Daigre, 60, was found dead in his home behind the Ursuline Convent where he lived alone. He was buried in Québec.

(Idem)

April 28th

A 16-year-old Illinois Indian woman, a captive of the Outaouais, was bought back from the Indians, returned to Québec and baptized. M. de Frontenac, Governor, and Mme. Marguerite Denis, wife of Thomas de la Nouguère (de la Naudière), named her Marie-Louise.

(Idem)

December 28th

We found the following notation in the Register of the St-François Parish on Île-d'Orléans: "His diebus visus est cometa magnus." ["A great comet has recently been sighted." Apparently a comet had been seen in the area and a brief notation made to the left in the *Registre*. This is a microfilmed copy of a portion of that entry blown up slightly to show the referenced words. The quality of this copy is fairly typical of the quality of many of the old records.]

HIS DIEBUS VISUS EST COMETA MAGNUS

MOVEMENT OF THE CATHOLIC POPULATION OF THE PROVINCE OF QUÉBEC 1671 TO 1680

	MARRIAGES	BIRTHS	DEATHS	OTHERS
1671	109	383	69	314
1672	68	401	61	340
1673	67	466	68	390
1674	31	424	54	370
1675	30	404	49	355
1676	45	442	72	370
1677	43	369	97	272
1678	47	451	71	380
1679	53	367	59	308
1680	65	386	100	286
TOTALS ➡	558	4093	700	3393
1608-1680	1582	7141	1607	5534

[Tanguay's "OTHERS" detail adds up to 3385 yet his 'TOTAL' is 3393.]

1681

The first few words in the l'Îslet Parish Register were:
> "Register of the baptisms, marriages and burials of the entire southern side, namely: Villieu, Côte-de-Lauzon, Beaumont, Ladurantaye, Cap-St-Claude, Berthier, Pointe-à-Lacaille, Rivière-du-Sud, Cap-Vincelet, Bonsecours, Îles-aux-Oies et aux-Grues, Rivière-des-Trois-Saumons, Langlais, St-Denis, Lacombe, La Bouteillerie, et Rivière-du-Loup...to begin on the 1st of January, 1681."

(Islet Register)

1682

May 7th
Romain Duval, 45, drowned in the Rivière-St-Charles.

(Québec Register)

NOTE: His brothers had also suffered tragic deaths: Pierre Duval had drowned in 1657; Martin Duval had been murdered in 1661; and Nicolas Duval had been burned on Île-d'Orléans in 1663.

1683

April 26th

Louis Lemieux, resident of Île-aux-Oies, gave his wife, Marie-Madeleine Côté, all of his belongings, before leaving for Outaouais country.

(Records of Duquet, p. 77)

June 9th

Isaac de l'Avant, 44, a native of Tours [in France], drowned near Québec.

(Québec Register)

October 28th

Louis Martin, 48, *serrurier* [locksmith] and native of *Ste-Radegonde-de-Poitiers*, drowned right across from *Cap-aux-Diamants*.

(Idem)

1684

[No specific date given.]

Several people were buried at about 9 PM in Champlain.
          Why?   An outbreak of smallpox.

August 25th

Louis Creste, 30, was buried after having died on Sieur Niel's boat on the very day of his return from France. He had been given the last rites of the church by M. Benoit Duplein, *chanoine* [canon] from Québec.

(St-Laurent-de-l'Île-d'Orléans Register)
[*Canons* were priests who were not allowed to teach or become parish priests. Their essential function was to pray together and, in a few cases, when they lived in a presbytery, to serve as missionaries.]

1685

April

Jacques Poissant dit Laseline, one of M. DeNoyan's soldiers, renounced his religion and entered into the bosom of the Catholic Church on Palm Sunday in the Pointe-aux-Trembles Church in Montréal.

(Pointe-aux-Trembles de Montréal Register)

August 13th

M. Richard Denys, Sieur de Fronsac, granted the land from Canseau to Cap-Desrosiers, Îles-du-Cap-Breton, St-Jean, etc., in the large St-Lawrence Bay, to the spiritual Directors of the *Séminaire-de-Québec*. He gave property in the name of his father, M. Nicolas Denys, gouverneur and lieutenant pour le Roi... namely:

...at Ristigouche, three *lieues* [abt 7.5 miles] by three [abt 7.5 miles] of frontage;
...on the Rivière-Ste-Croix, three by three *lieues* of frontage;
...on Île-de-Cap-Breton, three by three *lieues* of frontage.

(Records of Genaple, Royal Notary)

1686

Even before 1686, the seigniorial home of M. Cressé was used as the church where the [parish] baptisms were performed.

(Trois-Rivières Register)

July 22nd

Gilles Boivinet, 47, *agent général* for those interested in the *ferme du Roi* drowned near Québec when he returned from France.

(Québec Register)

[Ernest Gagnon noted that if one owned interest in the *ferme du Roi*, he would have exclusive rights to trade, hunt, fish and carry on commerce in the full expanse of the King's Domain from Île-aux-Coudres up to 2 leagues [about 5 miles] below Sept-Îles and in the following outposts: Tadoussac, Chicoutimi, Lake Saint-Jean, Nécoubau, Naskapis, Mistasasins, Papinachois, Rivière-Moisy and other locales ... exclusive rights to leases and other sources of revenue which did not fall under the Crown's normal administrative structure.]

September 6th

Thomas Bevin, 22, a native of London and soldier in M. DesBergères company, was found dead in the Canardière [in the outskirts of Québéc].

(Idem)

1687

Several victims of the Iroquois who were buried on the shores of Lac St-Louis in 1687 were found again in 1866. Human skeletons had been found in 1866 by several *cultivateur-propriétaires* [farmer-proprietors] of a piece of land, located on the shores of Lac St-Louis, above Île-de-Montréal. That information was immediately conveyed to the priest in that area, M. l'Abbé Chevrefils, who in turn volunteered to do all of the necessary research to uncover the names, ages, and burial date(s) for those individuals whose remains we had just uncovered. We found a crucifix with all the signs of being quite old[36] on one of the skeletons and that object alone showed that the human remains were very evidently those of several Christians.

After consulting the archives at Ste-Anne-du-Bout-de-l'Île Parish in Montréal, Father Chevrefils was still not able to locate any document which might have shown the existence either of a chapel or of a cemetery on that site, known as *Baie-d'Ursé*. The parish Register, first begun in 1704, also did not reveal any names or ages for the 10 individuals who had reposed there.

That valued colleague then wrote to me (Tanguay) hoping that my numerous statistical studies as well as my genealogical studies of the Registers themselves might perhaps have enabled me to resolve that interesting problem. I did not disappoint him. Indeed, I had the profound satisfaction of telling him that I had *all* of the documentation which he sought to answer his questions.

The 10 people buried on that site were French people who had been massacred in 1687 by the Iroquois and then buried by a Sulpician missionary, Father d'Ursé, near the site intended for the construction of St-Louis Church down from Île-de-Montréal[37].

Having received that information, the priest from Ste-Anne's was then able to commend the souls of the 10 individuals to the prayers of his parishioners on the following Sunday, with the names, ages and even the burial dates for each of them. Their remains, now kept together in a common grave, were returned to the Ste-Anne's church, and, after a solemn service, were once again buried but now with the benefit

---

36

The Reverend Father carefully preserved this old object.

37

The actual parish of Ste-Anne-du-Bout-de-l'Île would then, in 1687, have been dedicated to/called St-Louis, on the shores of the lake which carried that name.

of a Christian burial-service and in the presence of any of the parishioners who might have counted some of their ancestors among those unfortunate victims.

I had found the burial records for those 10 individuals in the 1687 Lachine Register: Claude DelaMothe[38], 40 years of age; J.-Bte. LeSueur[39], 21; Louis Jets[40], 24; Jean Vincent[41], 45; Jean DeLalonde[42], 47; Pierre Bonneau[43], 38; Pierre Perthuis[44], 24; Henri Fromageau[45], 27; Pierre Petiteau[46], 20; and Pierre Camus[47], 21.

(Tanguay)

February 12th
   Jean Balier, 45, *engagé* [under contract] with the Ursulines, died suddenly.

(Québec Register)

38

'Dit' the Marquis of Jourdis; a native of St-Leu in the diocese of Arras [France]; husband of Françoise Sabourin.

39

A native of Pont-Lévêque in the diocese of Lizieux [France].

40

A native of Courson in the Region of Aunis [France]; he was a miller.

41

A native of Conflans, in the diocese of Limoges [France]; he was found bruised from blows from the Iroquois.

42

'Dit' L'Espérance; husband of Marie Barbary from Havre-de-Grâce in the diocese of Rouën [Normandy, France].

43

'Dit' Lajeunesse; *caporal de milice* [corporal in the militia], husband of Marie-Madeleine Gignard from Tours in the diocese of Poitiers [France].

44

Native of Amboise in the diocese of Tours [France].

45

Native of LaRochelle in Aunis [France].

46

Native of St-Macaire in Brittany [France].

47

'Dit' Lafeuillade; soldier of M. de Cruzel; a native of Montesson [France].

April 12th

The burial of Pierre Salois, 15, the son of Claude Salois and of Marie Mabile, who had been killed by a falling tree.

(St-Laurent-de-l'Île-d'Orléans Register)

July 27th

An entire family of Ristigouche Indians was baptized in Québec. Jean, a Micmac Indian, 35, and his wife, Marie-Madeleine, 31, who both had Jean Bochart, a *chevalier* and *seigneur de Champigny*, as godfather and his wife as godmother. Jacques, 12; Charles-Gabriel, 8; and Anne-Josette, 18 months old all had Bouraillon, *capitaine d'Infanterie* [infantry captain]; the *chevalier* Charles Claude de Grays from Merville; and Joseph de Monic, *major des troupes* [company major], as their godfathers.

(Québec Register)

[For more information on titles, honors, decorations, etc. please see my comments after the entry dated November 24th of 1659.]

September 19th

Jean Noël, 15, who worked for M. Guillaume Chanjon, drowned.

(Idem)

December 31st

Although the annual number of deaths in New France had never surpassed 170, an increase in the number of Iroquois massacres in 1687 served to raise the total to 471.

1688

November 16th

The burial of Languedoc, a 25-year-old man who had died on the ship *Le Saint-Honoré*[48]. He was buried at Baie-St-Paul in the presence of Sieur Beaulieu, the *chirurgien-du-navire* [fleet-surgeon], and of Maret, the fleet's *charpentier* [shipwright].

(Baie-St-Paul Register)

[A shipwright is one whose occupation it was to construct or repair ships.]

---

[48]

The *capitaine de vaisseau* [ship's Captain] was Pierre Soumande, father of M. Louis Soumande, *chanoine* [canon] of the Québec Chapter; and of the first Superior at the Hôpital-Général in Québec.

(Dictionnaire Généalogique, V I, p. 552)

1689

July 12th

The burial of Jeanne Danny, 16, the daughter of Honoré Danny dit Tourangeau, who was killed by the Indians.

(Montréal Register)

On the same day, Pierre Hérou and Guillaume Beaulieu, both 25 and both soldiers with M. de Saint-Jean, were killed by weapons-fire.

(Idem)

August 5th

André Danny was killed by the Iroquois.

(Idem)

November 6th

The burial of Jacques Julien, 45, who was killed by the Iroquois who also then proceeded to burn the Church down.

(St-François-du-Lac Register)

A man named Lebasseur suffered the same fate.

(Idem)

The burial of Barbe Dodier, 24, the daughter of Jacques Dodier, and of Cathérine Caron, at the site set aside for the construction of the *Baie-St-Paul* church. Barbe had married Ignace Gasnier in 1680.

(Ste-Anne-de-Beaupré Register)

1690

January 26th

The burial of François Pougnet, 45, in the Church of Montréal. He had been murdered in his home.

(Montréal Register)

March 2nd

Mgr. de St-Valier baptized J.-Baptiste Ayegabouc, a Micmac Indian, 70, who had *Intendant* Bochart [Jean Bochart-Champigny] as his godfather and Françoise LeGardeur, wife of René D'Amours, the Sieur de Clignancour, as his godmother.

(Québec Register)

March 12th

The burial of an Abénaquise Indian woman, Jeanne Ontarimanouk8e, who died at St-François-du-Lac at 100 years of age.

(St-François-du-Lac Register)

[For information about problems encountered when spelling or pronouncing Indian names, please see my comments after the February 10th 1664 entry.]

March 14th

Joseph Morache, 36, the husband of Marie-Anne Aubert, was buried in Batiscan after he burned to death in a fire which also destroyed his home.

(Batiscan Register)

May 18th

The burial of Pierre Forcier, 42, and Jacques Vacher dit Laserte, who were both killed by the Iroquois.

(St-François-du-Lac Register)

June 8th

Paul Hus, a *cultivateur* [farmer] from Sorel and the husband of Jeanne Baillargeon, had his son, Paul, 6, buried after he was killed by the Iroquois.

(Sorel Register)

July 2nd

"An encounter between the French and Iroquois took place near a ravine on Jean Grou's land above Île-de-Montréal. Dead were Sieur Coulombe, *lieutenant réformé* [discharged lieutenant]; Jean Jalot dit Desgroseilliers, *chirurgien* [surgeon]; Larose; Cartier; Jean Beaudoin, the son; Pierre Masta, the son; Isaac, soldier; DeMontenon, Sieur de la Rue; Guillaume Richard dit Lafleur; and several others including Antoine Chaudillon, *chirurgien de la paroisse* [parish surgeon]. Since we were deathly afraid of the Iroquois, we very quickly buried all of the victims at that same site right after they were killed and it wasn't until the 2nd of November in 1694 that the remains were brought to and reburied in the Pointe-aux-Trembles de Montréal cemetery."

(Pointe-aux-Trembles de Montréal Register)

July 29th

The burial of Louis Marié, 30, who drowned in a pit into which he had accidentally fallen.

(Québec Register)

August 11th

Gédéon DeCatalogne married Marie-Anne Lemire in Montréal.

(Montréal Register)

NOTE: Gédéon DeCatalogne, the first of his name to have emigrated to Canada, was born in 1662 in Bresse, in the Béarn. He was the son of Gédéon and of Marie from Cap-de-Molle. While still young, he had entered the Engineers Corps and had become an officer; but not wanting to give up his Protestantism, as his oldest brother who was then *membre du Parlement* [a member of Parliament] in Navarre had just done, he planned to leave France after the repeal of the Edict of Nantes. As a matter of fact, he left for New France in 1685 with 120 of his *co-religionnaires*, who, wishing to follow his lead, accompanied him in his exile.

After a long and stormy crossing, their ship was caught by surprise at the mouth of the Gulf of St-Lawrence by a very violent storm which caused the ship to break up on the reefs which bordered Île-d'Anticosti. He suddenly realized that he was going to die and that only a superhuman force could save him. Since his very preservation might depend upon his recanting his Protestantism, he immediately promised to do just that and to join the Church if he escaped from death.

Seven of his companions made that same vow and Providence saved them all. Of the 120 passengers, they were *the only ones* who escaped from the tragic end of their unfortunate companions!

So, miraculously saved, Gédéon remembered his vow and upon his arrival in Québec, recanted his Protestant faith in the presence of Mgr. de St-Valier, the then Bishop of Québec. His companions did the same.

Scarcely back in his new country, Gédéon wished to give some proof of his courage and devotion. He took part in an expedition which was preparing to go to Hudson Bay on the Rivière-Ste-Thérèse to take back the fort which the French had built but which the English had since become masters of. In the company of M. de Troyes and M. Duchesnil, he took command of a detachment of 30 soldiers, whereas the three sons of Charles Lemoyne, from Iberville, Ste-Hélène and Maricourt, headed up 70 Canadians, true *coureurs des bois* [trappers and hunters] and accustomed to long hikes and prolonged fasting and able to withstand the rigors of the sharp cold in these remote regions. The expedition was a complete success for the small army.

[Coureurs des bois were men who traded without a licence or any other form of permission. Most of the time, they traded with the Indians. They were usually native born trappers or hunters and very familiar with the interior of New France.]

Gédéon de Catalogne authored: '*Recueil de ce qui s'est passé en Canada au sujet de la guerre tant des Anglais que des Iroquois, depuis l'année 1682.*' ['A Compendium of what has happened in Canada concerning war since 1682 - as much with the English as with the Iroquois.']   The Historical Society of Québec had this compendium printed, several years ago, omitting the name of the author – probably erased or destroyed.

'*La Collection de Manuscrits*', recently edited (1884) under the auspices of the Québec Legislature, attributed this collection to a M. de Léry, *ingénieur* [engineer].

"Yet, several quotations in this collection which I will permit myself to make here, will demonstrate, without question, I trust, that the writer who, in this collection expresses himself in the first person while relating events which took place between 1695 and 1712, is very likely the same as that which the historians referred to as *De Catalogne*. *It couldn't have been M. de Léry* during these years, since he was only 13 years old in 1695, and since his orders to leave for Canada were not given to him until the 23rd of June in 1716."

"On page 54 of the 4th Series of the same collection published in 1695 by the Historical Society, we find: "We sent 2 detachments to M. de Louvigny at Lac St-François, one commanded by M. de Repentigny *and I commanded the second*."

On February 24th, Montréal's Hôtel-Dieu [hospital] burned down. On the 28th, M. de Callières met with all of the principal residents of the parish to assign the work and contributions necessary to repair it. *"They made me responsible for overseeing the work of repairing the Hospital."*

> [Trudel notes: "In the beginning...education and hospitalization [were left to] the religious communities" AND "both seigneur and censitaire had to share certain duties, such as the repair or contruction of the church and...related properties" (*'Introduction to New France'*, Quintin Publications, 1997, pp. 179, 181, 251).]

Now let's look at an article about the life of Mlle. Mance which reads:

> "After the fire at the Hôtel-Dieu of Montréal, M. Gédéon de Catalogne came to the assistance of this afflicted community. A capable *architecte* [architect], he prepared the plans for the new hospital, directed the workers in the preparation of the wood necessary for its restoration, and, along with M. Pothier, a Montréal *marchand* [merchant], was entrusted with overseeing the work, this according to a decision made at a general meeting of the citizenry presided over by M. de Callières."
>
> "Those two men discharged the responsibilities of this honorable task with all of the diligence which we might have expected of such devoted men."
>
> *('Vie de Mlle. Mance'*, Volume II, p. 130)

> M. de Catalogne distinguished himself as *ingénieur civil* [civil engineer]. In 1714, he directed the work of fortifying Cap-aux-Diamant and Château-St-Louis. Later he supervised the fortification of Louisborg. He died there on the 5th of January 1729.

> His son Joseph, born in Montréal in 1694, married Charlotte Dubuisson in 1733, and is the *auteur* [author] of a paper on magnetic forces, which earned him a Chair with the Academy of Sciences in Paris. He was also decorated with the *Croix-de-St-Louis.*

> [Other than the above and to a claim by McLennan in his *"Histoire de la Nouvelle France"* (Louisborg, p. 49), there does not seem to be any evidence that Joseph ever wrote a treatise on the magnet, thereby gaining a seat in the *Académie de Science.*]

His descendants moved on to Martinique where they raised their families.

> (SEE: "*Étude sur une Famille Canadienne*" by Father C. Tanguay AND *"Mémoires de la Société Royale du Canada"*, Volume II, pp. 7 and following pages.)

October 23rd

> The burial of the Sieurs de Clermont, both Lieutenants, and Joseph de la Touche, who were all killed by the English in the battle of the 18th of October in 1690. They sacrificed their lives for their religion and for their nation.
>
> *(Beauport Register)*

December 3rd

We read this in the *Registre de LaPrairie-de-la-Madeleine*:

"This 3rd of December 1690, I, the undersigned *missionnaire* certify to having gone into the woods to find the remains of the late Bourbon, a resident of this parish, and of another one whose identity we were not able to determine since he had been so [badly] disfigured by the Iroquois. We believe that it was one of M. le chevalier Degrais' soldiers named Lamothe, and that they were both killed on the 4th of September in the aforementioned year, in the attack which took place at the crossroads at la-Prairie-de-la-Madeleine, with Jean Duval and Jean Barault, residents of the parish: and Latreille, Beaulieu, Larose, and d'Auvergne, soldiers with M. le chevalier Degrais. We have buried the remains of the above-named Bourbon and Lamothe, this 3rd of December, as we did with the bodies of Barault and Jean Duval, on the 4th and 5th of September, in the cemetery of the said parish, the others having been buried on the day of the battle, before my arrival.

In testimony whereof, I have undersigned,

L. Geoffroy, priest"

Both Collin, *interprète*[interpreter], and Labossière were burned to death by the Iroquois.

(*Extract from "Recueil de Gédéon DeCatalogne"*)

Gabriel Bouat, 19, was taken prisoner by the Iroquois and died of smallpox.

(*Idem*)

Between 1690 and 1700, a large number of young Englishmen and women who were captives of the Iroquois, were ransomed by some Canadian families, and baptized. The names of most of these young people are recorded in the "*Dictionnaire Généalogique*", Volume I, pp. 8, 9 and 10.

The number of deaths has greatly increased because of the war.

MOVEMENT OF THE CATHOLIC POPULATION OF THE PROVINCE OF QUÉBEC 1681 TO 1690

	MARRIAGES	BIRTHS	DEATHS	OTHERS
1681	73	456	133	323
1682	62	482	120	362
1683	76	494	146	348
1684	70	437	169	268
1685	80	419	130	289
1686	107	436	120	316
1687	123	482	471	11
1688	144	434	273	161
1689	140	482	220	262
1690	104	510	181	329
TOTALS ➡	979	4632	1963	2669
1608-1690	2561	11773	3570	8203

1691

January 9th

In the *Pointe-aux-Trembles de Montréal* Register, we find the following note: "At the baptism of Claude, on the 9th of January 1691, the son of Pierre Payet dit Saint-Amour, M. de Lamothe's *caporal* [corporal], and of Louise Tessier; the child is believed *posthume* [born after the death of his father] since we believed that his father had been killed by the Oneyouths. He had been taken prisoner and given over to that nation on the 2nd of July 1690 during the attack on the Coulée fort, one *lieue* [about 2.5 miles] below the Pointe-aux-Trembles de Montréal Church."

He returned to his family in the course of the year 1693 after obtaining his freedom and had his son, Jacques, baptized on the 17th of June 1694.

(Pointe-aux-Trembles de Montréal Register)

May 21st

At a ceremony presided over by Father Guybert de la Saudrays, we blessed a bell called '*Marie-Jeanne*' which had cost 200 *livres* [about $40.00].

(Boucherville Register)

[The first of eight such <u>bell-blessings</u> recorded in this book. Roman Catholics have a great deal of faith in the value of having things blessed. They themselves receive special blessings at the time of their baptisms and marriages and illnesses and deaths and ask for blessings for their throats...and their prayer beads...and their fishing boats...and their gifts... etc. etc. . And so it is not surprising that during a period when the Church was so important in the colonists' everyday lives, a time when they were too poor to be able to afford individual timepieces, that they had to rely on church or other public bells to keep track of the time of day. Bells signaled the start and close of religious ceremonies and of workdays. They tolled to warn of emergencies or to advise of deaths or of happier events. They summoned citizens to assembly or to prayer or to arms or to fight fires. They indicated when it was time to sleep ... and to awaken. They rang to let merchants know when they could open up their shops... and when they had to close them. The colonists would surely have insisted upon blessing the very bells which guided their daily activities since they were absolutely essential to the life of the community.]

June 27th

We buried several residents who were massacred by a band of Iroquois who had been laying in wait while the residents harvested their corn: J.-Baptiste Gourdon dit Lachasse, *marguiller-en-charge*[49]; René Huguet[50]; Jean Guignard dit L'Espérance; Jean Marin dit Latreille[51]; Pierre Blondeau dit Lajeunesse[52]; Joseph Jean dit Lagiroflée[53].

(Lachine Register)

[The *marguiller-en-charge* was the churchwarden currently responsible for the secular affairs of the parish. It was a position which was sought after by all and which "became a form of consecration for those who had not yet made their fortunes." Women were not allowed to become churchwardens.]

49

He was 47 years of age and the father of 7 children.

50

He was 40 years of age , the brother-in-law of Gourdon, and the father of three.

51

A soldier in M. Dumesnil's Company.

52

A soldier in M. Dumesnil's Company.

53

A soldier in M. Dumesnil's Company.

August 11th

The burial of Pierre Pinguet de Montigny, 33, the husband of Cathérine Tétard, killed by the English in the Laprairie engagement.

(Montréal Register)

Pierre Soumande, Sieur de l'Orme, was *lieutenant* on the Royal ship *Le Hazardeur* which arrived at the Port of Québec on the 12th of August.

(Records of Duquet, Royal Notary)

François Cibardin, married on the 9th of July in 1691, fell under the fire of the English at the battle of Laprairie. Pierre Cabassier, Nicolas Barbier, Louis Ducharme, Jean Leber dit Duchesne, Pierre Pinguet, Dosta, *capitaine réformé* [discharged captain], and 8 other French combatants also fell.

October 16th

Armand-Louis Delorndarce, the baron of Hontan-Herlèche, *Chevalier de l'ordre de Notre-Dame-du-Mont-Carmel*, and *capitaine d'un détachement de la marine* [Captain of a detachment of marines], served as a godfather in Québec.

(Québec Register)

[For more information on titles, honors, decorations, etc. please see my comments after the entry dated November 24th of 1659.]

November 27th

The first burial in the new Montréal cemetery was that of Charles Forestier, the child of Étienne Forestier and Marguerite Lauzon, and was made today.

1692

July 22nd

In an encounter with the French, a large party of Iroquois killed three officers: Jean-Baptiste leGardeur de Montesson, 26, the son of Jean-Baptiste DeRepentigny and of Marguerite Nicolet; De la Poterie[54]; Pierre de la Brosse[55],

---

54

Leneuf de la Poterie, son of Michel Leneuf, Sieur de la Vallière.

55

Sieur de Bocage, *lieutenant de la marine* [marine Lieutenant].

and four soldiers; Pierre-Nicolas Jetté[56], 23; Lavallée[57]; Joachim DeBoucherville[58]; and Vincent.

1693

April 19th

We found the body of Pierre Moret, 80, *ancien domestique* [an old domestic servant] working for the Ursulines. He was viewed as a perfect Christian.

(Québec Register)

July 5th

A tragic accident: Cathérine Dumets[59],18; Jeanne Bisson[60], 15; and Madeleine Moisson[61],14; all drowned while boating.

(Idem)

July 20th

On the subject of legal foundations set up by him in the colony, Mgr. de St-Valier stated that "in the event of invasion or destruction of the nation by its enemies, or of whatever other abandonment of the nation which might do away with the original reasons for having first established the foundations, he wished that he and his *successeurs* would dispose of those funds by whatever other religious works which might seem appropriate, always with the advice of the *ministre d'État* [Secretary of State or equivalent position] of whichever governmental administrative department might be heading up the nation."

(Records of Genaple, notaire royal [Royal Notary]*)*

56

The son of Urbain Jetté of Montréal.
57

Menuisier [carpenter] and one of M. de St-Ours' soldiers.
58

The son of Pierre Boucher and former Governor of Trois-Rivières.   (*Tanguay*)
59

The daughter of Jean and Jeanne Redié.
60

The daughter of Michel Buisson, from St-Cosme.
61

The daughter of Pierre Moisan, *pilote* [pilot], and of Barbe Rotteau.

1694

June 3rd

At the baptism of Pierre Richaume[62], the son of Jacques Richaume and of Marguerite Gratiot, it was mentioned that the father was being held captive in Iroquois country[63].

(Repentigny Register)

October 28th

A document dated the 28th of October 1694 written in the Lachine Register reads as follows:

"Today, the 28th of October, the Feast of St-Simon and St-Jude, by virtue of a mandate dated the 18th of June of last year from Monseigneur, the most illustrious and most reverend Bishop of Québec, signed by Jean, the Bishop of Québec, and countersigned by his secretary, Trouvé, and sealed with the Seal of his Arms, following the publications and announcements which we have made after the sermons on 2 consecutive Sundays, I, Pierre Rémy, *curé* [priest] at *Saints-Anges* parish in *Île-de-Montréal,* then came to the issue of the parish mass for the reburial of the bodies of several residents of the Parish which had [first] been buried on the 5th of August 1689 at which time they – as many men as boys, and women as girls – and their houses and barns had been taken, looted and burned by the Iroquois. They could not have been exhumed and then transported to the Parish's cemetery any earlier because of the frequency of the Iroquois' raids and because the deceased's flesh had not been fully consumed, but we have now done it and in the presence of several of our parishioners.

1. Near the home of Lalande, was the body of Jean Fagueret dit Petitbois, where after having dug near a large stone with a pickaxe, we found all of his bones – all of the flesh being consumed – which we removed from the earth.

---

[62]

We again find this Pierre Richaume established in Louisiana in 1724.

(Louisiana Census of 1724)

[63]

He was later ransomed and returned to his family.

(Repentigny Register)

2. At the dwelling of the late Jean Michau[64], we found the bones of the said Jean Michau, of his son, Pierre, 15, and of his wife's son, Albert Boutin, 18. [65]

3. At the dwelling of the late Noël Charmois dit Duplessis[66], we found the bones of the said Charmois and of André Danis dit l'Arpenty – both slaughtered and burned.

4. At the dwelling of André Rapin, we found 5 skulls in one hole, one of Perinne Filastreau[67], the wife of Simon Davaux dit Bouterain, with her bones; one with the bones of a young man whom we believe to be a soldier; two childrens' skulls and their bones; and the skull of Marie Cadieu, the wife of André Canaple dit Valtagagné[68] whose bones were found in a grave, at the foot of the Fort Rolland stronghold.

Along the water's edge, we also recovered some of the bones of 2 soldiers killed by the Iroquois on the 6th of August 1689 in the battle which the Iroquois launched against the French between the Church's fort and Fort Rolland, not being able to remove the rest of the bones because the water now overflows that area.

5. We sent 6 men beyond the small *Rivière-de-la-Présentation* onto the dwelling of the late René Chartier[69] where he and his 2 sons[70] and a small Indian, their slave from the Panis nation, had been killed by the Iroquois on the 5th of August 1689, and where several people have told us that they had seen their heads and their bones *on* the ground since

---

64

His real name was Michel, husband of Marie Marchesseau, widow of Pierre Boutin.

(Tanguay)

65

This is a mistake. Albert Boutin was 24, having been born on the 7th of September 1670.

66

He was 69 years old.

67

She was the daughter of Réné Filastreau, born in 1663 and married in 1677.

68

A *tonnelier* [cooper] who had only been married for one year before the massacre.

(Tanguay)

[A cooper is one who makes and/or repairs barrels and casks.]

69

He was 76 years old when he was killed. He was married to Marguerite Delorme.

70

The oldest, François, was 16; the other (unnamed) was probably 15.

they had died; but the grass had grown since then and they were now not able to find anything[71]; and it was almost sunset when we left the area, having had the remains placed in a boat which we had returned for, with the surplice and the black stole, at the ringing of the big bell, accompanied by acolytes in their surplices and carrying candlesticks, the cross and holy water, and singing Psalms in keeping with the practice of the Holy Church; and having them covered with hearth cloths, we had them brought to and put on deposit in the Church to have them buried in the cemetery on the following day: which we did with great solemnity after having celebrated a High Anniversary Mass over the bones, and offered all of the service with gifts of bread and wine.

And of the above, we have made this current record to serve and validate – at the proper time – that we have signed and had signed by André Rapin and Jean Paré, *anciens marguillers*, and Guillaume Daoust, *chantres* [cantors] for this Church."

[a) *Anciens marguillers* were individuals who had already served as churchwardens and as such were apt to be involved in advisory roles for their parishes once their terms had expired.
b) *Chantres* or *cantors* were involved in the choir of a church.]

"The signators were:
André Rapin, Jean Paré, Guillaume Daoust and Father Rémy, priest."

"As to the bodies of Vincent Alix dit Larosée, of Marie Perrin, his wife, and of some of their children who were burned by the Iroquois in their home on the 5th of August 1689, we found nothing since the fire had consumed both their flesh and their bones."

October 31st
Madeleine Boursier, an 11-month old child, was buried after being killed in the water by the Iroquois on the 5th of August, 1689.

(Lachine Register)

71

We buried some of the remains of the late René Chartier which we had had removed from his dwelling site in that Church on the 23rd of May in 1701.

1695

August 12th

Jean Deniau, 65, and his wife, Hélène Daudin, 49, were buried in Boucherville after being killed by the Iroquois.

(Boucherville Register)

August 22nd

The burial of Mathurin Richard des Sablons, the husband of Jeanne Bertaut, who was killed by the Iroquois.

(Idem)

September 29th

The burial of Christophe Février, 47, the husband of Claire Françoise Gautier, who was killed by the Iroquois.

(Idem)

October 16th

The *maître d'école* [schoolmaster] at the Boucherville parish was Jean-Baptiste Bau dit Lallouette, 41, the husband of Étienne Loré.

(Idem)

1696

April 3rd

All of the Montreal population was present at the *supplice-du-feu* [punishment by fire] of 4 Iroquois who were so condemned only a few moments after having being baptized.

(Montréal Register)

I found this in a batch of unpublished letters from 1701 which I had looked through: "When I first entered Montréal, it was by the St-François entryway. I noticed a man from my neighborhood who came to greet and to hug me. After we had greeted, he mentioned that he also belonged to my [military] company. As we spoke, he noticed that I was somewhat distracted by a large crowd which had gathered in the Jesuits' yard."

At that point, he said: "my goodness, you're arriving just in time to see four Iroquois burned alive: let's move forward", he continued, "right up to the Jesuits' front door so that we'll be able to see better." That bloody event was going to take place right at their front door ! I thought that the poor souls were probably going to be thrown into a fire but after looking around a bit I couldn't see any stakes for their sacrifice; so I then asked my new acquaintance what several small and evenly-spaced fires were for and he merely said: "patience - we'll have a lot to laugh about". Yet not everybody thought that it was funny.

The 4 Indian men – brothers – were perhaps the most handsome men that I'd ever seen. They were escorted to and then baptized by the Jesuits who then also gave them some short admonition, which, quite frankly, was comparable to rebuking a dead person.

Once the religious part of the service was completed, they were then subjected to torture which they might perhaps have been the first to use. They were tied, naked, to posts which had been driven 3 or 4 feet into the ground, and then they had each part of their bodies roasted with red-hot branding irons wielded by some of our *sauvages alliés* [Indian allies] and by several Frenchmen as well. The small fires which I'd noticed earlier were used as ovens or furnaces to heat up their vile instruments of torture, their branding irons.

The torture lasted for about 6 hours during which time the Indians never stopped singing their war chants, all the while drinking *eau-de-vie* [brandy] which seemed to flow through their systems as quickly as if we had poured it into a hole in the ground.

So ended the lives of these unfortunate individuals, with a steadfastness and an indescribable courage. I was assured that what I was witnessing was merely a small example of how the Indians themselves made us suffer when we were their prisoners."

D***

April 30th

A young Englishman who had been held captive by the Indians and ransomed by M. Pachot, was baptized and given the name François Philippe.
(Québec Register)
During the year, baptisms were conducted by the Côte-de-Lauzon missionary in the home of Pierre Lambert at Villieu.
(Idem)

1697

April 23rd

The burial of Pierre Hogue, 22, a native of Montréal, immediately after his body was recovered after he had drowned at Pointe-aux-Trembles.

(Pointe-aux-Trembles de Montréal Register)

September 8th

One of the royal ships arrived and spread smallpox to the Québec area. Its many victims included a nun named [Sister} Ste-Agnes who had devoted herself to the service of the sick[72] as a *religieuse hospitalière*.[73] She was buried on the 29th of October 1697.

(Québec Register)

[*Religieuse hospitalières* were religious women who devoted themselves to the running of the Hôtel-Dieu of Québec, a hospital for the sick.]

October 24th

The baptism of Guillaume Pagé's *trois jumelles* [*three twins* as these first recorded triplets were referred to]. This was the first such entry in the Québec Registers.

(Idem)

[The French word for twins is now bessons (m.) or bessonnes (f.); jumeaux (m.) or jumelles (f.). Triplets are now referred to as triplés (m.) or triplées (f.).]

1698

June 9th

The baptism of Thomas Williams at 14 years-of-age by Mgr. de St-Valier who had also expressed a desire to be his godfather and had then named him Joseph. A native of Jersey, Thomas had first been captured by the English when he was 2 years-of-age and had then been ransomed back by the French at Plaisance in 1696 where he was placed with M. Boucher de Montbrun.

(Boucherville Register)

NOTE: He is responsible for the continuation of the Ouilem de Boucherville families.

72

In 1740, the Royal vessel *"Le Rubis"* with more than 400 *soldats* [soldiers] and *matelots* [sailors], was infected by the same smallpox. The Bishop of Québec, Mgr. De Lauberivière, was the victim.

73

Angélique Tibierge, 20, daughter of Hypolite Tibierge, a Québec *marchand* [merchant], and Renée Hervé.

(Tanguay)

August 11th

A young man named Boulanger, 18, drowned while on his way to Beauport.

(Québec Register)

September 2nd

François de la Forest, *capitaine réformé* [discharged captain], seigneur for part of Illinois, sold one-half of his property in Louisiana, otherwise known as Illinois, to Michel Aco. The property had been sold to Sieur de Tonty and to the seller by His Majesty for 6000 *livres* [about $1200.00] worth of beaver skins, received in a place called *Les Chicagou*.

[Edna Kenton notes that *Les Chicagou* was an area named after Chicagou, Chief of the Illinois nation, who was one of 4 chiefs of Western tribes to travel to Paris in 1725 to meet (to be put on display would perhaps be more exact) with the King. ("*The Jesuit Relations and Allied Documents* ", Quintin Publications, 1998, pp. 426, 427).]

(Records of Rageot, notaire royal)

December 17th

Gabrielle Louise Braquil, a 16-year-old Englishwoman, was baptized in the Ursuline's church.

(Québec Register)

1699

January 3rd

The following (marriage) entry was in the Montréal Parish Register:

"I, François Dollier, *Grand-Vicaire* of the Bishop, declare that on Thursday night, the 1st of January, 1699, a man named Letendre dit St-Thomas[74] from M. de LaChassaigne's company, and Marie Morin[75], the widow of the late Testu[76], located me in the seminary, accompanied by Jacques Morin, the father of the said Marie, and by Pierre Hardouin, the brother-in-law of the said Marie, by a man

---

74

Thomas LeTendre, 24, was a native of Grimbouville in the diocese of Rouën. [in Normandy, France].

75

Marie Morin, 32, the daughter of Jacques Morin and Louise Garnier, had first married at 12 years of age a Jacques Vigor on the 16th of August 1679. After the marriage was nullified on the 15th of June 1695, she married a Jean Boutellier dit Testu from *Île-de-Rhé* on the 23rd of the same month in her second marriage. Widowed on the 4th of October 1698, she married a Thomas Letendre three months later.

DeLaChassaigne's company, and that the above-named St-Thomas told me that he, in the presence of the said above-named four witnesses, declared his love for and took Marie Morin, there present, as his wife; and Marie Morin then declared for and took him, the said St-Thomas, as her husband, there in the presence of the same four witnesses, notwithstanding what I might have been able to tell them about what could happen in this situation, the said St-Thomas, not really caring about the repercussions, provided that he *could* marry, to which I had raised objections, because the Governor and M. DeLaChassaigne, would have been reluctant to consent; now, all these things having been done, and omitting all of the Church's non-essential ceremonies, out of regard (for them), and not even taking up his surplice, I was satisfied by [merely] saying "ego conjungo vos" ["I marry you."] to them while making the sign of the cross over them; which I did, etc."

"Performed in the seminary, this 3rd of January 1699."

February 22nd

We found record of a baptism by a Brother Guillaume Bulfeau , a Récollet, whose name was not found anywhere else.

(Varennes Register)

[On page 184 of René Jetté's "*Dictionnaire Généalogique des Familles du Québec*", a Guillaume Bulteau (as opposed to Bulfeau) is now listed. He became a Récollet priest in 1689 in Flandre, arrived in Montréal in 1694, and died on 9 November 1716.]

May 5th

A Sergeant Dufeu drowned in Québec.

(Québec Register)

[René Jettés added that he had been a *sergent* [sergeant] in the Grais company.]

July 16th

The burial (after drowning) of Margaret Chapleau from Beauport. She had been married to a Noël Marcou for only 8 months.

(Beauport Register)

July 17th

The burial of André Parant, 37, who drowned in Beauport. The son of Pierre Parant from Perche, he had married Marguerite Côté in 1692.

(Idem)

October 10th

Claude de Ramezay, formerly the Governor of Trois-Rivières, and Charlotte Denis, his wife, sold some land, 42 *toises* and 4 *pieds* in width (about 273.2 feet) by 47 *toises* and 4 *pieds* in length (about 305 feet), located on the *Platon-de*-Trois-Rivières, (the Platon is the natural elevation which dominates the town of Trois-Rivières) along with a large two-story house and outbuildings, plus a new house built by the said sellers in the said Trois-Rivières, and outbuildings, with 50 *arpents* (about 9600 feet) of land to Mgr. de St-Valier, for 21,000 *livres* [about $4200.00].

(Records of Genaple)

[Based on a linear measure value of 191.8 feet per *arpent*. As was true of most French units of measurement at the time, however, the value of the *arpent* was not at all consistent and would often vary from one province to another.]

MOVEMENT OF THE CATHOLIC POPULATION OF THE PROVINCE OF QUÉBEC 1691 to 1700

	MARRIAGES	BIRTHS	DEATHS	OTHERS
1691	112	539	199	340
1692	98	574	165	409
1693	85	583	162	421
1694	157	627	196	431
1695	114	650	158	492
1696	138	657	143	514
1697	117	721	163	558
1698	186	797	213	584
1699	173	835	463	372
1700	172	907	350	557
TOTALS ➡	1352	6890	2212	4678
1608-1700	3913	18663	5782	12881

1700

January 17th

The baptism of a 16 year old Englishman at St-Joseph-de-Lévis by Father Bigot. The young man was a native of the Barbados who had been enslaved by the Abénaquis after being taken prisoner during a war. His godfather, M. Raymond

Martel, *marchand* [merchant], and his godmother, Charlotte Charets, the wife of Augustin LeGardeur from Courtemanche, named him Philippe.

(Québec Register)

October 18th

MM. de Callières and de Champigny wrote to France to report news of the death of Jolliet. The precise date of his death remains unknown but has been placed between 1698 and 1700 by various historians. Dwight H. Kelton, in his "*Annals of Fort Mackinac*", published in Chicago in 1882, repeated after Shea (on page 33) that Jolliet had very likely died in 1699. In a study entitled "*La Découverte du Mississippi*", Tanguay placed the date of his death at 1701. The uncertainty on this question has always been of interest to our historians.

In his "*Dictionnaire Généalogique*", M. l'Abbé Tanguay seemed certain that the famous discoverer of the Mississippi had died between May and October of 1700. When he was asked by the members of the press for the source of his information, he said that he knew of only one such official document regarding that highly contested date: it was the letter dated the 18th of October 1700 which M. the Chevalier de Callières and M. de Champigny had jointly sent from Québec to France and in which it was noted:
"Sieur Jolliet who taught [a class in] Hydrography in Québec, being dead, and the Jesuit Fathers offering to hold a class, we beseech His Majesty to make it easier for them by granting them the 400 *livres* [about $80.00] a year, which Sieur Jolliet had enjoyed ..."
(See the manuscripts in the Federal Parliament Library, Volume IX, Series II, p. 66.)

M. Margry, who had given a fairly extensive account of Louis Jolliet, wrote: "The last charts which we found regarding him [Jolliet] are, one of Anticosti in 1698, and another of the St-Lawrence River, addressed to M. de Villebois, on the 23rd of October 1699. Jolliet died some time after that as shown by the letter from both MM. de Callières and de Champigny, etc. My late and honorable friend, Father Ferland, assumed that he had died on his *Île-d'Anticosti*. Written evidence permitted me to state that he was buried in one of the Îles de Mingan, the one located at *le Gros Mécatina*." [on the shores of Labrador]

M. Tanguay's response was not long in coming: "Let us not forget", he said, "that MM. de Callières and de Champigny wrote to us on the 18th of October 1700 to let us know that Jolliet was dead. Check the 4th of May 1700 entry in the Notre-Dame de Québec Register and you will find among the witnesses to the marriage of Jérome Corda to Anne Normand dit Brière, the signature of '*Jolliet, the Royal Hydrographer*'[77]. Consequently, Joliette died between the 4th of May and the 18th of October 1700."

After that explanation, there was no possible doubt. Reverend Tanguay, addressing himself to M. Margry, the *conservateur des archives* [keeper of the records] of the *Ministère de la Marine* [Naval Admiralty] in Paris, who had mentioned a document which showed that the said Jolliet had been buried on one of the *Îles-de-Mingan*, the one located near *le Gros Mécatina* [on the shores of Labrador], continued: "In this case, we would have to conclude that Jolliet had died at a noteworthy time before the 18th of October and shortly after the 4th of May, so that M. de Callières and M. de Champigny could have known about it in Québec by the middle of October."

This was written in 1873, and the document referred to by M. Margry was never made public.

[The controversy continues...Lanctot in his "*A History of Canada*" (Clarke, Irwin & Company, 1963, p. 189) unequivocally states: "..some warriors struck down the man of God with a hatchet blow. This happened *on* October 18."]

77

Extract from the Register of baptisms, marriages and burials of Notre-Dame de Québec Parish, for 1700.
"On the 4th of May, 1700, after having obtained a dispensation from Monseignor l'Ill [sic], and the Reverend Bishop of Québec, by a mandate signed by his hand and by that of his Secretary, and sealed with his Official Seal, of three marital banns between Jérome Corda, the son of Isaac Corda and Jeanne, of the St-Eustache Parish in the Archdiocese of Paris, on the one hand, and Anne Normand, daughter of Pierre Normand dit la Brière, a citizen of the above-mentioned town in Québec, and of Cathérine Normand, and her father and mother, from this parish and archdiocese on the other hand; not having uncovered any impediments to their marriage, I, François Dupré, a parish priest in Québec, did marry them in the manner prescribed by our Holy Mother, the Church, in the presence of the said la Brière, the father of the bride, Charles Normand, of Sieurs Jacques Gourdeaux, Chambalon, royal notary, Charles Chartier. The said la Brière stated that he could not write; the others signed with the groom and the bride." (S.) Corda, Jolliet, the Royal Hydrographer; Anne Normand, Hugrunger, Depeiras, Jean Jacques Depeiras, Chambalon, J. Langlois, Chartier, Baudouin, lePailleur, A . DeLaborde, J. Thomas.

François Dupré.

Which extract, we, parish priest and pastor in Québec, the undersigned, certify to be true and consistent with the official Register, deposited in the Archives of the parish priest in Québec.

Forwarded to Québec, the 30th day of October, 1873.

J. Auclair, priest of Québec.

1701

January 5th

> A fire destroyed the home of Jean-François Hamel, a *cultivateur* [farmer] from Ste-Foye parish, who agonized as he watched his 5 young children perish in the flames.

> *(Ste-Foye Register)*

February 11th

> The baptism of Louis Marchand's 8-year-old Panis slave by M. Philippe Boucher, a priest at Lévis. Marchand lived in Lauzon when he bought the slave.

> *(Lévis Register)*

March 11th

> Claire Bissot, the widow of Louis Jolliet, conveyed ownership and possession of all of her businesses along the entire stretch from Mingan to Anticosti to her sons Charles Jolliet of Anticosti and François Jolliet of Baucour.

In the collection of unedited letters cited earlier, we found this description of the City of Québec:

> "When I first arrived, the City of Québec was located 2000 *lieues* [about 5000 miles] from France. It is divided between an Upper and a Lower City, in the latter reside the *marchands* [shopkeepers] and *les gens qui trafiquent à la mer* [those who make their money from the seas]; all of the houses are built comfortably strong, and made of a black stone which is just as attractive and hard as marble. Its anchorage is defended by a large platform [which has been placed] in the middle of the water [and] which lowers when the tide goes out, so that enemy vessels could not remain in the water without being very roughly tumbled about, as much by the cannon on the platform as by that in a fort overlooking both the City and the roads from one of the steepest locations.

From the Lower City to the Upper, there is a very slightly-winding road for carts and wagons which have their share of difficulty getting to the top, the Upper City being located at an extraordinary height.

FROM AN ENGRAVING BY RICHARD SHORT

The home of the Viceroy or Governor-General is in the Upper City, in a very conspicuous location. It is a two-story building, 120 feet long, with several pavilions which constitute the front and rear parts of the building, with an 80 foot terrace looking out over the Lower City and the river at its base, from which we can see as much as we could wish to see.

The *Gouverneur-Général*, who now lives in that home is M. le Chevalier [Louis Hector] de Callières, *cy-devant Gouverneur* [former Governor] of the City of Montréal, 60 *lieues* [about 150 miles] from Québec. He is respected, loved and cherished as much by the French as by the Indians, who all look upon him as the father of all those who live in Canada. It is to him that we should be grateful for all of the fortifications in our nation which were built under his care and direction. All of the *personnes de distinction* [people of good-breeding] also live in the Upper City.

The Bishop and *chanoines'* [canons'] Chapter house is quite nice: there is also a handsome seminary and several churches, among which those of the Jesuits and of the Récollets are the most attractive: that last one faces the Château and is looked upon as the most

LATE 16ᵀᴴ CENTURY-JESUIT & RÉCOLLET CHURCHES & CATHEDERAL (L TO R)

modern in the nation : the monastery of these fine Fathers has numerous windows – everywhere painted with the coats of arms of several of the benefactors of the house. Only the *Intendance* [the Administration building] is poorly placed on a shallow piece of land near a small stream.

>   [The *chanoines* ('canons') chapter house is the home of the members of the 'Chapter', the most distinguished group of clergy in New France principally because it was the closest to the Bishop. This 13-man group first appeared in 1684 and consisted of

contemplatives whose only role was that of prayer but who acted as the Bishop's Court and Council.]

"The City – both Upper and Lower – is situated between two tall mountains, one taller than the other. The first is called Cap-aux-Diamants because a large quantity of rocks which were almost as beautiful as the real thing – only the hardness being missing – had been found: the other mountain, the Saut-au-Matelot, was so-called because, during the first days of the French Settlement in this colony, there was a sailor, who, having stood too close to the edge, hurled himself from the top to the bottom in spite of himself. There is a small stream that winds towards the Administration Building near that second mountain."

D***

August 3rd

The burial of the Huron chief whom the historians called Kondiaronk in the church of Montréal. He was one of the most handsome figures in the Huron nation. Endowed with great intelligence, he conducted all of the affairs of his nation with caution and wisdom. He died a very strong Christian after a vehement appeal to the allied [Indian] nations which had gathered in Montréal. On his tombstone this short inscription was engraved: *"Cy gît Le Rat, chef Huron".* [78] ["Here lies Le Rat, Chief of the Hurons."]

(Ferland, Volume II, p. 35)

August 30th

The seigneurie of the fief of St-Luc, Rivière-du-Sud, belonged to Madeleine Morin, the widow of Gilles Rageot, *notaire* [notary], and to her niece Marie-Anne-Morin-Rochebelle, the wife of Jacques Pinguet de Vaucour. They ceded a 5 by 40 *arpent* [about 167 square-acre] parcel of land to Guillaume Blanchet.

(Records of Charles Rageot, 30 August, 1701)

[Based on a value of 5/6 of an acre per square *arpent*. As was true of all French measurements at the time, however, the value of the *arpent* was not at all consistent and could vary from one province to another.]

78

Kondiaronk is indeed the name by which our historians distinguish this noted chief; but if we look at his burial record, we will see that his real name was Gaspard Soiaga dit LeRat. He was the Chief of the Hurons of Michillimackinac, and was 75 years old when he died. *(Tanguay)*

1702

January 6th

The baptism of Jean Gautier's first child, Marie, at Kaskakia. The son of Pierre Gautier and Charlotte Roussel, Jean had married Suzanne Capei8svec8e, and was himself called Sakingoara.

(Kaskakia Register)

[The exact spelling of <u>Indian</u> <u>names</u> is almost impossible to determine since they were often so badly distorted both by the French and by the English who were all apt to phonetically transcribe the names which they learned from the Indians. One sound especially peculiar to the Algonquin language – although found in other languages as well – was the sound of an 8 or '*huit*, a whistling sound when pronounced in French. Many of the old names have retained the 8's in their spellings.]

June 19th

The stone-church built in the Pointe-aux-Trembles-de-Québec parish was today blessed and opened for worship.

(Pointe-aux-Trembles de Québec Register)

November 3rd

The Sieur de Sarrazin was the King's only *médecin* [medical doctor] in all of New France and his total annual fees only amounted to 600 *livres* [about $120.00], without fees from his patients.

(Letters of the Sieurs de Callières and de Beauharnois)

[New France ended up with a total of only four *médecins* (medical doctors) – numerous *chirurgiens* (surgeons) but very few doctors. Doctors were trained to take care of the sick by the Faculty of Medicine but really did not practice very much. The more-numerous surgeons – still only considered as craftsmen – were trained by the Society of Barber-Surgeons to perform several types of operations.. bleeding..lancing.. amputations .. (*without anesthetics*, of course) and substitute apothecary (druggist) tasks and they practiced accordingly. Their fees were very low whereas the more-expensive *médecins* could not even reset dislocated limbs which accounted for a great number of cripples. In effect, the *chirurgiens* were more valuable during this period.]

November 29th

The marriage of Louis LePoupet de St-Aubin, *chevalier*, Sieur de la Boularderie, and *enseigne du vaisseau* [ship's ensign], to Madeleine Melançon.

(Port-Royal Register)

[For more information on titles, honors, decorations, etc. please see my comments after the entry dated November 24th of 1659.]

December 5th

The burial of Marie-Anne Leneuf, the widow of M. René Robineau, *baron de Portneuf*, in the Récollets Church.

(Québec Register)

December 23rd

The *chirurgien* [surgeon] at Port-Royal was Jacques Pontif.

During 1702 and 1703, many people died from an *épidemie-de-variole* [a smallpox epidemic] in Québec as well as in a large number of parishes.
[Marcel Trudel notes that more than 2000 died in Québéc alone.]

1703

In 1662, a Frenchman, Laurent Dubock, born in St-Maclou in the diocese of Rouën in Normandy [in France] had married Marie-Félix, a Huron and the daughter of Joachim Arontio, in Québec. Joachim was the first Huron chief to have been converted to Christianity by Father de Brébeuf and was from a large village called Conception. Four sons, Joseph, Jean, Laurent and Philippe, and two daughters were born of this marriage. One of the 2 daughters, Marie-Anne, became an Ursuline nun by the name of Ste-Marie Madeleine, and the other, Louise-Cathérine, married a Jean Riddé, and includes the Viger families from Montréal among her descendants. It's very likely that the son of Joseph Dubock, *métis* [a halfbreed] married to a French-woman, was the one who became the hero of the terrifying drama told to us in the following letter:

Extract from a letter written in 1703 by M. Dubocq to his brother, a Franciscan priest: "He came to Montréal a few days after my arrival, a man whom History has made to seem more fable than truth, whom we called Dubock[79]. He was the son of an Indian and of a French woman. He was a *guerrier* [warrior] with great courage and extraordinary strength who has always been feared as the most noble partisan in the land.

He had been taken prisoner by the Iroquois at a battle near Orange[80] and had always dreaded that inevitable moment when he would be burned alive. One day while hunting with 8 warriors and 2 women, he was told that they would be staying in a cabin where there was a good supply of *eau-de-vie* [brandy]. Indeed, they found that precious cache as he had been told that they would; but the poor savages had no idea that their celebration would give rise to a bloody ending.

79

The grandson of Laurent Dubock.
80

Dubock, in a battle between the Mahingans and the Agniers, fell after an ambush near Orange. Out of sixteen, ten were killed: Dubock and three others were wounded and brought to Orange.

(Charlevoix, Book XVI, p. 199.)

After having eaten supper together, they began to sing and to drink in their usual manner which was to consume *eau-de-vie* more quickly and readily than we would drink wine at our most festive occasions. They invited the prisoner to keep up with their drinking spree. Dubock showed his gratitude by having several drinks of the liquor which had cost them quite a bit; it was then that they began to look upon him as a victim waiting to be sacrificed to the rage which they carried towards their enemies; it was, on the contrary, he himself who intended to kill them or to perish in the process, which to him seemed inevitable; but at that moment, merely all being friends merely enjoying themselves together, they began to sing songs of their victories over their enemies, and they sang to their heart's content; for one of the strengths of these people was to be able to thoroughly enjoy themselves once they took the time to do just that, and then only as a reward; and they were also so much more sober than all other people when it came time to fight or to hunt; that cache of *eau-de-vie* was the proof, since they had only visited it after returning from two marvelously successful military expeditions.

> [The Indians were very disciplined when it came to warfare. Here, they only chose to celebrate by going to and partaking of their cache of eau-de-vie after being victorious in two military expeditions.]

These infidels were very careful to hide their beverages and other supplies, and when it was necessary, not to carry anything other than their gun, axe, knife, club, powder and lead, with their quivers full of arrows, preferring to fast for seven or eight days or more, if necessary, than to carry the slightest thing which could have worked against them or been harmful to them.

Once their blood began to run boiling through their brains both from the *eau-de-vie* and from their songs of prowess in battle where they thought of the warriors whom they had killed or burned-to-death, several of them began to surrender themselves to slumber while those who were more aware of what was going on continued to force Dubock to drink; but as bad luck would have it, they had never used candles and had no other light in their cabin except for that which the [fireplace] fire furnished them: so, they could not notice that Dubock, although greatly inclined to drink, was not swallowing his *eau-de-vie*, and after having brought it up to his mouth, he would then merely let it slowly trickle out of his mouth down the full length of his stomach. So, by that method, he remained cold-blooded [sober] while the others became thoroughly inebriated, such that by the time the night was half over, there was only one of the warriors who was not asleep, and who was drinking all by himself; yet one moment later, he was caught up just like the others.

Would you believe what Dubock did? After ensuring himself that the ten others were truly asleep, he asked himself if he could profit more from his freedom simply by running away, or if he should send these others to their *pays des âmes* [land of the spirits or happy hunting grounds]. That's really how he thought. Finally, he decided on this last course of action, although sparing the two women, as an act of defiance, as if looking upon them as unworthy of his anger.

He started by tying the two of them up together, prejudiced as he was that having heads smaller than the men's, that they would be very drunk and so much more difficult to awaken. He tied them up like that, then took two smouldering-red logs in his hands, with which he was able to see the faces of the others, and no longer doubting their being asleep, he armed himself with a heavy axe, with which he saluted each of them, one after the other, with a strong and very quick blow to the head, and the first one who stirred was served with 2 or 3 blows which was enough to kill him, and his slaughter was done that way, and once the deed was done, he wished to awaken the two women, still without harming them; but was not able to do it and so, tired from tormenting them all, he resigned himself to spend the rest of the night smoking his pipe in the midst of this truly horrible spectacle.

The following morning, when the two Indian women awoke, he did not hesitate to make them aware that they were now widows, and had become his slaves, and finally that he had let them live providing that they would serve as witnesses to the truth; conditions which they accepted with all possible submissiveness; but, in addition, they knew fully right well that this bloody episode was not yet finished, and that the very last touch of inhumanity still remained. It is well, my dear brother, that you learn that when these people killed someone and on that very spot, they always brought the proof back with them, which was, according to them, a trophy which proved to the righteous their valor and courage. That unbecoming and shameful token is the human scalp which they removed as easily from the top of a head of a mortal being as we could remove the skin from a rabbit. They would cut the skin of the head down to the bone by starting in the middle of the forehead, while moving the hand from behind the ears, all the way around to where they had first started, and after some manual effort to begin to uncover the skull, they would turn the head backwards on their knees and, without releasing the skin, cause it to peel off as easily as a glove when we are trying to remove it from a hand; after which, they would sew it around a small circle of osier,

> [Picture the tough, fibrous branches of a willow (osier) tree ... the Indians used them to bind things together; as was the case here, they could also be woven together to form a band of twisted twigs.]

prepare it and pass it through to the side without any hair, all done as easily as they would do it with the skin of whatever-other-animal, and to finish this horrible masterpiece of cruelty, they would then comb them with some red pigment, and being attached to the circles of osier, as I have just said, they would place each of them at the end of a 10 to 12 foot long pole.

> [R. Douville and J. D. Casanova note that the scalping practice was an American-Indian phenomenon enabling the (new) owner of the scalp to add one eagle's feather per scalp to his war-bonnet.]

To return to our victor, after he had spent the time needed to do all of the above, he took the scalps in one hand and with the other, the two women who were tied together, and who didn't exactly have to be begged to walk; he brought them like that to the gates of Montréal and stopped there, as was usually done; he then let loose with 8 distinct death cries, to show that he had killed 8 men, according to the proof which he held in his hands.

> [These so-called death cries were really the 'scalp whoops' referred to in Howard Peckham's "*Captured by Indians*" and other works of 'captivity' literature.]

At those cries, each man from within hurried before him, believing that several warriors had arrived, about which they were very surprised and fooled when they saw Dubock alone. I wasn't one of the last to go to meet him, and since I knew him personally, I greeted him with great joy, while showing him how happy that I was with his success and at the happiness which he must have felt at having been able to escape from the cruelest men on this earth and from whom he could only have awaited some unheard-of treatment; I did not leave him until we got to the Governor's house, which he majestically entered holding in one hand 8 long poles at the end of which hung 8 long heads-of-hair, and in the other, his two prisoners whom he had had walk in front of him, tied together like children being lead by their leading-strings. [strings or straps used to guide and support a young child learning to walk].

M. de Callières received him very politely, and listened to his story with as much admiration as astonishment, all the more so because it was spoken in a very eloquent French – especially for a man who was half-savage – and spoken in the most natural of terms which one could express himself with. Then he gave him 240 *livres* [about $48.00], in merchandise, which was based on the 30 *livres* [about $6.00] which we ordinarily pay for each scalp which our Indians bring to us.

I, [Dubocq], embrace you with the most perfect friendship that one could have for a brother like you."

April 2nd

> The burial of Mme. DeGalifet[81], Mme. DeVilledonné[82] and Mme. Testard[83] in Montréal from among the families struck by the terrible outbreak of smallpox.

81

Cathérine Aubert, 21, the wife of François de Galifet, lieutenant du Roi.
82

Marie Damours, 28, wife of Étienne de Villedonné, *aide-major* [major's aid]   de Québec.
83

Marguerite Damours, sister of the above-named Marie, 26, wife of Jacques Testard de Montigny, *capitaine de la marine*. [naval Captain.]

[Louise Dechêne notes that a *maladie de petite vérole* and *flux de sang* or smallpox outbreak struck in January 1703, peaked in April, and dragged on until July, claiming 1000 to 1200 victims in the colony among the French and the Indians.]

We find the following note having to do with the outbreak of smallpox in the Ste-Famille Registers: "Grassante Boâ, sive Pabula, in eâ regione, ii omnes fatis occubuere eo morbo infecti."

["From the crawling serpent to the food we eat, all in that region infected by that disease succumbed to fate."]

July 24th

M. Mathieu DeGoutin was *lieutenant-général* at Port-Royal.

August 5th

Michel Bouvier, 57, *maître maçon* [master bricklayer], died when he fell from a staging on a house which was being built for M. de Senneville in an elevated location in Montréal.

(Montréal Register)

September 30th

Jacques Dejoncour commanded the royal ship *Le Faucon* which rested in the Port-Royal harbor.

(Port-Royal Register)

Patrice René, a Récollet, who had been *vicaire-général* and *supérieur* of the entire Mission in 1708, was now *curé* [priest] in the Port-Royal parish.

(Idem)

1704

January 10th

The baptism and naming of Cathérine, the child of William Parsons and of Anne Wheelright by M. Meriel, a priest from St-Sulpice in Montréal. She was born in Wells [Maine] in New England in 1701. She and her mother were kidnapped by the Indians from *Lac-des-Deux-Montagnes* on the 22nd of August 1703.

(Lac-des-Deux-Montagnes Register)

February 2nd

The first baptism recorded in the Détroit Register was of Marie-Thérese, the fifth child of Antoine DelaMothe-Cadillac, *fondateur* [founder] of Détroit, and of Marie-Thérèse Guyon-Desprès. Her godfather was Bertrand Arnaud, *marchand* [merchant], and her godmother was Geneviève LeTendre, the wife of Étienne Volant-Radisson. Father Constantin DeLhalle, a Récollet and first *aumônier* [chaplain] at Fort Pontchartrain in Détroit, performed the baptism and recorded it.

NOTE: See the notice dated the 13th of May 1723 regarding this Récollet Father.

February 12th

The name given to a hill in Montréal, the *Côte-à-Baron*, was explained by the fact that the owner of the Côte-de-Notre-Dame-des-Neiges was Jean-Baptiste Auger dit le Baron.

(Montréal Register)

June 15th

The baptism of Abigail-Marie-Élizabeth Nimbs, born on the 11th of June 1700 in Deerfield [Massachusetts], in New England. Her godmother was Demoiselle Élizabeth Lemoyne from Longueuil. After being kidnapped by the Indians on the 11th of March 1704, she lived in a small hut belonging to a *sauvagesse* [mountain-woman] called Ganastarsi.

(Montréal Register)

December 20th

The Royal vessel, *Le Lion* lost 3 of its crew-members: Ducorail, a *sergent* [sergeant]; Forest, *soldat de la marine* [marine]; and Jean Basque, *matelot* [sailor], while it stood anchored in the Port-Royal river basin from the 25th of October until today.

(Port-Royal Register)

December 26th

The burial of Pierre Tibodeau, husband of Jeanne Terriau, a *meunier* [miller] at Prée-ronde.

(Idem)

During the year, Mgr. De St-Valier was taken prisoner by an English fleet while returning from France to Canada on *La Seine, grande flûte du Roi* [a large royal merchantman] commanded by the Chevalier de Maupeau. He was then forced to spend 8 years in England.

(Archdiocesan Register)

1705

January 12th

The marriage of François Dupont-Duvivier, *enseigne du vaisseau* [ship's ensign] and the son of Hugues Dupont-Duvivier, seigneur de Serignac, to Marie Mius, the daughter of Jacques Mius, seigneur de Pobonkan, and of Anne Saint-Étienne.

(Port-Royal Register)

January 22nd

The burial of Mathieu Bosselet dit Jolicoeur, 40, soldier in M. de Beaucours' company, who was found dead on the ice.

(Montréal Register)

March 29th

The burial of Sieur Saint-Aubin, 85, seigneur of Pesmonquadis [s/b Passamaquoddy] or Rivière-Ste-Croix.

(Port-Royal Register)

May 22nd

The baptism of all the children – the oldest was 16 – from three families residing in Cap-de-Sable: François Amiraut had 8; Joseph Mius, 4; François Viger, 2.

(Idem)

June 10th

Marguerite Delajoüe, 18, drowned in Québec.

(Québec Register)

September 9th

The marriage of François Crepaux, Commandant of the frigate *La Bonaventure,* to Marie Mius, the daughter of Abraham Mius and Marguerite de St-Étienne.

(Port-Royal Register)

September 21st

François, the 14-year-old son of Pierre-de-Quatrebarbe, *capitaine réformé* [discharged captain] of the troops in M. DeLangloiserie's company, was buried after he had drowned in Québec [on the 19th]. His mother, Marie LeRoy, was referred to as *la jeune chevalière de Chambly* at his baptism at Pointe-aux-Trembles-de-Montréal in 1692 [22 January].

(Pointe-aux-Trembles de Montréal Register)

September 25th

The burial of Charles Calué dit Laforge, *habitant* [resident] of Beausoleil, above the River.

(Port-Royal Register)

October 3rd

The burial of Jacques-François DeBrouillant, Provincial Governor, who died on the 18th of September on the ship *Le Profond* one day away from Chibouctou. He was buried near the tall cross at the Cap, where we were planning to build a chapel.

(Idem)

October 19th

The marriage of Anne Hard to Sébastien Cholet dit Laviolette, *tisserand* [weaver] and native of Aubigny in Anjou [in France]. Born in 1681, she was the daughter of Benjamin Hard and Élizabeth Roberts from Chitcho near Dover, in New England. She had been taken prisoner by the *sauvages Loups* [Wolf Indians] in 1692.

(Montréal Register)

October 28th

The baptism of Marie-Madeleine Atchers, the daughter of Atchers and of Marie Oppen, who resided at the home of Mademoiselle de Sorel while a prisoner of war.

(Sorel Register)

December 31st

The burial of Robert Giffard, *chirurgien* [surgeon], and seigneur de Beauport. Born in France in 1587 and first buried in Québec on the 14th of April 1668, he was later transported from Hôtel-Dieu of Québec to the Cathederal *"pour libera"* ["for burial rite"] and then on to Beauport where he is now buried.

(Montréal Register)

1706

January 10th

The baptism of Mathias Farnet, who was born in 1680 in Groton [Massachusetts], New England. His godfather was Claude de Ramezay, the Governor of Montréal. He had been taken prisoner by the Indians on the 11th of August 1704 and brought to Canada. At the time that this entry was made in the Register, he resided in Notre-Dame-de-Lorette Mission on Île-de-Montréal.

(Montréal Register)

January 17th

The baptism of Thomas Hust who was born on the 3rd of June 1690 in Deerfield [Massachusetts], in New England. He was taken prisoner on the 11th of March 1704 and lived at the Notre-Dame-de-Lorette mission at the time that this entry was made.

(Idem)

SAINT NICHOLAS
SAINT-NICHOLAS CHURCH

March 16th

The baptism of a young English boy, Joseph, 8, at St-Nicholas. The boy had been kidnapped by the Indians during the war.

(St-Nicholas Register)

April 6th

The baptism of Marie-Françoise French, who was born in Deerfield [Massachusetts] on the 30th of November 1692 and kidnapped on the 11th of February 1704. She was the daughter of Thomas French and Marie Catlin and resided at the home of M. Jacques LeBé.

(Montréal Register)

April 24th

The baptism of Jean-Louis Dicker, 12, the son of Jean Dicker and Sara Teckel, *famille de pêcheurs* [family of fishermen] living in Hanzerbury on Île-de-Terreneuve. He was ransomed back from the Indians by M. Thomas de Joncaire, the *interprète du Roi* [King's Interpreter].

(Idem)

May 25th

The baptism of Guillaume-François Taylor, a native of Exeter [New Hampshire] in New England and later a prisoner of war who was in the service of Governor de Ramezay.

(Idem)

September 6th

The marriage of Louis Liénard de Beaujeu, son of Philippe, *chef du gobelet du Roi* [officer of the King's goblet], *guidon des chevaux légers de la Garde du Roi* [standard-bearer of the King's Light Cavalry], and of Cathérine Gobert from Versailles, to Demoiselle Denise-Thérèse Migeon de la Gauchetière[84], the widow of Charles Juchereau de Beaumarchais, Sieur Denis, still alive [as of the date of this entry in the Montréal Register], *conseiller du Roi* [royal counselor] and *lieutenant-général* of Île-de-Montréal.

(Idem)

[The *chef du gobelet du Roi* had the perilous responsibility of drinking any drink and eating any food which was destined for consumption by the King.]

September 12th

The baptism of Marguerite Huggins, the daughter of Jean Huggins and of Expatience Jones. Born on the 16th of March 1686 in Stonybrook, New England, she was taken prisoner by the Abénaquis at Parkamack near Northampton [Massachusetts] on the 23rd of May 1703 and then bought back by the Marquis de Crisaly, the Governor of Trois-Rivières.

(Idem)

84

Wet-nurse/babysitter for our seigneurs, the children of France. Born in Montréal on the 5th of February 1678, she had married – in a first marriage – a Charles Juchereau on the 21st of April 1692.

October 26th

The burial of Jacques Cosket de Luçon, 45, who died suddenly on the ship *Le Héron.*

(Québec Register)

November 16th

The burial of Daniel Galuccia, 54, a native of *Île-Jersey,* who had been taken prisoner in New England in July of 1706.

(Montréal Register)

1707

January 23rd

The baptism of Marthe French who had first been baptized in 1706. She was born on the 22nd of May 1695 and was a sister of Marie-Françoise. She had been given to the *Soeurs-de- la-Congrégation-de-Notre-Dame* by the Abénaquis Indians.

(Idem)

February 24th

The baptism of Joseph Stover, the son of Jean Stover and of Abigail from Cape Vadick, between York [Maine] and Wells [Maine] in New England. Born in 1690 and kidnapped by the Abénaquis in 1706, he was later ransomed by Françoise Domitilde, an Abénaquise woman who lived among the French and who sent him to Montréal.

(Idem)

March 8th

The marriage celebration of Anne Raté, the widow of Jacques DeTrépagny and daughter of Jacques Raté and Anne Martin[85]. The groom, a man named Jean from England, had been removed from England in his younger years and could no longer remember either the first or the family names of his parents.

(Château-Richer Register)

[According to Tanguay's "*Dictionnaire Généalogique des Familles Canadiennes*" (Volume 6, p. 512), Anne Raté's second husband was Jean Langlois.]

June 13th

The baptism of Marie-Françoise Hammond, born in 1688, and the daughter of Edouard Hammond and of Jane Montess from Kittery [Maine] in New England. Marie was captured by the Abénaquis on the 17th of May in 1705.

(Montréal Register)

85

Anne Martin was the daughter of Abraham Martin dit l'Écossais, the owner of the Plains of Abraham.

September 8th

Antoine de Vaillant, *enseigne des troupes* [ensign in the military], was killed while battling the English.

(Port-Royal Register)

September 11th

The baptism of Élizabeth Lamax who was born in 1698 of Nathaniel Lamax and Déliverance Clarke from Oyster River in New England. She had been taken prisoner by the Abénaquis on the 1st of June in 1707 and now lived in the home of M. Étienne Rocbert de la Morandière, *conseiller du Roi* [Royal counselor].

(Montréal Register)

October 31[s]

The marriage of the *baron* Anselme de St-Castin, the son of *baron* Jean-Vincent de St-Castin and of Matilde, an Indian woman, to Charlotte Damours, the daughter of Louis Damours, seigneur de Jemsec.

(Port-Royal Register)

November 6th

The baptism of Daniel-Louis-Philippe, the son of Sergent Dicker and Mary Oben. He was born in 1699 in New England and later kidnapped by the Abénaquis who then gave him to Governor Rigaud de Vaudreuil.

(Montréal Register)

1708

March 21st

The burial of Tobie Von, son of Tobie Von and of Sara Spark, who was born in 1690 and later taken prisoner on Île-de-Terreneuve. He belonged to M. de Montigny.

(Idem)

April 7th

The baptism of a 17-year-old English woman who was named Marie-Françoise. She was originally called Hélène Darvass, a native of the village of Jamesker in New England, and was kidnapped by the Indians during the war and placed with the Ursulines in Québec, where she died on the 30th of August 1710.

(Québec Register)

[Helen (Darvass) Davis was taken from her home in Jemaico (West Amesbury, Massachusetts) on August 9, 1704. She was later baptized as Marie Françoise in the Chapel of the Ursulines and had a Robert Drouard (of Jemaico) as her godfather and Marie-Jeanne W___[illegible], the wife of a Pierre Pilotte, as her godmother. She was buried on August 31st at age 19 by a Father Pacquet in the cemetery of the Hôpital with the name Heleine Da Wass. (Emma Lewis Coleman,"*New England Captives Carried to Canada - 1677-1760 - French and Indian Wars*", Southworth Press, 1925, pp. 127, 338 & 365) .]

May 6th

Mgr. Laval died in Québec at 85 years of age and was buried on the 9th of May in the Cathederal, under the first step of the main altar[86].

(Archdiocesan Register of Québec)

[People were rarely buried under the church. The privilege was reserved for priests who (ordinarily) had a place under the choir, and for seigneurs, under their seigneurial pews. Marcel Trudel noted that the custom eventually had to be limited because the graves were not dug very deep and 'pestilential odours' spread through the church.]

May 25th

The burial of Louis Richet, a 28-year-old Englishman, who drowned on the 1st of May while in a small boat belonging to Jacques Bernier. A good Catholic who was very faithful in receiving the sacraments, he had refused the English offers to leave so that he might remain in this nation and preserve his religion.

(Montréal Register)

May 28th

The baptism of Abigail-Marguerite, the daughter of John Stebbens and of Dorothy Alexander from Deerfield [Massachusetts]. Her godfather was Governor Rigaud de Vaudreuil and her godmother was Marguerite Bouat, the wife of Antoine Pacaud, who had been commissioned the *trésorier des deniers du Roi* [Royal Treasurer]. She was born in 1684 and married on the 14th of February 1704 by a minister in Deerfield [Massachusetts] after which she and her husband, Jacques Denoyon, came to live in Boucherville.

(Idem)

July 23rd

The baptism of Sara Tarbel, the child of Thomas Tarbel and Élizabeth Woods. She was born on the 9th of October 1693 in Grossen, New England, taken prisoner by the Abénaquis on the 20th of June 1707, and later ransomed to Canada where she lived with the Soeurs de la Congrégation de Notre Dame.

(Idem)

October 7th

The baptism of Philippe-Joseph Montaye, the son of Philippe Montaye and Jeanne Tourgis. He was born on the 25th of May 1683 at St-Oen, on Île-Jersey. On the 29th of March 1705, he was taken prisoner at Port Gravé, Île-Terreneuve where he lived in the home of M. Jacques Tétard.

(Idem)

86

In 1878, the body of Mgr. Laval was removed and transported, with great ceremony, to the chapel in the Seminary in Québec.

1709

January 1st

Joseph-Daniel Maddox, the son of Jean Maddox and Anne Witby, was born in Dover, in the county of Chester in England, and was garrisoned at St-Jean-de-Terreneuve at the time that the fort was overrun. He was sent to Montréal where he was baptized on the 26th of April 1710 with M. le Baron de Longueuil as his godfather. He worked the farm at the Séminaire-de-Québec at Île-Jésus, and was married twice, first to Marie Jetté in 1713, and then to Marie-Louise Lacelle in 1715. He died in Montréal in October of 1754.

January 21st

A disastrous fire at the home of Jacques Gaudry dit LaBourbonnière in which 4 of his children perished in the flames.

(Varennes Register)

May 20th

The baptism of several English captives who were ransomed from the Abénaquis Indians during this and the next few months.

(Québec Register)

June 2nd

Two women drowned while on their way to Mass on Pentecostal Sunday: Suzanne Mesny, 23, the daughter of Étienne Mesny and wife of Charles Croteau; and Marguerite Grenon, 27, the daughter of Pierre Grenon and wife of Jean Bergeron.

(St-Nicholas Register)

[Although originally an agricultural festival on which the people were expected to show gratitude to God for an early harvest, Pentecost later – at the time of Jesus Christ – began to have a less agricultural significance both to Christians and to Jews. For Christians, Pentecostal Sunday – the 7th Sunday (50 days) after Easter – memorizes the descent of the Holy Spirit on the Apostles empowering them to witness to Jesus Christ. For Jews, it is a celebration in observance of the giving of the Torah, the Jewish body of divine instructions, teachings and law, by Moses on Mount Sinai.]

On that same day, Marguerite DeNevelet, the widow of Abraham Bouat, entered the Soeurs-de-la-Congrégation-de-Notre-Dame convent in Montréal as a *pensionnaire perpétuelle* [permanent boarder]. She remained there until her death on the 11th of April in 1720 when she was 80 years old.

(Montréal Register)

June 3rd

The burial of Lorrain Pasquier, a member of the crew on the privateer *Morpain* and *filibustier* [pirate] from Santo Domingo Island.

(Port-Royal Register)

July 18th

The burial of Pierre Perthuis, the son of Pierre, who was killed in 1708 by the English in Deerfield [Massachusetts].

July 21st

The baptism of François-Jacques Havy, a 20-year-old Englishman, who had been held captive for 2 years.

(Québec Register)

On the same day, Joseph Benjamin Massy, a 19-year-old Englishman, was also baptized.

(Idem)

July 23rd

The baptism of Marie-Anne, the daughter of Jean Lalande, *interprète* [interpreter] for the English and Flemish in this area.

(Montréal Register)

August 12th

The burial of Jacques Raimbaut, a native of Nantes [in France] as well as a *filibustier du corsaire* [pirate on the ship] *Morpain*.

(Port-Royal Register)

That day, Peter DeMorpain, Captain in charge of *Le Marquis de Beaupré*, and the son of Jacques DeMorpain, *banquier* [banker] in Blaye in Guienne, married Marie-Joseph Damours, the daughter of Louis Damours, seigneur de Temsec.

(Idem)

September 30th

The burial of Jean Huillier, a native of the Havres and *lieutenant du vaisseau* [Lieutenant on the ship] *Le Corsaire dit Le-Paquet-bot*, commanded by M. DelaCroix.

(Idem)

October 10th

The burial of Guillaume Planty, a native of Angoulême [France] and *soldat du vaisseau* [soldier on the ship] *Le Corsaire dit Le-Paquet-bot*.

(Idem)

1710

January 31st

Thomas Jacob was the *maître canonier* [master gunner] at Port-Royal.

(Idem)

April 26th

The baptism of Daniel-Joseph, the son of Jean Maddox, born on the 4th of May 1697 in Dover, Chester County, in England. He was captured with the rest of the English garrison at St-Jean-de-Terreneuve on the 1st of January 1709 and now lives at the Séminaire-de-Québec farm on Île-Jésus.

(Montréal Register)

July 11th

The baptism of Jeanne Oardaway who was born in Newbury [Massachusetts] in January of 1687 and taken prisoner at Haverhill [Massachusetts] by the Abénaquis Indians in Bécancourt in March of 1704.

(Idem)

August 6th

Louis DeTrépagny, 19, the son of François DeTrépagny and Anne Lefrançois and *élève du Séminaire-de-Québec* [seminary student], drowned while swimming.

(Québec Register)

September 7th

The baptism of Richard Pears, the son of Nicolas Pears and of Mary Merson, who was born in 1680 in Cornwallis, England. He was taken prisoner by M. de St-Ovide at St-Jean-de-Terreneuve on the 1st of January in 1709 and then sent to Canada.

(Montréal Register)

September 22nd

Jesse Leduc, *procureur général du Roi* [the King's attorney general], had arrived in Canada early in the month but died and was buried in the church.

(Québec Register)

[People were rarely buried under the church. The privilege was reserved for priests who (ordinarily) had a place under the choir, and for seigneurs, under their seigneurial pews. Marcel Trudel noted that the custom eventually had to be limited because the graves were not dug very deep and 'pestilential odours' spread through the church.]

November 9th

Reference is made to a chapel dedicated to Saint Lawrence in the upper regions of the river[87].

(Port-Royal Register)

87

A portion of the upper waters was called Beausoleil.

MOVEMENT OF THE CATHOLIC POPULATION
OF THE PROVINCE OF QUÉBEC 1701 TO 1710

	MARRIAGES	BIRTHS	DEATHS	OTHERS
1701	143	861	224	637
1702	124	951	379	572
1703	155	680	1079	...
1704	145	1067	231	836
1705	144	788	226	562
1706	162	986	303	683
1707	111	978	280	698
1708	142	1013	485	528
1709	147	959	379	580
1710	189	1023	315	708
TOTALS ➡	1462	9306	3901	5405
1608 to 1710	5375	27969	9683	12286

[Tanguay's 'OTHERS' detail adds up to 5804 yet his 'TOTAL' is 5405.]

1711

January 7th

> The marriage of Jean Mouton, the son of Antoine Mouton, *maître d'hôtel* [head-waiter] for the Count de Grignau, to Marie Girouard, the daughter of Alexandre Girouard and Marie LeBorgne.

NOTE: The following was noted at the bottom of the marriage (certificate):
"Since the Governor [de Vaudreuil] maintains that I am not able to marry anyone without the authorization of the Queen of England, I have not yet decided whether I should publish the banns during the English invasion or not. I have therefore married Jean Mouton and Marie Girouard with clearly enunciated words in front of those here-present."

(SIGNED,)   Brother Justinien
                                            (Port-Royal Register)

February 16th

February 16th

A baptism was performed at Port-Royal by Bonaventure Masson[88], a Récollet.

(Idem)

December 1st

The marriage of Joseph Poupart dit Lafleur and Cathérine Juillet. His father, René Poupart, lived in Hill Water, near Orange [Massachusetts] in New England.

(Montréal Register)

December 27th

Father Justinien Durand, who had succeeded Father Pain as missionnaire to Port-Royal since 1704, was held prisoner in Boston [Massachusetts] for all of 1711. Once released, he remained at his mission until 1720.

(Port-Royal Register)

1712

June 13th

The baptism of an 18-year-old Englishwoman captured in a battle with the Indians from Deux-Montagnes. She professed to never wanting to leave the tribe which had adopted her.

(Lac-des-Deux-Montagnes Register)

Several Englishmen adopted by the *Lac-des-Deux-Montagnes* Indians were baptized but continued to live with them after their baptisms.

SEE: Claude, 2nd of July in 1759

Several Canadians have married Iroquois and Montagnais women.

SEE: Héry, Laforce, Normand
(Lac-des-Deux-Montagnes Register)

August 15th

The burial of François Fournier, nicknamed *Poignon* since he had no fingers on his left hand, after he and Jean Bois, his co-worker at the Hôtel-Dieu of Québec, had drowned.

(Baie-St-Paul Register)

August 31st

The burial of M. François Poncelet, 42, the premier *curé*[first priest] at *St-Laurent-de-l'Île- d'Orléans*, after he died of smallpox at the Hôtel-Dieu.

(St-Laurent-de-l'Île Register)

88

The name of this religious is not in the Index of Clergy.

September 10th

The baptism of Madeleine-Suzanne, the daughter of Vincent Henry dit Laforge of the diocese of Langres, and soldier in M. Sabrévois' Company. She was born in 1711 in Tsonnontouan, an Iroquois tribal home. On the 25th of December 1713, Father Pelfresne baptized a second child named François-Xavier at Fort Frontenac in Cataraquoi [Kingston, Ontario], but that baptism was not recorded in Montréal until the 30th of July 1714. Two other children were baptized in Lachine: Suzanne in 1718 and Vincent in 1720[89]; finally, Charlotte, born the 25th of May 1729 at the Tsonnontouan village, was baptized in Montréal on the following 12th of July.

(Montréal Register)

November 10th

Two little boys, François Grosleau, 12, and François Chaille, 9, disappeared and were never found. Their parents lived at Cap-de-Lauzon[90].

(Cap-Santé Register)

1713

January 5th

A fire at Intendant [Claude-Michel] Bégon's palais [mansion] took the lives of his *valet-de-chambre* [valet], Brisset, and of two of his wife's *filles-de-chambres* [chambermaids].

(Québec Register)

[As Intendant, Bégon was entitled to live at the Palais de l'Intendance in Québec.]

June 2nd

The burial of Pierre Doucet, 100, the first *centenaire* [centenarian] registered in Port-Royal.

In 1706, Michelle Aucoin, the widow of juge Boudrot, died at 95 years of age and Pierre Bézier died at 90 years of age; in 1709, Denis Godet died at 97 years of age.

(Port-Royal Register)

89

Entered in the Lachine Register.

90

The Cap-de-Lauzon (now known as Deschambault) is the high point of land on which the Deschambault Church is built.

1714

July 19th

The burial of Jacques Dupassage, 20, *écuyer* [squire] , seigneur Dupassage, after drowning at Pointe-aux-Trembles-de-Montréal.

(Pointe-aux-Trembles de Montréal Register)

September & October

Many children died during this two-month period.

(Québec Register)

[Trudel notes that the high birth rate in New France was often checked by the death rate which averaged 23.6 per 1000 and rose to 39.6 per 1000 in the years 1700-1770. During that period, as many as 246 per 1000 children died within the first year.]

1715

October 18th

The burial of Michel Ance, *étudiant en théologie* [theological student] who had also been the *organiste* in the Sibour Cathederal [in France].

(Idem)

The marriage of Joseph-Charles de St-Denis, the son of Charles Juchereau and of Denise-Thérèse Migeon, to Doña Maria, the first-born daughter of Don Pedro de Vilesca, *vice-roi* [viceroy] of Mexico.

(Margry, Part V, p. 535)

October 20th

Mgr. De St-Valier baptized and personally named Joachim, a 17-year-old Englishman and native of Boston.

(Québec Register)

1716

March 16th

The burial of Françoise Hébert[91], 78, the widow of Guillaume Fournier who was the *fondateur* [founder] of St-Thomas Church [in Montmagny].

(St-Thomas Register)

[Jetté notes that he was also one of the parish's *pionniers* (pioneers) and notes further that she – a grand-daughter of Louis Hébert – was a politically active woman in her parish. Their children helped to lay the foundation for the many Hébert descendants in Canada and in the USA.]

91

She was the grand-daughter of Louis Hébert, the first permanent settler in Canada.

September 6th

Bernard Aristoille was the *chirurgien du navire*[ship's surgeon] on the *Heureuse de Bayonne* which was at anchor in the Port of Québec.

(Québec Register)

October 10th

The departure from Mobile of Gabriel Baudreau dit Graveline along with his *société de commerce*[his Canadian business associates], MM. de St-Denis, de Léry, LaFresnière, Beaulieu and Derbanne, who had invested 60,000 *livres* [about $12,000.00] for merchandise for resale in the stores of a M. Croissat who, in 1713, had received the King's right to trade in Louisiana for a ten-year period. They hoped to be able to sell their goods to the Spanish in the new kingdom of Léon. Gabriel was born in Montréal in 1666, was the son of Urbain Baudreau and of Marguerite Julliet, and – in 1701 – had married Cathérine Forestier, also in Montréal.

(Historical Journal on the Establishment of the French in Louisiana, by Bernard de la Harpe, pp. 374-6)

1717

February 15th

The home of Pierre Yvon[92] collapsed under the weight of the winter's snow and his two children[93] perished in the ruins.

(Québec Register)

March 14th

The baptism of Marie-Madeleine in the palace chapel. She was the child of Pierre Méchin de Frontigny, *greffier de la maréchausée* [clerk for the police constabulary], and of Madeleine Delajoue. Intendant Bégon named her.

(Idem)

[Since Intendant Bégon was entitled by his office to live in the *Palais de l'Intendance* in Québec and since he seemed to have been personally interested in this particular baptism not to mention the fact that his own daughter was being baptized on that same day (next paragraph), the reference to a palace here is perhaps to his own 'Palais' or mansion. It is also possible, however, that the reference is to the Bishop's 'Palais' since the baptism was, of course, a religious service and also since the Bishop outranked the Intendant in order of importance.]

92

A resident of Québec and husband of Marie Massard. His real name is Pierre Yves LeBer, a native of the diocese of Léon in the Province of Tours [in France].

93

Pierre, 19, and Charlotte, 15.

On the same day, the baptism – in the palace chapel – of Jeanne-Élizabeth, born on the 27th of August 1715, the daughter of Claude-Michel Bégon, Intendant, *chevalier, capitaine des troupes* [company captain], and *seigneur de la Picardière*, and his wife, Jeanne-Élizabeth DeBeauharnois. Jean Martel, seigneur of the Rivière St-Jean in Acadia, stood-in as godfather in place of M. François Bégon, chevalier, conseiller du Roi, and *grand-maître des eaux et forêts de France*. [Minister of the Woods and Forests of France.]
[For more information on titles, honors, decorations, etc. , please refer to my comments after the entry of November 24, 1659.]

On the preceding 28th of February, Mgr. de St-Valier had baptized their son, Michel, whose godfather was M. [Philippe de Rigaud de] Vaudreuil, the Governor.

1718

March 13th
Pierre Choret, a native of Charlesbourg, was the *contremaître*[foreman or overseer] of the *ménagerie-des-pauvres* near Montréal.

(Montréal Register)

What is a *ménagerie des pauvres*? [Tanguay's question.]

[P. G. Roy notes that (animal) *ménageries* were not at all uncommon for the wealthier people in Europe during this period. Seigneurs or princes were apt to keep all types of wild and exotic animals as much as a show of their wealth as out of a sense of curiosity. The *ménageries de Versailles* or *de Vincennes* or *de Meudon* were examples of these and were very popular places to visit. The *ménageries-des- pauvres*, however, were more geared to feeding and caring for the animals belonging to poor people.]

During the year, we baptized several Panis Indians who had been brought from Louisiana as slaves for some Québec families.

(Québec Register)

April 30th
The burial of the 16-year-old son of Sieur Louis Daillebout de Coulonges, at Ste-Anne-du-Bout-de-l'Île. He had been mortally wounded by the Iroquois.

(Bout-de-l'Île-de-Montréal Register)

September 25th

Two children from Québec, J. Baptiste and Louis-Étienne Lafleur[94], were found in a canoe on the beach, apparently dead from cold or hunger.

(St-Pierre-de-l'Île-d'Orléans Register)

September 29th

The burial of Jean-Baptiste, the 18-year-old son of Sébastien Hervé from Québec who had drowned during the previous night while crossing from Lévis to Québec.

(Québec Register)

October 12th

Martin Leclerc, *bienfaiteur de l'église* [church benefactor], had originally been buried on the 8th of March 1703 but his remains were now moved into the new St-Pierre Church on Île- d'Orléans.

(St-Pierre-de-l'Île-d'Orléans Register)

1719

May 13th

The burial of Gabriel Nolin, 35, who was killed by a falling tree.

(St-Pierre-de-l'Île-d'Orléans Register)

November 5th

Québec's *première centenaire* [first centenarian] was buried and recorded in the Registers as Marie Bérard, the widow of Pierre Pivain dit Larécompense.

(Québec Register)

Philippe-Pierre Sauvenier de Coppin, *missionnaire* in Ste-Anne-de-la-Pocatière parish, made the following note in the Rivière-Ouelle Registers: "I performed a baptism in the Ste-Anne chapel of the Notre-Dame-de-la-Boutellerie parish."

(Rivière-Ouelle Register)

1720

94

I believe them to be the children of Jean-Frs. Dussault dit Lafleur.

(Tanguay)

January and February

Timothy Sullivan, *chirurgien* [surgeon], born in 1696, the son of Daniel Sullivan and Élizabeth Macarthy, came from St-Philbert in the diocese of Cork (Ireland). He had married Marie Gautier, the widow of Christophe Dufros de la Jemerais at la-Pointe-aux-Trembles in Québec sometime in 1720[95].

QUEBEC IN 1720

June 29th

The burial of the parish priest, M. François Dupré, in the church sanctuary. Jesuit Father Lebrun officiated at the services and was duly assisted by some of the parishioners.

(Lorette Register)

95

The marriage records in the Pointe-aux-Trembles Register do not mention the specific date of the month but it was written between the 24th of January and the 5th of February. The entry had escaped the scrupulous and incessant historical searches surrounding the mother of Mme. [Marguerite] D'Youville, the founder of the Grey Nuns in Montréal. An invaluable document which establishes the nobility in Timothy [O'] Sullivan's genealogical lines can be found in the Genealogical Dictionary, Vol I, p. 555.

[The specific problem encountered in trying to locate the marriage information for Mère d'Youville's mother's second marriage to a M. O'Sullivan was simply that they were wed at la Pointe-aux-Trembles near Québec despite both being from the Montréal area and this wasn't realized for some time. Also, we know that Mère d'Youville herself was only proclaimed a saint of the Catholic Church on December 9, 1990 and since the process for being declared a saint (called the canonization process) is a *very thorough* and usually *very long* and detailed review of the lives of candidates for sainthood, it could only have added further to the '*incesssant historical* searches' referred to by Fr. Tanguay).]

Jacques de Pensens, *chevalier-de-St-Louis,* and *capitaine* d'une *compagnie de la marine* [Captain of a company of marines under the Naval department] at the Port of Toulouse on Île-Royale, was listed as René-Ovide Hertel (from Rouville's) godfather.

SEE: the Hôpital-Général of Montréal's 1759 Register
[For more information on titles, honors, decorations, etc., please refer to my comments after the entry dated November 24, 1659.]

August 13th

The burial (in Trois-Rivières) of Philippe-Cochon Laverdière, the son of René, *chirurgien* [surgeon] on Île-d'Orléans, after he had drowned in the rapids at Trois-Rivières. He was born in 1685, married Marie-Anne Dupuis-Lagarenne in 1716, and settled near the Petite-Rivière-de-Yamachiche. His daughter, Marie-Antoinette, married Pierre-Joseph Millet in Deschambault in 1735.
[Philippe Cauchon dit Laverdière settled near the present-day town of Nicolet.]

MOVEMENT OF THE CATHOLIC POPULATION OF THE PROVINCE OF QUÉBEC 1711 TO 1720

	MARRIAGES	BIRTHS	DEATHS	OTHERS
1711	186	1002	507	495
1712	233	1082	345	737
1713	181	1147	405	742
1714	146	1179	871	308
1715	204	1127	628	499
1716	240	1229	482	747
1717	200	1269	631	638
1718	292	1232	487	745
1719	242	1346	433	913
1720	207	1341	426	915
TOTALS ➡	2131	11954	5215	6739
1608 to 1720	7506	39923	14898	25025

1721

January 17th

Louis Pillard, *frère hospitalière* and *missionnaire*, was a *maître d'école* [school teacher] in Boucherville.

(Boucherville Register)

March 23rd

Louis Bélanger, 31, a very pious man who never missed reciting his prayers to the Blessed Virgin, died while hunting marten [sable] 25 lieues [about 62.5 miles] up the Rivière-Noir [Black River].

(Islet Register)

April 21st

Robert-David Gotteville-Belisle, *chevalier, lieutenant de vaisseau* [ship's Lieutenant] and *capitaine d'une compagnie de la marine* [Captain of a company of marines], was also *Gouverneur* of the Îles-St-Jean [Prince Edward Island], Madeleine, Brion and Laramée. He was a *témoin* [witness] at a marriage celebrated at Île-St-Jean on the 21st of April 1721.

(Île-St-Jean Register)

Intendant Bégon gave Pierre-Thomas DelaNouguère (DelaNaudière) the contract to deliver the mail between Québec and Montréal for a 20-year period with rates based on a scale of graduated charges based on distance. <u>This was the first postal service in Canada.</u>

(Garneau, Volume II, 3rd Edition, p. 159)

June 11th

The baptism of Pierre-Robert-François, the son of François Pestureau, *directeur-général des vivres* [Supply-Master], who was named by the Très-Haute et Puissante [Most High and Powerful] Dame Louise de Kervin, *dame d'honneur* [lady in waiting] of the Duchesse d'Orléans, and wife of the Lord Pierre de St-Pierre, His Royal Highness' *premier écuyer* [first squire], and seigneur of the Îles-St-Jean, etc. .

(Île-St-Jean Register)

The death and burial in Louisiana of Louis-Hector Bizard, son of Jacques Bizard, *major* [military rank] at Montréal, and Jeanne-Cécile Closse, and Commandant at Fort Yasous, who was born in Montréal on the 3rd of December 1684. Charlevoix noted: "They tell me some extraordinary things about his religion, his piety and his zeal, which he had been a victim of. We all miss him as a father [misses his child], and all those who live in this colony have suffered an irreplaceable loss."

(Charlevoix, Volume II, p. 413)

July 3rd

The burial of Rouminia, 30, a native of Dol and Sieur de Boissière.

(Île St-Jean Register)

August 11th

Michel Duperroy piloted the *flûte du Roi* [Royal merchantman] *Les Quatres Frères*.

(Idem)

August 30th

The burial of Leon Dubroque de Bayonne, *matelot* [sailor] on the barge *La Janette* out of Martinique. The barge was owned by M. Lecompte-Dupré.

(Montréal Register)

September 16th

Philippe Meunier, only 23 and a *matelot* [sailor] on *Les Quatres Frères*, drowned in St-Pierre Harbor.

(Île St-Jean Register)

François Sellier, 45, was found dead in his home after having been shot.

(Idem)

1722

January 28th

The following *résidents notables* [prominent residents] resided on *Île-St-Jean* [Prince Edward Island]: Michel Haché, Captain of Port Lajoie; Louis DelaBretasche, *officier major du Port* [Medical Officer of the port]; and 2 *chirurgiens* [surgeons], Pierre Grandpré and Gabriel Delabonne.

(Idem)

March 3rd

Alexis Blais and Lawrence Bransard, the son of Lawrence Bransard and Marie Casset from Batiscan, were killed by the Chicahas Indians on the Mississippi River.

(Kaskakia Register)

June 22nd

One of the burial notices in the Kaskakia Registers was for the family of Jacques Nepveu. which had moved West to join him while he pursued his business. The Reverend Father de Beaubois noted:

"On the 22nd of June 1722, we held a memorial mass for Michelle Chauvin, 45, the wife of Sieur Jacques Nepveu, a *marchand* [merchant] in Montréal, for Jean-Michel Nepveu, her son, 20; and for daughters Suzanne Nepveu, 18, and Élizabeth, 13. They were all killed by the Indians, four *lieues* [about 10 miles] this side the of Wabash[96]. We believe that Sieur Jacques Nepveu[97] was captured and held captive with Provost, a 9-year-old, non-baptized slave."

(Kaskakia Register)

NOTE: This tragic end to a Canadian family was unknown even to other family members and friends in Montréal.

December

The *Jubilé* established by Pope Innocent XIII was celebrated in the Lorette Parish.

(Lorette Register)

[In the Roman-Catholic Church, the *Jubilé* represented a year in which Roman Catholics could obtain special remission of punishment for their sins by complying with certain conditions and performing certain acts. First established by Pope Boniface VIII in the year 1300, it was celebrated at the beginning of each succeeding century, later reduced to every 50 years and now to every 25 years.]

1723

April 19th

Jean-Baptiste Cauchon, a *cultivateur* [farmer] at *Château-Richer*, was married to Louise Pinguet dit Laglardièr[98] – his 5th marriage.

(Québec Register)

96

The Wabash River was also called the St-Jérôme River.

(Map of New France, by Bellin, 1755)

97

Jacques Nepveu married Michelle Chauvin in Montréal in 1695. According to the Louisiana Census of 1724, his 3 brothers, Joseph, Louis and Nicolas under the names Joseph Chauvin de Léry, Louis Chauvin de Beaulieu, and Nicolas Chauvin de la Fresnière had settled in Louisiana.

(Tanguay)

98

This is the only example in this century of a spouse in his 5th marriage.

(Tanguay)

-134-

A FARM IN CHATEAU-RICHER

FROM A 1787 WATERCOLOR BY THOMAS DAVIES

May 13th

In the Détroit (Fort Pontchartrain) Register is found the following note:

"On the 13th of May 1723, at the request of Reverend Father Bonaventure, a Récollet and missionnaire at the Détroit Mission on Lac Érie, we, the undersigned, state that we were brought to the site of the Church where the late Reverend Father Constantin[99], a Récollet, had been buried. At the time of his death, he had been performing the duties of both priest and missionary at the said outpost. After having examined the general burial area and based on instructions from Sieur Delisle, who had helped to bury him, we, Father Bonaventure and the 2 men whom he had hired to do the actual digging, found Father Constantin's casket while there was still plenty of light to search by. His body was identified by the following features which each of us saw: his skull-cap, several pieces of fabric from his frock, the semblance of a decorative ribbon on his body and of a hair-shirt with clearly differentiated hair. After that examination, the said Reverend Father Bonaventure had the corpse removed and brought to Church. In testimony whereof, we warrant this, our true statement, to whomever it might apply."

99

The Récollet Father Nicolas-Bernandin-Constantin DeLhalle, arrived in Canada in 1696 after having ministered in Longueuil and St-François-de-Sales-de-l'Île-Jésus (St-Françis-de-Sales-de-l'Île-Jésus) parishes, he made his way to Détroit in 1703, and was the first chaplain at Fort Pontchartrain, where he performed the first baptism on the 2nd of February 1704. Two years later, on the 1st of June 1706, he was killed by the Outaouais Indians who were in pursuit of the Miamis at the very moment when they – the Miamis – were about to take refuge in the Fort at Détroit with their missionaries.

(Charlevoix, V. II, # XIX, p. 309)

Executed at the Détroit Outpost on Lac Érie, on the 14th of May 1723.

(SIGNED,)   Henry Campeau
                  Charles Chesne
                  Paul Hubert-Lacroix
                        and Rocquetaillade."

"I the undersigned Récollet priest, performing the function of parish priest at the Détroit Church, certify to having buried the corpse of the Reverend Father Constantin DeLhalle, missionnaire Récollet at this post, under the stairs of the altar of the said church, in the presence of M. de Tonty, the King's *commandant* for the said post, and of M. de Rocquetaillade, who have signed with me, on this 14th of May 1723."

(SIGNED,) Tonty,   Rocquetaillade, Father Bonaventure, Récollet, missionnaire."

(Détroit Register)

[People were rarely buried under the church. The privilege was reserved for priests who (ordinarily) had a place under the choir, and for seigneurs, under their seigneurial pews. Marcel Trudel noted that the custom eventually had to be limited because the graves were not dug very deep and 'pestilential odours' spread through the church.]

July 1st

The burial of Hector-Louis Daillebout de Perigny, 23, *cadet des troupes* [young gentleman in training to be an officer in a company of troops], who was found at *Pointe-de-Nicolet* after drowning near Montréal.

(Trois-Rivières Register)

July 31st

The burial after drowning of François Combray dit Léveillé, a soldier in M. Péan's company.

(Québec Register)

August 19th

The *missionnaire* at Île-St-Jean was Louis Barbet, *cordelier* [Franciscan Friar] and *aumônier* [chaplain] from Donjon.

(Île-St-Jean Register)

August 23rd

A *marinier* [marine] named Nicolas Tangui was on the ship *La Chymène* from Brest.

(Idem)

October 12th

We could see the ship *La Sainte-Anne* in the Québec Harbor.

(Québec Register)

November 23rd

> Six *matelots* [sailors] from the ship *Les Quatres Frères* were drowned.
>
> *(Île-St-Jean Register)*

1724

January 31st

> Busquet, *capitaine du vaisseau* [captain of the ship] *Le Cheval Marin*, spent the winter at St-Laurent on Île-d'Orléans.
>
> *(St-Laurent-de-l'Île-d'Orléans Register)*

February 28th

> The [re] marriage of Jean Desnoyers to Marie-Thérèse Menard in Boucherville. They had married [*à-la-Gaumine*] several years earlier while their *missionnaire*, M. de Francheville, celebrated Mass.
>
> *(Boucherville Register)*
>
> [A marriage *'à-la-Gaumine'* was a plan-of-action used in New France in the first years of the 18th Century. A couple who for some reason or other had been refused the right to marry would make their way to Church in secret, together with two witnesses, at the hour when Mass was to be celebrated by the parish priest. Then, at the solemn moment of consecration, the couple would declare aloud their intention to take each other as wife and husband without further ceremony. This practice became so fashionable that the Bishop, supported by the administrative authorities (since the male partners in most such marriages were soldiers), excommunicated those who had contracted marriage in this way. André Lachance attributes the practice to a M. Gaumin who first conceived of the procedure in France. Also, according to Lachance, it never really became a matter of excommunication simply because the church and civil authorities always ended up by authorizing the marriages but due to the Council of Trent's indirect interpretation of *'à-la-Gaumine'*, the parties who were guilty of being 'married' in that fashion could certainly have found themselves excommunicated.]

April 12th

> Pierre Durant, 25, was killed by the *sauvages Renards* [Fox Indians].
>
> *(Kaskakia Register)*

June 6th

> The drowning of Félix Nicodinot, *patron de la chaloupe de la flûte* [skipper on the cargo-boat] *Les Quatres Frères*.
>
> *(Île-St-Jean Register)*

June 26th

> The burial of Lacroix, *contremaître* [first mate] on the ship *Le Dragon-Volant* at St-Jean, on Île-d'Orléans after he had drowned on the 16th of the month. The ship was owned by M. de la Minotière.
>
> *(St-Jean-de-l'Île-d'Orléans Register)*

September 3rd

Jacques Hervé, 45, drowned and was buried in the Beauport cemetery.

(Beauport Register)

October 15th

The burial of Jean-Baptiste Blondeau, *pilote du vaisseau* [pilot on the ship] *Le Vigilant.*

(Québec Register)

CANADIANS IN LOUISIANA
(ACCORDING TO THE 1724 CENSUS)

In one of the oldest censuses of Louisiana – 1724 – which we found in Paris and which is still unedited, we've run across a certain number of Canadian families already well established in Louisiana. Here is that list of Canadians:

1. Jacques l'Archévêque, born in Québec on the 4th of May 1694, the son of Jean l'Archévêque and Cathérine DeLaunay, settled in New Orleans on property owned by M. de Bienville. A hard-working *briquetier* [brick-maker], he had three negro slaves and one Indian to assist him.
2. Joseph Larche (l'Archévêque), born on the 4th of July 1696 in Québec, the brother of the preceding.
3. Étienne LeRoy, born in Montréal on the 8th of January 1691, the son of Pierre LeRoy and Cathérine Ducharme and nephew of M. Chauvin.
4. Joseph Chauvin, a native of Montréal, son of Pierre Chauvin and Marthe Autreuil.
5. & 6 Louis, and Nicolas, brothers of Joseph Chauvin. All three were very rich *propriétaires* [property-owners] with more than 175 slaves – blacks or Indians.
7. Joseph Verret, a native of Charlesbourg and son of Michel Verret and Marie Galarneau.

8. Jean-Baptiste Petit-LeVilliers, born in Boucherville on the 28th of November 1700, the son of Charles Petit-LeVilliers, *Captaine d'un détachement de la marine* [Captain of a detachment of marines] and of Madeleine Gautier de Varennes.

9. Étienne Daigle dit Malborouk, a native of Charlesbourg and son of Jean Daigle dit Lallemand and Marie-Anne Croteau.

10. Louis Viger, born in Boucherville on the 21st of November 1685, the son of Désiré Viger and Cathérine Moitié. These last two may include the Honorable Denis-Benjamin Viger and Commander Viger as their descendants.

11. Pierre Richaume, born in Repentigny on the 3rd of June 1694, the son of Jacques Richaume and Marguerite Gratiot.

The *Régistres* of the Grey Nuns (Hôpital-Général in Montréal) which were opened on the 7th of February 1725, contained a very large number of burial notices of old French soldiers from the colony. The first recorded burial was that of Jean-Claude Durand, 84 years old.It is truly strange to see how old these older retired-military really got to be !

Those same *Registres* furnished an important bit of information on the number of children left at the Hospital.

Several individuals of some distinction are buried in the Hospital chapel, and that doesn't even include all of the religious belonging to the community.

(Tanguay)

1725

April 11th

Anne Maurice, the wife of Charles Souhé, gave birth to a daughter in the forests of Illinois, near Wabash. She was baptized on the 25th of June in the Boucherville parish church.

(Boucherville Register)

May 16th

Joseph Lamy, a native of Sorel and husband of Marie-Anne Provost, was killed near the village of Kaskakia by a party of Indians. He had been *marguiller-en-charge* for the year.

(Kaskakia Register)

[The *marguiller-en-charge* or churchwarden was the individual currently responsible for the secular affairs of the parish.]

May 19th

Intendant Bégon was the godfather for a 17-year-old English woman, the daughter of Joachim-Michel Tacar.

(Québec Register)

May 27th

Marie-Marguerite Seaman, a 14-year-old English girl, recanted her Protestantism in the Ursulines Chapel at Trois-Rivières. At that time, she lived with Demoiselle Marguerite LeBoulanger de St-Pierre. In 1740, the young girl married Louis Godfroy, Sieur de Tonnancour, *subdélégué de l'Intendant*. She died on the 11th of September 1746 and was buried on the 13th.

(Trois-Rivières Register)

[The *subdélégué-de-l'Intendant* was a representative of the Intendant for civil affairs. Keep in mind that the Intendant was perhaps the most important individual in New France whose jurisdiction included justice, police and finance.]

August 25th

Le Chameau, a Royal vessel bound for Québec, broke up and sank off the coast of Louisborg. Not a single man survived. Among the victims were: M. de Chazel, who was due to relieve Intendant Bégon; M. de Louvigny, who had just been named *Gouverneur* of Trois-Rivières; M. de la Gesse, *capitaine* and son of M. de Ramezay, the *ancien Gouverneur* [former Governor] of Montréal, who had died the previous year, and several other officers, clergymen, Jesuit and Récollet priests.

(Charlevoix, Volume II, Book XX, p. 409)

October 11th

Anne Jousselot, who had outlived 4 husbands, was married for a fifth time. Born in 1659 of the marriage of Pierre Jousselot and Ozanne Drapeau, she first married Joseph Galois in 1677 [February 9]; her second one was to Toussaint Dubeau on the 23rd of May 1678; her third was to André Duval on the 21st of July 1698; her fourth was to Jean Maranda on the 13th of June 1712; and finally, her fifth was to Claude Dubreuil. She lived until the 13th of January 1743[100].

(Charlesbourg Register)

100

It is also the only example in this [the 18th] century of a wife in a fifth marriage. Her death record showed her to be 92 years of age, but she was really only 84 since the 1681 Census showed her to be 22 years of age.

1726

July 23rd

The body of M. Charles Hazeur-Desormeaux, priest at St-Thomas de Montmagny, had been buried on the 6th of June 1715 in the *ancienne église* [old church], but was now exhumed in order that it might be transported and buried in the *nouvelle église* [new church] in that same parish.

(St-Thomas Register)

August 6th

Michel Chabot[101], 63, and his 2 sons, Pierre, 22, and Augustin, 15, drowned while crossing from Beauport to Île-d'Orléans.

(St-Pierre-de-l'Île-d'Orléans Register)

August 13th

Charles Cauhet married Marie-Charlotte Laroche at Pointe-aux-Trembles de Québec. He had already signed the marriage contract yet reasonable doubt regarding the death of his first wife arose and so Marie-Charlotte was prohibited from living with him as of the 30th of October 1725 until definite proof of her death could be presented by Cauhet.

(Pointe-aux-Trembles de Québec Register)

September 21st

We blessed the bell for the Grondines church. *(Grondines Register)*
[For more information on this the second of eight such instances recorded in this book, please see my comments on page 90, after the entry dated May 21st, 1691.]

1727

April 22nd

The burial of Nicolas Rochon, 33, the son of Gervais Rochon and Madeleine Guyon. He had been lost on the ice near Montréal and was buried at St-Thomas. [formerly Pointe-à-Lacaille]: "On the said body", added pastor Lelièvre, "was a hat made of chinchilla fur, a jacket made of a white fabric, a coarse-canvas vest on the front of which was a blue and red piece of Indian fabric, a scapular, malamute leggings, white stockings, shoes, an Indian belt, a cotton handkerchief, a small empty purse, a tin cup, a knife, a peace pipe, and two small money-box keys attached in the buttonholes of the said vest. His hair was held in place by a black ribbon". *(St-Thomas Register)*
[Shortly after the 1st printing of this translation in July of 1998, a reader posted this information to the Internet's list of Revolutionary War and French & Indian researchers and re-enactors. An immediate question was received as to just how 'chinchilla' fur might have made its way to the wilds of Canada at that time. My response, which came from Agnes C. Laut's, "*The Fur Trade in America*", MacMillan Company, New York, 1921, was: "Chinchilla fur as you are aware is principally from the Southern Hemisphere or it certainly was in the earlier days when they were more plentiful in the wild. In addition, it was never known for its durability since a chinchilla is a fragile animal as is a fox or a muskrat or a mole or a squirrel. It is not likely, therefore, that Rochon's cap was made of real chinchilla fur.

101

Michel Chabot was the brother of M. Antoine Chabot, priest at Ste-Anne's parish.

141

For some reason or other, dyed white rabbit fur has apparently often been mistaken for chinchilla. In 1887, the London Chamber of Commerce, which - I gather - was one of the agencies governing fur trade at the time, ruled as non-permissible the use of several descriptive names for specific and somewhat rarer animal furs. Sure enough, they ruled that the use of 'white rabbit, dyed 'was no longer a permissible name for chinchilla. At about the same time, the Canadian Conservation Report was recommending that the name 'rabbit, white, dyed' be abolished since it - here again - was supposedly being used either to describe or in place of chinchilla. Since the position that they'd taken above left some kind of a void, the London Chamber of Commerce apparently recommended that the terminology 'chinchilla cooney' be used in place of 'rabbit, white, dyed ' or 'white rabbit, dyed ' so quite obviously there had been some connection between dyed rabbit fur and chinchilla fur for quite some time. Now, keeping in mind that many people had apparently been led to believe that 'dyed white rabbit' fur was chinchilla fur - undoubtedly the reason for the above-referenced actions having been taken - I suspect that good Father Lelievre was also so confused. After all, if - as in later years - people who knew their furs were so easily mistaken, then couldn't a missionary from an earlier period possibly make the same mistake especially since he was merely trying to describe the outfit worn by a person who had frozen to death out in the wilderness?

Another point to consider is based on today's definition of coney (or cony) as in 'chinchilla coney' above. The word apparently has several definitions but 3 of those definitions are of particular interest here: (1) a rabbit; (2) rabbit fur, and (3) a gullible person. The connection with the first two is obvious but I suspect that the latter definition might have come about because people were consistently being led to believe that some 'dyed white rabbit ' furs were chinchilla furs. Why? Strictly dollars-and-cents since one would have had to pay considerably more for a supposed 'chinchilla' fur than they would ever have had to pay for any kind of rabbit fur.

I trust that this might explain just how poor Nicolas Rochon could end his days on this earth wearing a 'chinchilla' cap."

May 2nd

The baptism of a child who had been secretly brought to the home of Agathe, an Abénaquise woman in Bécancourt, and then to *Lieutenant-Général* M. Godfroy de Tonnancour. His godparents, M. Louis-Joseph Gatineau and Mme. Véronique Petit, held him over the baptismal font while they named him Louis-Bonaventure.

(Trois-Rivières Register)

June 10th

The burial of Joseph Héroux, 20, who perished in a shipwreck on Lac-St-Pierre.

(Ste-Anne-de-Yamachiche Register)

July 29th

Jean-Baptiste Sabourin, *capitaine de milice* [captain who lead his parish militia] at Lac-des-Deux-Montagnes, married a 17-year-old English woman named Sarah Enneson who was born near Boston. For some time after, she was called Cathérine Kigilekok8e by the Algonquins or Iroquois-du-Lac. Today's Raizenne and Séguin families include her among their ancestors. *(Lac-des-Deux-Montagnes Register)*
[For more information regarding problems encountered when spelling or pronouncing Indian names, please see my comments on page 107 - immediately after the entry of January 6th 1702.]

December 18th

The remains of Jesuit Fathers Pierre-Gabriel Marest and Jean-Jacques Marmet were transported to the church in Kaskakia. Father Marest was a native of Fresnes in Champagne [France] who, in 1694, had been taken prisoner by the English while a *missionnaire* at Hudson Bay and then brought to Plymouth. Once free [circa 1700] he moved on to Illinois where he died on May 15th, 1727. *(Kaskakia Register)*

December 23rd

While Father Gervais Lefebvre, a native of Batiscan, celebrated a Low Mass, Sieur Daniel Portail, from Gevron, the son of Daniel Portail, *maire perpétuel* of the town of St-Florent-le-Vieil in the diocese of Angers, married Marie-Anne Antoinette Langy de Levrard '*à-la- Gaumine*' and that [was done] without the priest's knowing about it. They had their marriage reinstated on the 8th of September 1728.

(Batiscan Register)

[a) Maire perpétuel or mayor for life is comparable to honorary titles which are awarded in the USA.

b) For more information as to just what a marriage '*à-la-Gaumine*' is, please refer to my comments after the February 28th of 1724 entry.]

c) A Mass is a church celebration as well as a sacrament in the Roman Catholic Church consisting of a series of prayers and ceremonies. A High Mass is celebrated by a priest usually assisted by a deacon – in former years a sub-deacon as well - with music and incense. A Low Mass is celebrated by 1 priest with no music and little ceremony.]

December 26th

Mgr.-de-St-Valier died at the Hôpital-Général at 74 years of age. He was buried on the following 2nd of January in the same community church that he had founded in 1688[102].

(Archdiocese of Québec Register)

1728

February 9th

In the Ste-Anne-de-la-Pérade Register we read the following: "Louis Guillet from the newly-established parish of Ste-Geneviève." Father LeSueur, a Jesuit, officiated in the chapel of the said Ste-Geneviève-de-Batiscan [parish].

(Ste-Anne-de-la-Pérade Register)

February 18th

The burial of Guillaume Taillon, 52, husband of Anne Gagnon, who died on the ice after having been surprised by the bad weather and nightfall.

(Château-Richer Register)

April 13th

The burial of Nicolas Gronier, 20, the son of Nicolas Gronier and Anne Chrétien from Ste-Famille-de-l'Île-d'Orléans parish. He was killed in the woods and buried at Longue-Pointe near Montréal.

(Longue-Pointe de Montréal Register)

102

The record of his burial adds "that he was buried in a tomb dug out by the said seigneur Bishop in the parish church at the Hôpital Général in Québec."

April 21st

The burial of Pierre, 7, the child of Pierre Morin and Thérèse Pelletier, who was lost on the icy Rivière-du-Sud on the 5th of October 1727, and found by his father on the banks of the St-Lawrence River.

(St-Thomas Register)

June 19th

Antoine Bilodeau, husband of Angélique Lepage and father of 6 children was struck by lightning in his home at around 6:00 in the evening. He had worked as a *cultivateur* [farmer] in Berthier-Sur-Mer. His burial record notes: "We all have good reason to look ahead to our salvation after having led a good life. He especially showed much fervor during his lifetime, by often taking part in the Sacraments, to the point where he was genuinely missed by *all* of the members of the parish who assisted in his burial."

(Berthier Register)

July 7th

The burial of Jacques Salé who drowned while crossing from Québec to Lévis.

(Lévis Register)

September 15th

The burial of Jacques Lalande, 50, a native of Dieppe [France] and *matelot* [sailor] on the barge *La Reine Esther.*

1729

February 4th

The burial of Louis Héros, 38, a native of Bordeaux [France]. This pious young man had dedicated himself to charitable work by becoming a *hospitalier* known by the name of Brother Jérôme.

(Montréal Register)

[The *Frères Hospitaliers-de-la-Croix et de Saint-Joseph* [Charron Brothers] was founded in 1692 by François Charron de La Barre. They devoted themselves to the running of an asylum and the Hôpital-Général in Montréal. They also taught school and for a time operated a real trade school. In the end, they were forced to dissolve because they were too few in numbers and because of poor administration, quarrels and defections.]

LeBeau, a *commis* [clerk], the son of a bourgeois from Paris, arrived in Canada this year and lived for some time with the Indians. He returned to France and published the story of his adventures. Don't believe everything that you read, however. [Tanguay's comment]

(Rameau, "Les Canadiens", Part II, p. 71)

April 24th

We often found the name *'Cap-à-l'Arbre'* [now known as St-Jean-Deschaillons] in historical documents whose readers were often left with serious doubt as to its exact geographical location. Among others, the *"Journal des Jésuites"* dated the 6th of November 1646 mentioned the wreck of a barge near *Cap-à-l'Arbre* which had been going up river from Québec to Trois-Rivières. Yet was this *'Cap'* to the north or to the south side of the River ? ... and at what distance from the two cities ?

We believe that we can answer that question and define precisely where the site called *Cap-à-l'Arbre* is located. We consulted the Marriage Register for the Ste-Anne-de-la-Pérade parish and found an entry dated the 24th of April 1729 in the marriage record for Robert Houy and Louise Pilotte in which it was noted that he resided at *Cap-à-l'Arbre* in the Lotbinière parish, which is known today as the *Pointe-de-Saint-Jean Deschaillons.*

An entry dated the 14th of April 1734 in that same Register furnished us with the burial information for Joseph Boisverd who lived in the fief Deschaillons at the *Cap-à-l'Arbre.*

In the first St-Jean Deschaillons parish Register, we read: "Register of baptisms, marriages and burials of the St-Jean Baptiste parish, *dite le*[also called the] *Cap-à-l'Arbre,* for the year 1741."

(Tanguay)

1730

January 7th

The marriage of Charles-René Gaudron de Chevremont, *sécrétaire* for the Marquis of Beauharnois and son of M. Nicolas Gaudron, Sieur de la Bossière, to Marie-Bénigne Derome.

(Québec Register)

May 31st

The blessing of a bell for Ste-Anne-de-Beaupré parish by M. Girard de Vorlay. The bell was named *'Marie-Joseph-Ignace'* by M. Perthuis and Marie-Anne Roussel, the wife of M. Louis Beaudoin.

(Ste-Anne-de-Beaupré Register)

[The third of eight such bell-blessings recorded in this book. For more information on these blessings, please refer to my comments after the entry for September 21st, 1726.]

July 6th

The burial of Jérome Michau, resident of Kamouraska, who drowned while swimming in the Rivière-Boyer.

(St-Valier Register)

During this and the following years, the Trois-Rivières Registers recorded a large number of baptisms and burials of Panis slaves belonging to the leading families of the city[103].

(Trois-Rivières Register)

Many children from Québec and its neighboring parishes died from measles and whooping-cough this year.

(Québec and Lorette Registers)

MOVEMENT OF THE CATHOLIC POPULATION OF THE PROVINCE OF QUÉBEC 1721 to 1730

	MARRIAGES	BIRTHS	DEATHS	OTHERS
1721	235	1343	476	867
1722	272	1404	574	830
1723	262	1442	581	861
1724	261	1516	587	929
1725	254	1453	564	889
1726	254	1484	577	907
1727	315	1593	744	849
1728	311	1709	795	914
1729	353	1867	836	1031
1730	382	1910	1173	737
TOTALS ➡	2899	15721	6907	8814
1608 to 1730	10405	55644	21805	33839

1731

March 25th

We celebrated Easter today, on Annunciation Day.

103

In 1754 we find a tabular listing of families with slaves.

April 12th

Étienne Tibaut and Louis Dolbec, residents of St-Augustin, had noticed a man's stocking hanging from a fir branch about *40 feet high [!]* while walking in the forest at the seigneurie of Maure and had then felled the tree and found that the stocking held 18 foot bones as well as a toenail from a big toe. The stocking and bones were recognized as belonging to Philippe Gasse[104] who was lost in the forest around the 3rd of December 1729. His bones were buried in the cemetery on the 13th of April. On the 4th of June and the 29th of September, more of his remains were buried in the cemetery and blessed by the priest of St-Augustin, M. Auclair-Desnoyers.

(St-Augustin Register)

[Philippe Gasse *had to* have been wearing red !]

May 13th

The burial of Gui Rozé, a 25-year-old *matelot* [sailor] who had been part of the crew on the ship *La Manon* commanded by M. Lemoyne.

(Baie-St-Paul Register)

May 24th

Claude Boissel, 25, was accidentally killed with his own gun.

(St-Pierre-de-l'Île-d'Orléans Register)

June 11th

The burial of Nicolas, a 60 year old bachelor who, for 50 years, had served the missionaries by example and with a fervour and faith worthy of our first Christians.

(St-Thomas Register)

July 23rd

A 23-year-old man, Jacques Guillemet, drowned while swimming.

(Lévis Register)

Guillaume Verrier, *procureur général* [attorney general] of the *Conseil Supérieur* of Québec, carefully reviewed the old notarial records. His research began in December of 1731 and continued until August of 1732 and served as the basis for *"L'Extrait des Minutes des Notaires"*, on file at the *Ministère de la Marine* [Naval Admiralty] in Paris. It covers the period from 1637 to 1714.

(Documents – "Notaries")

104

Philippe Gasse, 37, was married to Marie Saloir.   *(Genealogical Dictionary)*

1732

May 23rd

Rosalie Brunet, the daughter of François Brunet and Anne Tibaut, was the first child born in the Ste-Claire[105] parish, commonly known as *Les Plaines*.

(Terrebonne Register)

June 2nd

The burial of the bodies of Louis Dubois and Joseph Branchaux, who both drowned on May 1st in the Rivière-Etchemins.

(Lévis Register)

July 7th

The burial of Louis Hervé, a *matelot* [sailor] on the ship *l'Amazone du Désert*, commanded by M. Girard de la Soudrais. He also drowned on that same day while his ship was at anchor in the port of Québec.

(Beauport Register)

November 13th

The burial of Charles Poirier and of a Saint-Jean, *cordonnier* [a shoemaker], who both drowned.

(Beaumont Register)

[Charles was born on the 13th of October 1710 and married on the 30th of June 1730 to Marie-Anne Casse. The Saint-Jean who drowned with Charles lived in the home of a M. Beauséjour in Lévis.]

Louis Bourassa, 40, and his son Jean, 14½, were struck and killed by lightning while returning from Québec. Another of his children had been baptized on that very same day.

(St-Nicolas Register)

1733

February 26th

Isabelle Dugas, the wife of Pierre Aubois, drowned with 6 of her children, between the two crossings.

(Port-Royal Register)

April 5th

Easter Sunday.

105

That name no longer exists. It is now known as Ste-Anne-des-Plaines parish.

(Tanguay)

This year, smallpox took the lives of a large number of people in most of the parishes and especially at Trois-Rivières.

(Trois-Rivières Register)

November 4th

A violent storm caused a schooner to sink in the *Anse de Berthier* [a small Berthier cove], [on the] Rivière-Bellechasse. Six people drowned. They were: François Caron; his wife, Françoise Paré; Françoise Boirie; Marie-Joseph Bourassa, wife of Louis Bossé, (her second marriage); Marie Dubeau, wife of Marois of Québec; and Jean Labranche.

November 5th

The six people who drowned on the 4th were buried in the Berthier parish cemetery.

(Berthier Register)

1734

February 11th

Germain Lepage, entitled by the proxy of Louis Lepage[106] to a parcel of land in the interior and along the entire front of the seigneurie-de-Terrebonne.

"There has come before me, Gilles Hocquart, *chevalier* and *conseiller du Roi* while the Council was in session in our town hall, the *Intendant de justice, police et finance* in New France, Germain Lepage; Sieur de St-François, *capitaine de milice* [captain who led his parish militia] of the settlement at St-Louis and seigneurie-de-Terrebonne, established under the personal signature of Sieur Louis Lepage de Ste-Claire, seigneur de Terrebonne-des-Plaines and a priest, on the 15th of this month, remaining annexed to those now present, which the said Sieur de St-François told us that he had come to render and deliver in our hands the *foi et hommage* which the said Sieur Lepage de Ste-Claire is expected to render and deliver to His Majesty at Château St-Louis in Québec, because of the seigneurie of a parcel of land of two leagues [about 5 miles] to add to the non-ceded lands in the interior and along the entire front of the said seigneurie-de-Terrebonne, and has given as proof of ownership for the said parcel of land, the *brevet en original de concession* which had been made to him by His Majesty, on the 10th of April 1731, to be enjoyed by him, by his heirs or – with cause – as their own, and then according to the same rights which are attached to the said seigneurie and for the same fees, clauses and conditions which are also so

---

106

Priest and seigneur of Terrebonne, he was the son of Sieur René Lepage, seigneur of Rimouski. All of the Lepage families from Rimouski, Île-d'Orléans and Ste-Anne des Plaines consider him as one of their ancestors.

attached, requiring the said Sieur de St-François in the previously spoken name which it pleases us to receive the said *foi et hommage* for the said Sieur de Ste-Claire, and at once having placed himself in the role of servant, bare-headed, with neither sword nor spurs, one knee to the ground, would have stated in a loud and clear voice that he rendered and delivered the *foi et hommage* to us as the said Sieur de Ste-Claire is expected to render and deliver to the King, at Château St-Louis in Québec, because of the said seigneurie of the said two league [about a 5-mile] parcel of land, to which *foi et hommage* we have received and do receive by these present the said Sieur de St-François in the previously spoken name except for the rights of the King and others in all things, and took an oath to well and faithfully serve His majesty and to warn us and our successors if he learns of something against him, and we have dispensed him for this time only from going to the said Château St-Louis in Québec and from the charge of giving and furnishing his *aveu et dénombrement* during the 40 days, following the custom of Paris, of which and of all the said Sieur de St-François in the previously spoken name, has required us to do something which we have granted him and which he signed for [agreed to] with us."

HOCQUART
Lepage from St-François

[For this or any other somewhat bewildering legal document pertaining to the seigneurial system, it is important that one first understand that the seigneurial system itself is the body of law and practice pertaining to the distribution and ownership of property in New France. The rest will then fall into place provided the reader clearly understand the definitions for the various parts of the system and is ready to break the document down into those component parts. Richard Harris' "*The Seigneurial System in Early Canada*" by McGill-Queen's University Press is but one of many publications which might be helpful for someone wishing to study the geographical aspects of the system.]

Authorization from Sieur Lepage of Ste-Claire to Sieur Lapage of St-François:
"I, the undersigned, seigneur de Terrebonne-des-Plaines, etc., give the power to my brother at St-François, to render for and in my name *foi et hommage* which is due the King for the contract of the new seigneurie which His Majesty accorded me on the 10th of April 1731, and moreover again render another new *foi et hommage* for the seigneurie-de-Terrebonne, if need be, promising to agree to and ratify all which he might do in my name for this purpose."

Given at Terrebonne this 11th of February 1734.

Lepage from Ste-Claire
(Registre des actes de foi et hommage, Volume III, pp. 5, 6 and 7)

April 12th

The following is from the *St-Jean-de-l'Île-d'Orléans* Parish Register:

"I appointed myself godfather after having refused Simon Campagna because of his obvious and blatant ignorance when I asked him some basic catechism."

      (SIGNED,)   René Portneuf, Priest

NOTE: M. René Robineau of Portneuf was the parish priest at St-Jean-de-l'Île-d'Orléans. Later, he moved on to become the *curé* at St-Joachim. He was killed by the English on the 23rd of August 1759.

July 28th

The corner-stone for the Nicolet Church was laid today. That first stone was placed in the circular area on the epistle side [front, left] by M. Thierry-Hazeur, *chanoine* [canon] and *grand pénitencier* of the Québec Chapter[107].

                                             (Nicolet Register)

[A *grand pénitencier* is a member of the Bishop's advisory council (*chapitre*) who was especially appointed to hear confession.]

August 24th

The blessing of a bell named *'Geneviève'* which had been given to the St-Thomas parish by M. Yves Arguin, *marchand* [merchant] in Québec, and Geneviève Côté, his wife.

                                             (St-Thomas Register)

[The fourth of eight such <u>bell-blessings</u> recorded in this book. Roman Catholics have a great deal of faith in the value of having things blessed. They themselves receive special blessings at the time of their baptisms and marriages and illnesses and deaths and ask for blessings for their throats...and their prayer beads...and their fishing boats...and their gifts... etc. etc.. And so it is not surprising that during a period when the Church was so important in the colonists' everyday lives, a time when they were too poor to be able to afford individual timepieces, that they had to rely on church or other public bells to keep track of the time of day. Bells signaled the start and close of religious ceremonies and of workdays. They tolled to warn of emergencies or to advise of deaths or of happier events. They summoned citizens to assembly or to prayer or to arms or to fight fires. They indicated when it was time to sleep ... and to awaken. They rang to let merchants know when they could open up their shops... and when they had to close them. The colonists would surely have insisted upon blessing the very bells which guided their daily activities since they were absolutely essential to the life of the community.]

107

Marcel Trudel notes that the 'Chapter' was the most distinguished group of clergy in New France principally because it was the closest to the Bishop. This 13 man group first appeared in 1684 and was composed of contemplatives whose only role was that of prayer but who acted as the Bishop's Court and Council.

The burial of Pierre Fluet, *cultivateur* [farmer] from Lorette, after he drowned at Pointe-Lévis.

(Lévis Register)

1735

June 26th

The burial of Jean Piochau, a member of the crew on *Le Comte de Toulouse*.

(St-François-Xavier-de-la-Petite-Rivière Register)

1736

The *directeur des forges* [manager of the iron works] of St-Maurice, Pierre-François, Sieur d'Olivier DeVezain, made an entry in the Trois-Rivières Register.

(Trois-Rivières Register)

January 19th

From burial records, we were able to determine the address of Pierre Latour, 70, of Québec who had had a clock-making business in the colony. He died in Montréal.

March 26th

The burial of Élizabeth Perrin, wife of Jean Lalande, *interprète* [interpreter] for the English and Flemish in this area.

(Montréal Register)

May 26th

The burial of Marie Gendron, a 16-year-old girl, who drowned along with 2 other people when their canoe broke up while shooting the Sault St-Louis rapids.

(Longueuil Register)

July 6th

Two children of the late Antoine Bilodeau, Isidore, 13 and Marie-Louise, 9, drowned in front of their home. Their father, a *cultivateur* [farmer] in Berthier-sur-Mer, had been killed in an electrical storm on the 19th of June 1728.

(Berthier Register)

July 12th

Jacques Dupont, *originaire* [native] of Grandville, and *aumônier* [chaplain] on the ship *Le Phénix* located on the Gaspé coast, today baptized Augustine DuPaul, 4. Gaude Hugon, *capitaine et armateur du navire* [captain and owner of the ship], was the godfather.

(Rivière-Ouelle Register entry dated the 4th of December 1736)

-152-

August 26th

Noël Alard drowned while trying to board the ship *La Ville de Québec* and was buried at Beauport.

September 27th

The burial of Jean Catreville, *maître du vaisseau* [boatswain] on *Le Montréal* commanded by M. DeBeauvais.

(Québec Register)

November 3rd

The ship *La Renomée* commanded by Sieur Joseph Damours de Fréneuse departed from Québec.

("*Voyage au Nouveau Monde*" & "*Histoire du Naufrage de Père Crespe*", Amsterdam, 1757)

December 19th

The elevated point on which the Deschambault Church is built is described as follows: "The Church of St-Joseph, at Cap-Lauzon, under the small pine trees, in the seigneurie Deschambault."

1737

May 27th

The burial of Jacques Tremblay, 20, in the Saint-Paul Bay cemetery. He had been electrocuted in his home during a thunderstorm.

(Baie-St-Paul Register)

June 9th

The burial of Langevin, a 35-year-old *maître corroyeur* [master leather-worker], who drowned while traveling to Trois-Rivières after his canoe smashed against the rocks at Grondines. He was found and buried on the same day.

(Grondines Register)

July 17th

Michel Haché, *captaine* of Port-Lajoie, was found after he had drowned after becoming mired in the mud near the mouth of the *Rivière-du-Nord* on the 10th of April 1737.

(St-Jean Island Register)

August 25th

Le Comte de Matignon, a ship commanded by Sieur Pierre Pigneguy, was one of the vessels at anchorage in the harbor at Québec.

(Lévis Register)

1738

The marriage of of Claude-Charles LeRoy de la Poterie, *conseiller du Roi* and *contrôleur de la marine et des fortifications* [he looked after the military storehouses and fortifications], and Élizabeth de St-Ours. We found the names and locations of 3 of their children in the *Régistre des actes de foi et hommage.*

1.   Charles-Augustin, chevalier, seigneur de Bacqueville and de la Touche, in Touraine [France] , and co-seigneur of St-Ours, Canada, in 1738, *capitaine aide-major* [Captain, major's aide - part of Governor's General Staff] for the King on the Île-de-la-Guadeloupe. He forwarded a *procuration* [procurement papers] with his 2 brothers to Henry Hiché for the seigneurie of St-Ours. Charles Augustin resided in the Bailly district of the St-Dominique parish on the Île-de-la-Guadeloupe.

2.   Marc-René, brother of the preceding individual, and *conseiller du Roi* at the *Conseil Supérieur* of Guadeloupe, lived in the *quartier des vieux habitants* [the elderly residential area] at St-Joseph-de-la-Guadeloupe.

3.   Pierre-Denis LeRoy of la Poterie des Manvilles, *chevalier* and *ancien lieutenant de la marine* [former marine Lieutenant], lived in the Deshays district of St-Pierre parish, on Île-de-la-Guadeloupe.

(Régistre des actes de foi et hommage, V. II, pp. 119 & 123)

[At the end of the 17th century, when the King of France no longer allowed Canadians to become nobles, only one important honor remained, *l'Ordre-Royal-et-Militaire-de-Saint-Louis*. That military order was divided into 8 Grand-Croix, 24 commanders and an unlimited number of *chevaliers* and was the only military order in which New France had the honor of taking part. To obtain the decoration, one had to be an officer in the regular forces which immediately eliminated the entire parish militia system and other ranks. Also, one could only serve the King of France in order to qualify.]

June 26th

Charles Corvoisier was an *instituteur* [school-master] at Ste-Anne-de-la-Pérade.

(Ste-Anne-de-la-Pérade Register)

June 28th

Louis-Frédéric Bricault, 47, Sieur de Valmur and *sécrétaire* of the Intendant [Hocquart], was buried in the archway of the Cathederal of Québec.

(Québec Register)

July 7ᵗʰ

The burial of Joseph Gagnon, 22, son of Jean-Baptiste Gagnon, who drowned along with his young brothers in the river in front of his father's home. He was buried on that same day at Saint-Roch-des-Aulnets.

(St-Roch-des-Aulnets Register)

July 15ᵗʰ

The completion and solemn blessing of St-François-Xavier Church at la-Petite-Rivière. Work on the church had begun on the 19ᵗʰ of June 1738. In the cornerstone had been placed the first stone which had been blessed 3 years prior. Scratched on it were the names of MM. Abrat and Navières, priests who had left more than 3 years earlier.

M. Flamand, *entrepreneur* [contractor] from Québec, had supervised the work. The *marguilliers de l'Oeuvre* [those who attended to the business affairs of the church's construction] were Louis Tremblay, Antoine Bouchard and François Bouchard, and the *missionnaire*, M. Louis Chaumont from la Jannière.

(St-François-Xavier-de-la-Petite-Rivière Register)

July 17ᵗʰ

The burial of Pierre Bernier, a resident of St-Joachim, whose body was found on shore near Sault-Montmorency.

(l'Ange-Gardien Register)

August 29ᵗʰ

Marguerite Roy, 28, wife of Pierre Valade, and resident of Charlesbourg, was killed in a thunderstorm.

(Charlesbourg Register)

December 5ᵗʰ

Charles Valin , 22, son of Nicolas Valin and Anne Trud, from Lorette, was beaten to death with sticks and spears by several soldiers.

(Québec and Lorette Registers)

1739

The *maître-serrurier* [master locksmith] at the St-Maurice Ironworks was Pierre Beaupré.

(Trois-Rivières Register)

May 5ᵗʰ

The burial of Julien Fortier dit Tranchemontagne, 30, a soldier in M. de St-Ours' Company after he was found dead.

(Montréal Register)

June 11th

The burial of Jacques Delestre dit Vadeboncoeur, 25, a soldier in M. Contrecoeur's Company, who had drowned on the 1st of June.

(Idem)

July 2nd

At the Feast Day for the dedication of churches in the diocese of Québec, M.Hazeur, *chanoine* and *grand pénitencier* , blessed the church at *Pointe-du-Lac* after calling upon the Visitation of the Holy Virgin, the first patron saint, and upon St-Charles, the second. Present were: Dame Marguerite Ameau, widow of René Godfroy, the *seigneur* of Tonnancour; Roch de Ramezay, *capitaine*, and Louise Godfroy, his wife; Marguerite-Charlotte de Ramezay, their daughter; Godfroy de Tonnancour, *subdélégué de l'Intendant*, and Chefdeville, *curé*.

POINTE-DU-LAC - CHURCH OF THE VISITATION

(Pointe-du-Lac Register)

[a) <u>Canons</u> were priests who were not allowed to teach or become parish priests. Their essential function was to pray together and, in a few cases, when they lived in a presbytery, to serve as missionaries.

 b) A *pénitencier* was one who was especially appointed to hear confessions whereas a *grand pénitencier* was that but also a member of the Bishop's advisory council or *chapitre*.

 c) The *subdélégué-de-l'Intendant* was a representative of the Intendant for civil affairs. Keep in mind that the Intendant was perhaps the most important individual in New France whose jurisdiction included justice, police and finance.]

October 1st

The blessing of *'Marie-Claire-Joseph'*, the Deschambault church bell.

(Deschambault Register)

[The fifth of eight such <u>bell-blessings</u> recorded in this book. For more information on these blessings, please refer to my comments after the entry for August 24th, 1734.]

December 12th

Chirurgien [surgeon] Phlem from Ste-Anne-de-la-Pérade housed the patients with dropsy in his own home so that he might be better able to care for them. Those patients included: Paul Desmarets, a resident of Verchères, who was buried today, and Gabriel Desmaisons, a resident of Bécancour who married Isabelle Dehornay in 1737 and was buried on the 22nd of February 1742.

(Ste-Anne-de-la-Pérade Register)

1740

February 9th

Jacques Ourson, 45, *boulanger* [baker] and a native of the Tours diocese [in France], perished wretchedly in a bakery-fire at the seminary at St-Sulpice.

(Montréal Register)

May 30th

Nicolas Baillargeon, 28, drowned on the night of the 10th while trying to cross the Rivière-du-Sud alone.

(St-Thomas Register)

July 4th

Louis-Joseph Rivard dit Bellefeuille, 56, husband of Louise Lesieur, was killed during an electrical storm.

(Yamachiche Register)

On the same day, we buried Faucher Chateauvert from la Pointe-aux-Trembles who had drowned at St-Joseph-de-Lévis.

(Lévis Register)

August 7th

M. Jacques-Joseph Masson from Montbrac, a 26 year old priest at St-Sulpice, was buried in the Kamouraska church, on the epistle side [front, left]. He contracted a dangerous contagious disease while he was on the Royal ship *Le Rubis*, commanded by M. de la Saussaye. He was brought ashore at Kamouraska and died on the 6th of August.

(Kamouraska Register)

[People were rarely buried under the church. The privilege was reserved for priests who (ordinarily) had a place under the choir, and for seigneurs, under their seigneurial pews. Marcel Trudel noted that the custom eventually had to be limited because the graves were not dug very deep and 'pestilential odours' spread through the church.]

August 16th

Michel Maray, Sieur de la Chauvignerie, married Marie-Joseph Raimbaut. He was the son of Louis, Sieur de la Chauvignerie, *officier de la marine* [marine officer], and was himself an *interprète* [interpreter] of the Iroquois language.

(Verchères Register)

August 20th

Mgr. François-Louis Pourroy, 29, from Lauberivière, the 5th Bishop of Québec, died after a 6-day illness which he contracted while caring for the sick on the Royal ship *Le Rubis* which brought him to Québec[109].

109

A book about Mgr. Pourroy, "*Documents Annotés*", appeared in Montréal in 1885.

Joseph Tessier was buried on the same day at Ste-Anne-du-Bout-de-l'Île de Montréal after having drowned on the preceding 20th of June at Long-Sault while en route to Michillimakinac.

(Bout-de-l'Île-de-Montréal Register)

A fever which spread to Québec from the infected ship *Le Roulier* caused many deaths.

September 5th

Michel Berthier, *chirurgien du Roi* [royal surgeon], fell ill while caring for his hospital patients, many of whom had become ill on the infected ship *Le Rubis.* He died and was buried on the same day.

(Québec Register)

November 15th

The burial of Savade Guillomètre, 38. He was a native of St-Jean-de-Luxe and a *matelot* [sailor] on *La Marianne*, a ship commanded by Georges Tanqueray.

(St-François-Xavier-de-la-Petite-Rivière Register)

MOVEMENT OF THE CATHOLIC POPULATION OF THE PROVINCE OF QUÉBEC 1731 TO 1740

	MARRIAGES	BIRTHS	DEATHS	OTHERS
1731	404	1959	960	999
1732	330	2126	872	1254
1733	333	1955	2025	...
1734	369	2285	870	1415
1735	360	2195	786	1409
1736	388	2255	895	1360
1737	324	2322	894	1428
1738	369	2207	900	1307
1739	386	2355	861	1494
1740	406	2420	941	1479
TOTALS ➡	3669	22079	10004	12075
1608 to 1740	14074	77723	31809	45914

[Tanguay's 'OTHERS' detail adds up to 12,145 yet his 'TOTAL' is 12,075.]

1741

June 9th

The burial of Laurent Béni, 26, at Baie-St-Paul. He had died onboard the ship *Le Saint-Louis* while en route to France. M. Dugard from Rouën [Normandy, France] owned the company which owned the ship.

(Baie-St-Paul Register)

July 15th

Jean Gourau, *matelot* [sailor] from the ship *Le Saint François*, drowned. He was a native of Dompierre in the diocese of LaRochelle.

(Lévis Register)

July 17th

Jean-Baptiste Laville, a native of St-Nicholas-de-la-Rochelle was buried at Beaumont. He was the charpentier du navire [ship's carpenter] on *La Reine Esther.*

(Beaumont Register)

October

The Commandant at Fort Cahokias was a man named Santilly.

(Cahokia Register)

November 20th

We transferred the bodies which had been buried in *l'ancienne chapelle seigneuriale* [the old seigneuriale chapel], *Chapelle St-Antoine,* to the Deschambault church. Until then, the chapel had been used by the family of François Chavigny de la Chevrotière and had been interdicted by the Bishop. The bodies of M. de Chavigny, of his son Augustin, and of his grand-son, François, were not however reburied until the 2nd of November 1745.

(Deschambault Register)

DESCHAMBAULT - CHURCH OF SAINT JOSEPH

[a. An <u>interdict</u> is a Church ruling by which the faithful of the Catholic Church are forbidden from performing certain church offices, sacraments, or privileges, including burials. The fact that this chapel had been interdicted meant that it could no longer be used for burial services – among other things – without the express approval of the Bishop. Doing something against the express wishes of the Bishop could have led to being excommunicated by the Church and very few Catholics – if any – would have chosen that alternative.

b. People were rarely buried under the church. The privilege was reserved for priests who (ordinarily) had a place under the choir, and for seigneurs, under their seigneurial pews. Marcel Trudel noted that the custom eventually had to be limited because the graves were not dug very deep and 'pestilential odours' spread through the church.]

1742

March 29th

The burial of a soldier named Jean-Louis Pelletier dit Larose, a member of M. DeNoyon's company. "Accisus à concilio belli, tanquam Desertor exercitus, justa placita regia."
["Cut off from the Council of war, like a deserter from the army, he was cut off from life's pleasant things."]

(Trois-Rivières Register)

June

Mgr. Pontbriant, the 6th Bishop of Québec, made his first pastoral visit to Longue-Pointe and confirmed the children who were up to 2 months of age[110].

(Longue-Pointe Register)

LONGUE POINTE - ST. FRANCIS OF ASSISI CHURCH

110

During that visit, Monseigneur verified the healings brought about by the intercession of the late Monseigneur de Lauberivière.

[In light of the fact that young Catholics were *ordinarily* only confirmed after having had a chance to study catechism and that they were usually also required to know their prayers from memory before being confirmed, any mention of confirming children who were 'up to 2 months of age' is suspect although the Bishop clearly had the power to decide on a different age if he had felt that there was a danger of death – certainly not unknown for the times – or if a grave reason suggested that it should be done.]

June 6th

M. François St-Michel, Sieur de Gourville, *lieutenant des troupes* [lieutenant in an infantry company], was the Commandant at Fort Niagara.

(Montréal Register)

September 5th

The burial of the Marquis Durfort, *garde-marine* [honor-guard] of the Rochefort Province. The Commandant on His Majesty's ship *Le Rubis* assisted at his burial ceremony as did MM. de Beauharnois and Hocquart.

(Québec Register)

September 30th

The burial of Pierre Chaillot, *ouvrier* [worker] at the Saint-Maurice iron works. A native of Sueur-sur-Saone in the diocese of Dijon [in France], he had been crushed by a falling tree while in his cabin.

(Trois-Rivières Register)

1743

June 18th

The burial of Jean-Baptiste Hayot, 74, who fell onto the rocks, 6 *arpents* [about 1152 feet] beyond the Cap-Santé church.

(Cap-Santé Register)

[Based on a linear measure value of 191.8 feet per *arpent*. As was true of most French units of measurement at the time, however, the value of the *arpent* was not at all consistent and would often vary from one province to another.]

October 2nd

The burial of Louis Dechone who drowned at 11:00 at night while trying to cross the Rivière-du-Domaine (Rivière-Boyer) on horseback.

(St-Valier Register)

November 29th

The burial of François Grouard, 81, in the chapel at Hôpital of Québec. Born in Québec in 1662, he had received the *ordre de sous-diaconat* [he had been an exemplary sub-deacon] and assumed the responsibilities of *chapelain* of the *chapitre* of Québec.

(l'Hôpital Général de Québec Register)

[a) A *sous-diaconat* or sub-deacon was a clergyman who ranked below a deacon who in turn ranked just below a priest. The position of sub-deacon no longer exists in the Catholic Church but the deacons may and do give most of the sacraments.

b) This *chapitre* was perhaps the most distinguished group of clergy in New France principally because it was the closest to the Bishop. A 13-man group, it first appeared in 1684 and was composed of contemplatives whose only role was that of prayer but who acted as the Bishop's Court and Council.]

1744

March 27th

In the Bécancour Registers we read:

"The child, François-Xavier Provancher, died on the 10th of March 1744, and had been laid out in the *ancien chapelle de l'Île* by his father, Louis Provancher – this without the appropriate approvals and against the wishes and regulations of the Bishop. The chapel had been interdicted for burials as long ago as the Summer of 1743 and so once he, His Lordship, the Bishop, was informed of what was happening, he forbade that the child be buried anywhere but in the new cemetery. Based on that, the body was brought back and buried in the new cemetery, after the normal [religious] burial ceremonies." G. Marcol, S.J.

(Bécancour Register)

[The fact that this chapel had been interdicted for burials meant that it could no longer be used for Catholic burial services and being buried without the proper burial services prevented one from gaining the rewards of Heaven - not a very comforting thought for Catholics.]

April 17th

The burial of Marie Cardinal, the wife of Jean-Baptiste Menard, who drowned on the 12th of November 1743 but whose body had just been recovered from the banks of the St-Lawrence River.

(Longueuil Register)

June 24th

Jacques Auger, *pilote du navire* [pilot on the ship] *Le Caribou*, drowned.

(St-Pierre-de-l'Île-d'Orléans Register)

July 3rd

Mgr. Pontbriant confirmed 530 people of all ages, even one-month-old children, at St-Thomas. On the 11th of July 1750, he confirmed 169 more, also of all ages.

(St-Thomas Register)

[Again, in light of the fact that young Catholics were usually only confirmed after having had a chance to study catechism and that they were ordinarily also required to know their prayers from memory, any mention of confirming 'even one-month old children' is suspect although - again - the Bishop could have decided on a different age if he had felt that there was a danger of death – certainly not unknown for the times – or if a grave reason suggested that it should be done.]

December 21st

The burial of Pierre Patry, the son of Jean Patry and of Cathérine Vanasse of St-François-du-Lac, on the same day that he was found dead in his bed.

(St-François-du-Lac Register)

1745

May 19th

Joseph Brault dit Pominville, son of Jean-Baptiste and Élizabeth Brunet-Bourbonnais, from Lachine, was killed by the Sioux. He was married in Cahokia in 1743.

(Cahokia Register)

In the course of the year, Bellin, *ingénieur du Roi et de la marine*[Royal and naval engineer], had published a map of the Eastern part of New France. Ten years later, he published a second map of that same area. On that last one, he had designated the *Rivière-Ouabache* (Wabash) as the *Rivière-St-Jérôme* where the mission and Fort Ouiatanon are located.

(The Archives of the Ottawa Agriculture Department)

During the year, several Frenchmen were taken to Boston as prisoners of war.

(Québec Register)

June 24th

Jean-Baptiste Dubé and Marie-Anne Rasset had both of their twins baptized; two others were baptized on the 15th of March 1751; and another two on the 11th of January 1754.

(Québec Register)

Married in 1737, Dubé died in 1780 at 70 years of age; his wife died in 1797 at 80 years of age after having given birth to 19 children. Being very fertile certainly does not always lead to a premature death.

(Tanguay)

1746

March 24th

The baptism of Amédée-Constantin-Brice-Siméon-Richard, child of Nöel Bouchard. This was the first recorded case of 5 baptismal names being given to 1 child.

(Baie-St-Paul Register)

October 3rd

The burial of Marie-Joseph, 29, daughter of Pierre Verville, who drowned in the *Rivière Bécancour*, opposite her father's property.

(Bécancour Register)

October 5th

The burial of Louis Burdairon dit Jean Guy, *maître de barque* [master on a small boat or barge], who drowned 5 months ago at Long Sault as he went up to Fort Frontenac. His body was just recovered at Île-aux-Hérons.

(Montréal Register)

October 17th

Le Fourneau, a ship commanded by Guillaume Compiaux, was at anchor in Québec.

(Québec Register)

1747

January 16th

The marriage of LeGallais, *second maître* [petty officer] on the frigate *La Marthe.*

(Idem)

April 7th

The burial of Nicolas Varin, 44, who had been lost on the ice during a snowstorm at the beginning of the year.

(Montréal Register)

May 21st

The burial of Jacques Simonet, *écuyer* [squire] , Sieur d'Albergemont, *directeur intéressé dans les forges Saint-Maurice* [manager and iron-master with an interest in the Saint-Maurice Ironworks]. He was the son of Jean-Baptiste Simonet, Sieur d'Abergemont, *conseiller* and *secrétaire du Roi,* and of Dame Élizabeth Berauilt, from Dompierre in the diocese of Langres. His first marriage was to Marie Foissey and his second to Geneviève Boucher of Grand-Pré, widow of Charles Hertel – this latter on the 17th of November 1738.

(Trois-Rivières Register)

June 5th

René-Joseph Patry, 23, son of René Patry and of Cathérine Girard, drowned in the Rivière-Méchatigan[110] and was buried in the St-Joseph-de-la-Nouvelle-Beauce cemetery.

(St-Joseph-de-la-Nouvelle-Beauce Register)

June 25th

M. Pierre-René LeBoulanger, 68½ years of age and a *curé* in Charlesbourg, was buried in the church along with M. Alexis Leclerc, 40, *missionnaire* at St-Joseph parish, seigneurie of Fleury.

(Charlesbourg Register)

July 1st

The burial of Michel-André DeMoyres, 60, a native of Anjou [France], and *supérieur des frères charons* [Superior of the Charron Brothers] at the Hôpital-Général in Montréal.

(l'Hôpital-Général de Montréal Register)

August 8th

The burial of Madeleine Jarret from Verchères in the Ste-Anne-de-la Pérade church. She was the wife of Pierre-Thomas Tarieu, Sieur de la Pérade.

SAINTE-ANNE-DE-LA-PERADE CHURCH

[Madeleine Jarret de Verchères was 14 when, in the absence of her parents, the Iroquois raided their seigniory on the St-Lawrence River on the 22nd of October 1692. With the aid of her 10 and 12 year old brothers, a servant and 2 soldiers, she fought off the (45) Indians who attacked their fort until she was relieved 8 days later. In 1706 she married Pierre-Thomas Tarieu de la Pérade whose life she saved in 1722 when he was attacked by an Indian.]

September 1st

Jacques Taychaten, 25, a Huron chief at Détroit, was buried in Montréal.

(Montréal Register)

October 27th

The burial of Jean-Baptiste Ki8et, 84, an old Algonquin chief who killed and scalped *La Chaudière Noire*, the chief of the Iroquois who had devastated Canada with his raids when he was only 18-years-of-age.

(Trois-Rivières Register)

110

Méchatigan, by corruption 'Saint-Igan', is the Indian name for the 'Rivière Chaudière'.

[The exact spelling of Indian names is almost impossible to determine since they were often so badly distorted both by the French and by the English who were all apt to phonetically transcribe the names which they learned from the Indians. One sound especially peculiar to the Algonquin language – although found in other languages as well – was the sound of an 8 or *'huit'*, a whistling sound when pronounced in French. Many of the old names have retained the 8's in their spellings.]

October 30th

The marriage of Jean Dubois, an *officier de la frégate* [officer on the frigate] *La Marthe.*

(Québec Register)

1748

May 1st

The burial of M. Claude-Michel Bégon, 65, *chevalier*, Governor of Trois-Rivières, and husband of Jeanne-Élizabeth DeBeauharnois.

(Montréal Register)

June 24th

The *meunier du Roi* [King's miller] at Fort Frédéric was Jean-Baptiste Desraby.

(Québec Register)

[A miller is a person who owns or operates a mill, especially a flour mill.]

July 4th

A young daughter of Pierre Dubreuil and Marie Vaudray drowned at Pointe-aux-Trembles de Montréal.

(Pointe-aux-Trembles de Montréal Register)

August 8th

The burial of 5 soldiers who were killed somewhere between Yamachiche and la-Pointe-du-Lac while escorting 3 Outaouais and Sauteux Indians to prison in Québec.

(Trois-Rivières Register)

August 12th

The marriage of Mathurin Chapelet, a native of Plerin in the diocese of St-Brieu, and Angélique Demitre, daughter of Jean-Robert Demitre.

(Québec Register)

In the *Registres des procès-verbaux [Official Statements] de liberté* we find that Angélique Demitre received permission to marry Pierre Batz on the 4th of June 1764, after having furnished evidence that her husband, Chapelet, had died at the St-Pierre Hospital in Martinique.

(Register of the 'Procès-verbaux' [Official Statements] of the Archdiocese of Québec)

August 13th

The marriage of Jacques Franchères, the *second chirurgien* [junior surgeon] on the *Fleuve-St-Laurent,* to Élizabeth Boissy.

(Québec Register)

August 20th

Jean Diau, the *second canonnier* [back-up gunner] on the same ship, was also married in Québec.

(Idem)

August 23rd

M. De la Villangevin, *vicaire-général,* in his pastoral visit to St-Pierre-les-Becquets, directed that two copies of [all of the Parish] Registers be made and that they be filed in the appropriate places.

(St-Pierre-les-Becquets Register)

November 13th

For the second time in Canada, 5 baptismal names were given to a youngster[111], Louis-Augustin-René-Brice-Sauveur, the son of Augustin Balard, *armurier* [gunsmith], and of Victoire Tremblay, at the paroisse Éboulements.

(Éboulements Register)

1749

January 18th

In the Register of Cap-St-Ignace, we found the following note:
"From the present death record to the 10th, inclusively, I failed to specify on each death certificate that the said body had previously been buried without benefit of religious services, by several residents, in an interdicted cemetery, and it is in all fairness that they were removed from the said cemetery: and that's what we gleaned from the Registers......that the burials were made a long time after the deaths of those individuals."

(SIGNED)   Curot, *curé'*
(Cap-St-Ignace Register)

NOTE: MM. Hiché, *procureur du Roi* and Louet, *greffier de l'admirauté* [clerk of courts for the Admiralty Court] of Québec, were witnesses to the transfer of the bodies, the burials of which dated from the 30th of September 1748 to the 13th of November of the same year.

(Idem)

111

See the entry for the 24th of March 1746.

[As previously alluded to, the very powerful belief at the time was that being buried forever in an <u>interdicted</u> cemetery prevented one from gaining the full rewards of Heaven - not a pleasant thought for Catholics.]

April 27th

The burial of Raphaël, 16, and of his brother Stanislas, 14, children of Alexis Sauvageau, who both drowned in the Rivière-Lachevrotière.

(Deschambault Register)

June 14th

The marriage of Pierre-François-Olivier, Sieur de Vézin, son of Hugues Olivier, seigneur de Lyonne, in Bassigny, and of Dame Louise Leroux of Dinjolincour, diocese of Toul , to Marie-Joseph Gatineau-Duplessis, the daughter of Sieur Jean-Baptiste Gatineau. M. Vézin was the *grand-voyer* [official in charge of the care of roads] of the province of Louisiana and was the first one to be sent to this nation by the King specifically to set up the furnaces and ovens at the St-Maurice Ironworks and to serve as its [first] manager.

(Trois-Rivières Register)

August 19th

The burial of Joseph Héroux, 18, who died after having been struck by lightning. He was the son of Pierre Héroux and Angélique Carbonneau.

(Ste-Anne-de-Yamachiche Register)

Simon Aubry, husband of Marie Beaudet, drowned while trying to cross the icy waters of the Rivière-Cap-Rouge at St-Nicolas.

(Register of the 'Procès-verbaux' [Official Statements] of the Archdiocese of Québec, 1750)

At some time during the year, Pierre Bouet dit Lalancette, *canonnier* [gunner], arrived in Québec and took up residence near the citadel.

(Register of the 'Procès-verbaux' [Official Statements] of the Archdiocese of Québec, 1766)

1750

June 17th

Mgr. Pontbriant visited St-François-Xavier-de-la-Petite-Rivière, near Beaupré.

(St-François-Xavier-de-la-Petite-Rivière Register)

The St-Pierre-du-Sud church was interdicted this year. Why? [Tanguay's question.]
SEE: The St-François-du-Sud Register for the 8th of September 1750.

[An interdict is a Church ruling by which the faithful of the Catholic Church are forbidden from performing certain church offices, sacraments, or privileges - including burials. The fact that a church is interdicted meant that it could no longer be used for burial services – among other things – without the express approval of the Bishop. Doing something against the express wishes of the Bishop could have led to being excommunicated by the Church and therefore possibly losing the rewards of Heaven - not an attractive possibility for Catholics.]

July 30th

Michel de Sallaberry[112], son of Martin de Sallaberry and Marie Michelance, from Cibour in the diocese of Bayonne, was married for a second time, this time to Madeleine-Louise Juchereau. He was an officer on the frigate *Anglezea*. Two years later, he was *capitaine de la flûte du Roi* [Captain of the Royal ship] and commanded *Le Chariot Royal* .

M. Gomain, *lieutenant des vaisseaux du Roi* [lieutenant of the royal vessels] and *commandant* on the frigate *Anglezea*, was a witness at the marriage of M. de Sallaberry.

(Beauport Register)

August 11th

The burial of Gabriel Latreille, 26, *homme de l'équipage* [member of the ship's company] on the brigantine *La Louise* commanded by Denis Larche.

(St-Thomas Register)

September 14th

The baptism of Joseph-Nicolas, son of Kionhatonni, *orateur sauvage* [Indian spokesman] in the new Présentation-de-la-Rivière-Hoegatsi settlement, and of Onhatsouaten, *dame du conseil* [lady counsellor] of the said establishment.

(Montréal Register)

October 1st

M. Koseph Gaillard, *chanoine* [canon] *of Québec*, is named *seigneur* of the *Île and comté* of St-Laurent.

(St-Pierre-de-l'Île-d'Orleans Register)
[*Canons* were priests who were not allowed to teach or become parish priests. Their essential function was to pray together and, in a few cases, when they lived in a presbytery, to serve as missionaries.]

112

His grand-son, Charles-Michel, was the '*Héros de Châteauguay*'.

ILE d'ORLEANS
SAINT-LAURENT CHURCH

November 5th

> François Nicou, the *contremaître* [first mate] on the ship *Le Saint-Joseph* from Nantes [France], was buried today in the cemetery at St-Laurent-de-l'Île-d'Orléans. Captain Fontaine was that ship's *commandant.*
>
> *(St-Laurent-de-l'Île-d'Orléans Register)*

December 5th

> The burial of François Delsol-Desnoyers, who died on the schooner *La Trompeuse*, commanded by Denis DeVitré.
>
> *(Île St-Jean Register)*

December 30th

> M. Pierre-Joseph Tarieu de la Naudière and Marie-Joseph Gastineau were the sponsors of Ste-Anne-de-la-Pérade's parish bell which was blessed today by M. Louis-Eustache Chartier de Lotbinière, an *archdiacre* [archdeacon].
>
> *(Ste-Anne-de-la-Pérade Register)*
>
> [The sixth of eight such bell-blessings recorded in this book. Roman Catholics have a great deal of faith in the value of having things blessed. They themselves receive special blessings at the time of their baptisms and marriages and illnesses and deaths and ask for blessings for their throats...and their prayer beads...and their fishing boats...and their gifts... etc. etc. . And so it is not surprising that during a period when the Church was so important in the colonists' everyday lives, a time when they were too poor to be able to afford individual timepieces, that they had to rely on church or other public bells to keep track of the time of day. Bells signaled the start and close of religious ceremonies and of workdays. They tolled to warn of emergencies or to advise of deaths or of happier events. They summoned citizens to assembly or to prayer or to arms or to fight fires. They indicated when it was time to sleep ... and to awaken. They rang to let merchants know when they could open up their shops... and when they had to close them. The colonists would surely have insisted upon blessing the very bells which guided their daily activities since they were absolutely essential to the life of the community.]

MOVEMENT OF THE CATHOLIC POPULATION OF THE PROVINCE OF QUÉBEC 1741 TO 1750

	MARRIAGES	BIRTHS	DEATHS	OTHERS
1741	425	2379	1104	1275
1742	422	2529	1134	1395
1743	418	2467	1348	1119
1744	426	2546	1436	1110
1745	438	2626	1150	1476
1746	418	2702	1275	1427
1747	513	2737	1717	1020
1748	614	2784	2031	753
1749	664	2810	2210	600
1750	619	2974	1879	1095
TOTALS ➡	4957	26554	15284	11270
1608-1750	19031	104277	47093	57184

1751

May 7th

> The burial of Joseph Germain, 32, who drowned while hunting. He was *marguiiller-en-charge* at Cap-Santé.
>
> *(Cap-Santé Register)*

[The marguiller-en-charge was the churchwarden currently responsible for the parish's secular affairs.]

CAP SANTE
SAINTE-FAMILLE CHURCH

May 23rd

    Charles Beausoleil left Terrebonne to escort M. Lacorne's boatload of flour but he drowned and was buried at Pointe-aux-Trembles.

(Pointe-aux-Trembles de Montréal Register)

June 15th

    François Dugal, a 30-year-old *matelot* [sailor] from Brittany [in France], drowned and was buried at Beauport.

(Beauport Register)

June 21st

    Louis Bourassa and his 16-year-old son, Jean, were buried after being struck by lightning on their way back from Québec to St-Nicolas.

(St-Nicolas Register)

June 24th

    Antoine Vermandois drowned and was later found on the beach and buried in Berthier-sur-Mer.

(Berthier Register)

July 16th

    Mgr. Pontbriant ordered that a small register be maintained of the burials of children born dead.

(Lorette Register)

September 22nd

    Pierre Petit, a Frenchman, drowned at Pointe-aux-Hurons in Lotbinière.

(Lotbinière Register)

November 24th

    Ignace Guay, 45, drowned near Québec City and was then buried.

(Lévis Register)

December 8th

    Jacques Chaperon, 50, drowned at Pointe-aux-Trembles de Montréal and was buried at Varennes. He had married Françoise Auger in a second marriage on the 19th of April of that same year.

(Varennes Register)

During that year, François Moreau, a native of Thionville, arrived in Québec on the *Angélique* commanded by M. Vitray.

(Register of the 'Procès-verbaux' [Official Statements] of the Archdiocese of Québec)

The year's *Registre des procès verbaux de liberté* [of Liberty] mentioned that Marie-Joseph, the daughter of Jacques Fournel and Marie-Joseph Pelletier from Pointe-aux-Trembles de Québec, was born in 1738, and abducted by Daniel Hardiment, a Jewish person, when she was 13. *(Idem)*

1752

January 31st

The record of the marriage of Jean Girard from Ange-Gardien did not mention his wife's nor their parents' names. We might have concluded that Jean Girard had married himself ! [a Tanguay witticism]. Fortunately, his wife's name did show up on their childrens' baptismal and burial records. *(Tanguay)*

April 23rd

Charles Goguet, a *cultivateur* [farmer] from Longue-Pointe, was buried in the forest after being crushed by a tree which he had felled. *(Longue-Pointe Register)*

May 13th

Jean Favre and his wife, Marie Bastien were buried after being murdered in their home on the night of the 11th of May 1752. They were both 60 years of age. *(Montréal Register)*

We read the following in the Rimouski Chronicle (Volume I, pp. 67- 84):

"In the Fall of 1755, a French frigate was transporting some troops to Québec. The ship broke up on one stormy night at Gros Mecatina off the coast of Labrador. The ship's 300-man crew was able to salvage a portion of the sails and of the rigging and had hurriedly rigged up the hull of another brig of 100-or-so tons which had also run aground at that same location several years previously. It was called *"Le Saint-Esprit"* and had belonged to M. Jean Taché, forefather of the Messrs. Taché of Kamouraska. This improvised ship which the crew called *"l'Aigle"* or *"Le Sneau"*, sailed up the river towards Québec but ran right into another storm near Rimouski. During a truly frightening and stormy late-November night, very heavy seas carried a portion of the mast away and tossed the ship up onto the northeastern point of l'Île-de-St-Barnabé. Toussaint Cartier, the Hermit of St. Barnabé, spotted the shipwreck at dawn while leaving his humble home on the Île and ran as quickly as he could to the site of the wreck. He found victims freezing to death and several who had already died. He took the survivors to his home but since it was much too small to hold them all he immediately signaled for help from the residents of Rimouski. Several hours later, some of the area's able-bodied men were already helping the survivors to get to their village although some of the victims were so weak from hunger, cold and exposure, that they weren't even able to survive that short trip! MM. DeLoubarat, the Commandant; DeCondamin, the First Lieutenant; DeSouvenier, a surgeon; and Reverend Joseph Chesnot, a chaplain, were some of the very few who survived."

The author of this interesting account allowed us to correct several errors in dates and names, mistakes which we had noticed while comparing the account to an authentic document on file in the Archives of the Archdiocese of Québec:

"A man named Pierre Brunet, a native of Niort in the diocese of Poitiers, had embarked on the ship "*l'Aigle*" at Brest while he was still a boy of about 16. The ship, commanded by M. DeRoboras, arrived in Canada in 1752 after having been ship-wrecked in Mécatina, on the shores of Labrador."   *(Register of the Procès-verbaux de liberté', 1767)*

It was thus in 1752 and not 1756 that "*l'Aigle*" was shipwrecked and the name of the Commandant was '*DeRoboras*' and not '*DeLoubarat*'.

June 11th

    Nicolas Claude, a native of St-Nicolas parish in the diocese of Strasbourg, Alsace, recanted his Lutheran religion and, on the following day, married Geneviève Bouleau at Ste-Geneviève parish in Montréal.   *(Ste-Geneviève de Montréal Register)*

August 28th

    Mathieu Hianveu, 28, a native of Gisors, a town in the diocese of Rouën, Normandy, married Marguerite Pépin in Charlesbourg. A young soldier in M. Marin's Company, Mathieu, AKA 'Lafrance'. In 1759, Father St-Pé, the superieur général [Superior-General] of the Jesuits, appointed him notaire royal [royal notary] for the seigneuries belonging to the Jesuit Order in New France. He died in Québec and was buried on the 7th of March 1793. His descendants almost all distinguished themselves as very skillful relieurs [bookbinders] and especially as model citizens and Christians in Québec. [AKA (Also Known As) was used here since 'Lafrance' could have been translated here either as a surname or as a nickname. Since there is an obvious distinction between the two in the English language, AKA was appropriate.]

1753

February 16th

    The burial of Louis Dechau who was crushed to death by a falling tree.
                                                 (Nicolet Register)

April 21st

    Renunciation of his old faith and baptism into the new of Valentin Jean-Baptiste Cole, an Englishman, at St-Antoine-de-Tilly.   *(St-Antoine-de-Tilly Register)*

May 28th

    The residents of Nicolet parish exhumed all of the bodies from the old cemetery to transport and rebury them in the new one.   *(Nicolet Register)*
    [Transfers such as this one to consecrated grounds were usually done for Christians who had been buried quite hurriedly in unconsecrated land such as at the site of a continuing battle at which they might have been killed.]

June 10th

    The death and burial of Pierre Brose, homme de l'équipage [crew-member] on the ship Le Saint-Esprit which was at the Gaspé. Commanded by Sieur Pierre Bérade, the ship originally came from Bayonne.

June 24th

Pierre Daigneau and Louis Roulette were struck and killed by lightning while sailing on Lac-St-François.

(Soulanges Register)

August 6th

Pierre Buisson, 18, a native of Dinan, drowned. He was the aide-canonier [assistant gunner] on the Royal vessel *Le Tigre* commanded by M. De la Villeon.

(Québec Register)

August 25th

François Coiteux, 23, was buried at Fort Presqu'ile, in the *pays d'en haut*, by Brother Denis Baron, a Récollet, and aumônier [chaplain]. Proof of his burial can be found in the Longue-Pointe de Montréal Register.

(Longue-Pointe Register)

[The *'pays d'en haut'* was the area above the Saint Lawrence River which included the Great Lakes area. Détroit was the center of the *pays* with Michilimackinac serving as its ecclesiastical capitol.]

September 24th

A case of *superfétation.* [A second conception during a pregnancy from an earlier conception.] Michel Hunaut-Deschamps and Marie-Charlotte Cuillerier had their daughter, Marie-Françoise, baptized after being born on the 23rd of September 1753. Another daughter, Marianne, was born on the 13th of May 1753 and baptized in that same year.

(Ste-Anne-du-Bout-de-l'Ile Register)

[There is some disagreement on the current definition ot *superfétation.* " Stedman's Medical Dictionary – 25th Edition, 1990 " specifies that the 2 fetuses of different ages are not twins and that the concept is an obsolete one whereas Joseph Segen's 1995 "Current Med Talk, a Dictionary of Medical Terms, Slang and Jargon" notes that the concept serves as a theoretical explanation for the difference in times of delivery of fraternal twins.]

October 29th

We found a record of the burial of the chevalier de la Margue[113] in the Fort Duquesne Register along with the following notation: "Died in the Fort at Rivière-aux-Boeufs but buried by the name of Mr. Pierre Paul, *écuier* [squire],

---

113

NOTE: The chevalier Marin de la Margue, born in Montréal in 1692, had married Mlle. Marie-Joseph Guyon-Desprès in Montréal in 1718; her cousin had married Antoine Lamotte [s/b Lamothe] Cadillac, the founder of Détroit. One of the daughters of the *chevalier* of la Margue married Charles-René de la Roche-Vernay in 1755.

(Tanguay)

Sieur de Marin, Chevalier de l'Ordre Militaire et Royal de St-Louis, *capitaine d'infanterie* [infantry Captain], and *commandant-général de l'armée de la Belle-Rivière."* [commanding general of the Belle-Rivière army]

(Fort Duquesne Register)

[At the end of the 17th century, when the King of France no longer allowed Canadians to become nobles, only one important honor remained, *l'Ordre-Royal-et-Militaire-de-Saint-Louis*. That military order was divided into 8 Grand-Croix, 24 commanders and an unlimited number of *chevaliers* and was the only military order in which New France had the honor of taking part. To obtain the decoration, one had to be an officer in the regular forces which immediately eliminated the entire parish militia system and other ranks. Also, one could only serve the King of France in order to qualify.

The first person to receive the decoration in Canada was Callières, the Governor of Montréal, who received it in 1694, and the first Canadian chevalier was Pierre le Moyne d'Iberville who attained that distinction in 1699. From 1693-1760, *only about 145 men* were so decorated in Canada whereas France decorated 12,180 of its citizens from 1814-1830 alone. After the Conquest, only about a dozen of these *Chevaliers-de-Saint-Louis* remained in Canada and about 6 of those eventually took an oath of alliegance to the King of England, thereby severing their alliegance to Canada and France.

The glory and prestige of the decoration still remains in Canada because of its rarity whereas comparatively little value remains to the holders of the French decoration.]

1754

February 15th

The marriage of Pierre Benard and Cathérine Laviolette who married *'à-la-Gauminé'* during the elevation of the Holy Host. By edict of M. Lenormant, vicaire-général of the Diocese, a mandate against those 'marriages' was read at the Sermon on Sunday the 24th of the same month by Mgr. de St-Valier. As a result, the so-called married couple was excommunicated.

(Pointe-aux-Trembles de Montréal Register)

[A marriage *'à-la-Gauminé'* was a plan-of-action used in New France in the first years of the 18th Century. A couple who for some reason or other had been refused the right to marry would make their way to Church in secret, together with two witnesses, at the hour when Mass was to be celebrated by the parish priest. Then, at the solemn moment of consecration, the couple would declare aloud their intention to take each other as wife and husband without further ceremony. This practice became so fashionable that the Bishop, supported by the administrative authorities (since the male partners in most such marriages were soldiers), excommunicated those who had contracted marriage in this way." André Lachance attributes the practice to a M. Gaumin who first conceived of the procedure in France. Also, according to Lachance, it never really became a matter of excommunication simply because the church and civil authorities always ended up by authorizing the marriages.]

May 22nd

Cassegrain dit Laderive, 19, a native of Notre-Dame-de-Chartres and soldier in Rousseau's Company; Sieur Dorfontaine; and Jacques Bau-dit-Vadeboncoeur, 19, from Poitou [France] – all three drowned.

(Île-St-Jean Register)

Joseph Belletête, 18, a native of St-Jacques de Dieppe in Picardy [France], arrived in Québec in 1754 on the ship *Le Dauphin*, commanded by his uncle, Captain Durand. He was married in 1768.

(Register of the 'Procès-verbaux' [Official Statements] of the Archdiocese of Québec)

August 23rd

The burial of Joseph Baudoin, 28, who drowned at Cap-Santé.

(Cap-Santé Register)

November 21st

The burial at St-Thomas of Louis Chel-dit-St-André, 52, after he was accidentally shot-to-death.

(St-Thomas-de-la-Pointe-à-Lacaille[114] Register)

December 30th

Pierre Dalserie, 40, a native of Brittany [in France], was found frozen-to-death on the ice and was buried in Sorel.

(Sorel Register)

1755

SLAVES

March 13th

We found the burial certificate for Louise, a 27-day-old Negress who belonged to M. Deschambault.

(Longue-Pointe Register)

1756

November 4th

The baptism of Marie-Judith, 13, a Panis Indian who belonged to Sieur Preville.

(Longue-Pointe Register)

114

Now known as St-Thomas-de-Montmagny.

1757

January 22nd

    Lieutenant-General Guiton of Monrepos sentenced Constant, a Panis slave belonging to M. de St-Blain, *officier d'infanterie* [infantry officer], to one day of *la peine du carqan* in the Public Square on a day when the markets were open; futhermore, he was banished forever from the Province of Montréal.

                               (Montréal Records)

[Being sentenced to one day of *peine du carqan* meant that one would have to stand in the Public Square in an iron collar which was attached to a pole, possibly with weights attached to his feet, for the prescribed amount of time]

    It's impossible to deny that slavery existed in Canada both before *and* after the surrender of the colony. It existed not only *en fait* [in fact] as the listing furnished a little bit later will prove; but also *en droit* [in law], or even better, *d'après la loi* [according to the law], as Commander Jacques Viger demonstrated in a report published by the Historical Society of Montréal.

There are three documents which prove that slavery was introduced in Canada in 1688 or shortly thereafter:

1.   The Raudot Ordinance of the 13th of April 1709, which, at the pleasure of the King, ordered that all of the Panis Indians and Negroes which had been or which would later be purchased as slaves, would belong entirely to those who had purchased or would purchase them as slaves.

2.   The Hocquart Ordinance of the 1st of September 1736, which declared nul and void all emancipations of slaves not recorded before notaries, for which [emancipations] minutes had been maintained and recorded in the Office of the Clerk of whatever Royal jurisdiction [that this might be happening in].

3.   The Decree dated the 23rd of July 1745 by the King's *Conseil d'État* which stated that "the Negroes who escaped from the colonies which were enemies of the French colony, and their belongings, would belong to His Majesty, the *King Très Chrétien*".

    [*King Très Chrétien* here was actually King Louis XVI who reigned from 1715 to 1774. This title was one bestowed by the early Popes on the kings of France.]

Those three documents established three phases of slavery in Canada. The first legalized what was still but an abuse; the second merely stated what actually was and established a very formal procedure for doing it the right way; and the third was the final one which was needed to deal with the extreme situations.

We prove it again with Article XLVII of the Surrender of Québec[115]:
> "The Negroes and Panis of the two sexes shall remain as slaves in the possession of the French and Canadians to whom they belong; they will be free to keep them in their service as slaves in the colony or to sell them; and they could also continue to raise them in the Roman religion, except for [any of] those who might have been imprisoned."

In the Québec Gazette of the 18th of March 1784 we read the following advertisement:

> FOR SALE   A Negro woman who is presently [living] in town.
> Contact Mme. Perrault for the price.

In the issue dated the 25th of March in that same year:
> FOR SALE   A Negro man, approximately 25, who has had smallpox.
> For more information, please contact the printer."

On the 9th of June 1783, Elias Smith sold James Finlay, *Juge de Paix* [justice of the peace], a Negress whom we called Peg. On the 14th of May 1788, the said Finlay resold her to Patrick Langan. In both instances, the slave had a value of 50 *livres* [about $10.00].

In 1793, in the Parliament of Lower Canada, a bill to abolish slavery in this Province was introduced but the motion was not seconded. It was taken up again by Parliament in 1799, and in 1803 the question was newly discussed again without a firm resolution. It was only by the Act of 1833 that slavery was definitively abolished.

115

The surrender of Québec, as we know it, was signed by General Amherst, commander-in-chief of the troops and forces of His British Majesty in North America and the Marquis de Vaudreuil, Governor and Lieutenant-General for the King in Canada.

The following table is based on information from various *Registres* and should be of interest:

TABLE OF FAMILIES WITH SLAVES FROM THE PANIS NATION

FAMILY NAME	SLAVES' NAMES	BORN	DIED	DIED WHERE	AT AGE
MM. Leschelle	Marie-Louise	1737	1754	Hôpital-	17
MM. Senneville	Marie-Anne	1732	1754	Général	22
MM. Felta	Marie	1748	1754	of	6
Demoiselle Desrivières	Marie	1748	1755	Montréal	7
MM. Vien, Jean	Charlottte	1742	1782	"	40
MM. Adhemar, A.	Marie	1763	1781	"	18
Dame Cuillerier	Joseph	1680	1755	"	75
MM. DeBaune	Joseph	1737	1755	"	18
MM. Perigny	Joseph	1755	1755	"	?
MM. Réaume, Simon	Joseph	1730	1755	"	25
MM. Ducharme	Marie	1730	1755	"	25
MM. Lacoste	Marie	?	1755	"	?
MM. Laplante	Marguerite	1720	1755	"	35
Dame Linctot	Marie	1710	1755	"	45
MM. de la Vérandrie	Joseph	1736	1755	"	19
MM. de la Vérandrie	Marie	1736	1756	"	20
Au Roy	Marie	1744	1756	"	12
Au Roy	Louise	?	1756	"	?
Au Roy	Two Girls	?	1756	"	?
Au Roy	Marie	1737	1757	"	20
MM. Feltz	Marie	1749	1757	"	8
MM. Godet	Marie	1741	1757	Hôpital-	16
Au Roy	Marie	1732	1757	Général	25
Au Roy	Marie	1748	1757	of	9
Au Roy	Joseph	1733	1757	Montréal	24

FAMILY NAME	SLAVES' NAMES	BORN	DIED	DIED WHERE	AT AGE
Au Roy	Joseph	1747	1756	"	9
Dame DesLignery	Marie	1745	1757	"	12
Demoiselle Monier	Marie	1743	1757	"	14
MM. de la Corne (*chevalier*)	Marie	1712	1757	"	45
MM. de Vaudreuil	Marie	1712	1757	"	45
MM. Lacroix, Hubert	Marie	1712	1757	"	45
MM. Chenneville	Marie	1730	1757	"	27
MM. Messière-Lahaye	Louis	1750	1758	"	8
MM. Giasson, Jean	Joseph	1750	1758	"	8
Dame Couteraux	Louise	1742	1758	"	16
MM. Baron, Ant.	Marie	1743	1758	"	15
MM. d'Aguille	Cathérine	?	1758	"	?
MM. Pillamet	Joseph	1750	1759	"	9
MM. Leschelle	Marie	1743	1759	"	16
MM. de la Ronde	Marie	1744	1759	"	15
MM. Feltz	Marie	1725	1759	"	34
MM. Corporon	Joseph	1749	1759	"	10
Au Roy	Marie	1719	1759	"	40
MM. Perthuis, Iroquois Interpreter	Marie	?	1759	"	?
MM. de Bleury	Marie	1743	1759	Hôpital-	16
Au Roy	Marie	1747	1759	Général	12
M. Gagné	Joseph	1748	1760	of	12
Dame de la Naudière	Marie	1740	1760	Montréal	20
Au Roy	Marie	1755	1760	"	5

FAMILY NAME	SLAVES' NAMES	BORN	DIED	DIED WHERE	AT AGE
M. Perrault	Marie	1745	1760	"	15
Dame Giasson	Marie	1748	1760	"	12
Dame de Perigny	Marie	1740	1760	"	20
DeQuiensek, chief of the Algonquins	Joseph	1725	1760	"	35
MM. Saint-Dizier	Marie	1736	1760	"	24
MM. Deschambault	Marie	1745	1760	"	15
MM. Réaume, Simon	Marie	1740	1760	"	20
MM. Deschenaux	Antoine	1738	1760	"	22
MM. de Lessard	Marie	?	1760	"	?
MM. de la Garde, Iroquois missionary	Anselme	1749	1760	"	11
Dame de Lignerie	Marie	1739	1760	"	21
Dame Benoit	Marie	1736	1761	"	25
Dame Delisle	Joseph	1752	1761	"	9
MM. Brossard, Paul	Jean-Baptiste	1746	1761	"	15
MM. de Bleury	Joseph	1745	1761	"	16
MM. de la Corne	Joseph	1743	1763	"	20
MM. Ferrière	Angélique	1748	1763	"	15
MM. Volant, Frs.	Jean-Baptiste	1707	1766	"	59
MM. d'Auterive	Marie	1719	1769	Hôpital-	50
Demoiselle Guyon	Marie	1748	1769	Général	21
Demoiselle DeBlainville	Marie-Joseph	1723	1769	of	46
MM. Carignan	Joseph	1752	1769	Montréal	17
MM. Côté, traveler	Charlotte	1762	1775	"	13
MM. Dauby	Charlotte	1752	1776	"	24

FAMILY NAME	SLAVES' NAMES	BORN	DIED	DIED WHERE	AT AGE
MM. Lemoine-Despins, Jacques	Claire	1769	1776	"	7
MM. Saint-Luc-Lacorne	Marie-Joseph	1747	1777	"	30
MM. Bernard (Anglais)	Joseph	1764	1778	"	14
MM. Adhémar, Jean-Baptiste	Marie-Joseph	1770	1778	"	8
Dame D'Auteuil	Marie-Joseph	1699	1799	"	100
Dame de Clignancour	Marguerite	1714	1794	"	80
MM. Gamelin, Ignace [Wed to MM. De Longueil (below)]	Jacques-César (noir)	W e d	i n	L o n g u e u i l	
MM. de Longueuil	Marie (noire)		on	5th of January 1763	

June 1st

Another case of *superfétation*. [A second conception during pregnancy from an earlier conception.] François Thibaut and Marie-Anne Richard from St-François-du-Sud parish, had their son, Nicolas, baptized shortly after he was born. He died on the 8th of August. On June 27th of that same year, they had another son who was born, baptized and died on the same day. He was buried on the 28th.

(St-François-du-Sud Register)

[There is some disagreement on the current definition ot *superfétation*. "*Stedman's Medical Dictionary – 25th Edition, 1990*" specifies that the 2 fetuses of different ages are *not* *twins* and that the concept is an obsolete one whereas Joseph Segen's 1995 "*Current Med Talk, a Dictionary of Medical Terms, Slang and Jargon*" notes that the concept serves as a theoretical explanation for the difference in times of delivery of *fraternal twins*.]

June 23rd

> Father Duvau, ship's *aumônier* [chaplain] on the Royal ship the *Opiniâtre'*, blessed the grave of Jean Loiselle, 24, *partie de l'équipage* [a member of the crew] on that same ship, who was a native of Ploûeve in the diocese of St-Malo. Jean was buried in Lévis.
>
> *(Lévis Register)*

June 25th

> The burial of Mathurin Lemaître, 25, a native of St-Malo, and crew member on the ship the *Opiniâtre* .
>
> *(Lévis Register)*

June 28th

> Antoine Mercier, a *cultivateur* [farmer] who lived in Les-Écureuils, *drowned in the Rivière-Jacques-Cartier.* He had only been married for 5 months.
>
> *(Écureuils Register)*

July 20th

> The burial of Jean-Baptiste Polemond, 43, *ancien chirurgien-major* [former head-surgeon] in Douay, Flanders and *chirurgien-major* [head-surgeon] of the French troops in Canada, who had drowned the night before in the Rivière-Duchesne.
>
> *(St-Jean-Deschaillons Register)*

July 27th

> A solemn blessing for a bell named *'Marie-Joseph'*.
>
> *(Deschambault Register)*

> [The seventh of eight such bell-blessings recorded in this book. For more information on these blessings, please see my comments after the entry of December 30th, 1750.]

1756

January 15th

Ruette D'Auteuil.

"A real copy of a will made before Ferdinand Ximenès de Pineda, *notaire* in the town of Cartagine and witness, on this day, for Ignace Auteuil[116], *chevalier*, seigneur d'Auteuil, in the town of Monceraire, eldest son and ½-heir of François Madeleine Ruette, *écuier* [squire], Sieur of Auteuil and of Monceaux, and of Dame Marie-Anne Juchereau, by which it appears that all that it would be possible for her brother-in-law, M. De Muy[117] to find, on deposit and in trust, as part of the interest and inheritance which his deceased father had left him, he ceded him willingly and graciously, in addition to 1000 piastres given on the goods of his estate which he had bestowed upon him and left him as a legacy in the best manner that it could rightfully be done."

[For more information on titles, honors, decorations, etc., please refer to my comments after the entry dated October 29th, 1753.]

April 2nd

Jérôme Dufix, a native of Carepras in the diocese of Nîmes in Languedoc [in France], and a soldier in Guiana, renounced his Calvinism.

(Longue-Pointe Register)

Jean-Baptiste Joseph de Roche de Beaumont was the Commandant of the Cahokias in 1756.

(Cahokias Register)

May 20th

The burial of François, a French *matelot* [sailor], who died on board *La Sirène* and was buried at St-Michel de Bellechasse.

(St-Michel Register)

A large number of English soldiers from Boston were buried at the Hôpital-Général.

(L'Hôpital-Général de Montréal Register)

116

Ignace-Alexandre was born in Québec on 9 June 1688.

117

Jacques-Pierre Daneau de Muy, the grandson of Governor Pierre Boucher had married Louise-Geneviève Ruette D'Auteuil in Montréal in 1725. She was born in Québec on the 5th of August 1696.

June 6th

The Reverend Father Quoad, 38, a Jesuit and *missionnaire* for the Indians at Rivière-des-Caps (St.-André-de-Kamouraska) was buried in the church at Kamouraska.

(Kamouraska Register)

June 27th

Jacques Horne and Françoise Savary, recent arrivals in Québec from Île St-Jean, [Prince Edward Island] had their son, Louis, baptized. He was born on the 13th of the month on the same boat which had brought them over.

(Québec Register)

The ship *Le Dandanais*, commanded by Captain Fayal, was at anchorage in Québec. Guillaume DeLugas who had married Marie-Joseph Sasseville in 1762 was a member of the ship's crew.

July 20th

François Leclere, a young soldier and native of Dol in Franche-Comté, drowned at Cap-Rouge and was buried in the Notre-Dame-de-Ste-Foye cemetery.

(Ste-Foye Register)

August 19th

While looking through the Fort St-Frederic Register, I (Reverend Tanguay) ran across the name of one of my grandfather's brothers, a member of the militia who died in the Fort. Here is a copy of this young soldier's burial record:

"In the year 1756, on the 19th of August, by me the undersigned, the King's chaplain at Fort St-Frederic[118], was buried Jean Tanguay[119], a militia man from the Saint-Valier parish with the usual ceremonies, in the Fort's cemetery. He was 18 or so, and fortified with the sacraments of Penance and Extreme Unction."

In testimony whereof I have signed,

Father Didace Cliche, curé, Récollet"

---

[118]

Fort St-Frederic was located at the head of Lac Champlain.

[119]

Born the 7th of October in 1735 in Saint-Valier, the son of Jacques Tanguay and Geneviève Mercier.

Antoine Chevalier, 25, a native of St-Project in Bordeaux [France], arrived in Québec from Marseilles on *Le Fortuné*, commanded by Captain Daniel.

(Register of the 'Procès-verbaux' [Official Statements], 1761)

Pierre Chevely, 16, a native of the parish of Bidac in the diocese of Bayonne, arrived in Québec on the ship *Le Victoire*, commanded by Captain Fosselave.

(Register of the 'Procès-verbaux' [Official Statements], 1761)

DeBougainville, *Chevalier de St-Louis*, General Montcalm's *aide-de-camp*, set fire to a small English fleet while Commander-in-Chief at Île-aux-Noix. After 1763, he was the chef d'escadre [chief of a naval squadron (equivalent to a rear admiral)] at several naval battles during the American War of Independence, and Governor of Brest in 1790. He died on the 31st of August 1811 at age 82.

December 26th

René Lavoie's child was the first birth recorded in the new church as well as the first burial in the new cemetery.

(Baie-St-Paul Register)

1757

February 28th

The burial of Simon Berquin dit Labonté, the *bédeau* [sexton] at Beauport.

(Beauport Register)

[A *bédeau* or beadle or *verger* is an official who takes care of the interior of a church whereas a sexton (or *sacristain*) is an officer of the church whose duty it is to take care of the building, vessels, vestments, to ring the bell, to attend on the officiating clergyman or minister, and sometimes to dig the graves in the churchyard.]

The Register noted that his body was buried under the bell and that – according to Reverend Tanguay – "is where it really belonged".

March 3rd

The burial of Joseph Lavalée, a native of Île-d'Orléans, who was employed by Sieur Ganier as *commis* [clerk] in the King's store. He was found frozen to death.

(Longueuil Register)

March 30th

M. Gaspard Dufournel, 94, one of the first priests in the parish, was buried in the sanctuary at the Ange-Gardien church.

(l'Ange-Gardien Register)

April 18th

The marriage of François Estève, 30, a native of Montpelier, to Élizabeth Bissonnet, the daughter of René. He was secretary to the Marquis de Montcalm.

(Montréal Register)

May 18th

The burial of Jean-Baptiste Robida[121], 55, in Nicolet. Although he had drowned last Fall, his remains had just been found at the Pointe-aux-Sables. He had married Marie-Joseph Pepin-Laforce in 1722.

(Nicolet Register)

May 30th

The burial of Pierre Bertaut, 45, Captain on the schooner *La Salée Robin*, one of the ships in the Marquis Des Gouttes' squadron.

(Île St-Jean Register)

The *chevalier* Gabriel Rousseau, Sieur de Villegouin, commanded Île-St-Jean in 1757. He was married to Barbe LeNeuf from la Vallière.

(Île-St-Jean Register)

Julien Cadet, the husband of Marie-Louise Chatel, was *maître d'équipage* [boatswain] on the schooner *La Thérèse* , commanded by Captain J. Marchand, when he died at Cap-St-Domingue in 1757.

(Register of the 'Procès-verbaux' [Official Statements] of the Archdiocese of Québec, 1757)
[A boatswain was a warrant or petty officer who was in charge of the deck crew, rigging, etc. .]

Joseph Baris dit Namur, 27, a native of Namur in Belgium, arrived in Québec in 1757 on *Les Ficheurs* and established himself on the Cul-de-Sac road.

(Register of the 'Procès-verbaux' [Official Statements] of the Archdiocese of Québec, 1766)

July 13th

Fort Machault, at the mouth of the Rivière-aux-Boeufs below Niagara, was built by M. de la Jonquière. The St-Antoine-de-Tilly parish Registers mention this Fort, while also giving the name of the *chirurgien du Roi* [royal surgeon] ... *La Crouzette*.

(St-Antoine-de-Tilly Register)

121

The families from this line also include that of Manseau.

(Tanguay)

July 27th

The *flûte du Roi* [Royal merchantman], *La Fortune*, was in Québec harbor near Île-d'Orléans.

(St-Laurent-de-l'Île-d'Orléans Register)

Father Boyer, the *aumônier*[chaplain] on the Royal vessel *Le Célebre*, performed a baptism while the ship was at anchor at Île-aux-Coudres.

(Île-aux-Coudres Register)

September 27th

Dominique des Sombres from St-Christophe and Jean Gautier from Larochelle both drowned after the ship *l'Hirondelle* broke up on the rocks at Beaumont.

(Beaumont Register)

October 18th

The baptism of Governor Pierre François de Vaudreuil [Cavagnial]'s slave, a 6-year-old Indian child who was named Joseph-Adrien by M. Adrien Gourdeau.

(Trois-Rivières Register)

November 12th

The *chevalier* François LeMeslier, the son of M. Nicolas François LeMeslier, *Capitaine au régiment Agenois* [Captain in the Agenois regiment], and of Lady Charlotte LeRebours, was born on the 29th of December 1722, in Caudebec near Rouën, Normandy [France], and was baptized today in the Bishopric of Québec.

(Caudebec in the Bishopric Register, p. 127)

Paul Navarre, a native of St-Sauveur in Cayenne, *chirurgien-major* [head-surgeon] on *'King Très Chrétien's* frigate *Le Favory*, perished in a shipwreck on the Terre-Neuve coast. His widow, Geneviève de la Roche, miserable because of her loss, was able to salvage a few of their more-precious belongings from the wreck and ended up in Montréal where she married Raymond Menard on the 28th of September 1768.

SEE: 1768 Entries.

[*King Très Chrétien* here was actually King Louis XVI who reigned from 1715 to 1774. This title was one bestowed by the early Popes on the kings of France.]

During 1757 and 1758, many Acadian refugees died in Québec because of all of the [various types of] suffering which they had had to endure.

(Québec Register)

[H.H. Walsh tells us that 400 victims died of the plague at the General Hospital in 1757 and an additional 300 in 1758. Also, famine was stalking the land and it was then followed by Wolfe's devastation of the countryside and his persistent bombing of the citadel of Québec.]

1758

January 31st

The burial of Chrystophe DuPuy in the church. He had been the *capitaine-au-régiment-du-Languedoc* [Captain in the Languedoc regiment] and had died on the 29th of January while wintering at Ste-Croix. Frichingen, a *lieutenant-des-troupes* [lieutenant in an infantry company], was at the service.

(Ste-Croix Register)

April 22nd

Hilarion Landry, the husband of Marie Taphorin, was attacked and killed by the Indians while returning by boat from the *Rivière-aux-Boeuf* to Fort Duquesne. He was only about 6 *arpents* [about 1152 feet] away from the Fort.

(Register of the 'Procès-Verbaux' [Official Statements] of the Archdiocese of Québec)

[Based on a linear measure value of 191.8 feet per *arpent*. As was true of most French units of measurement at the time, however, the value of the *arpent* was not at all consistent and would often vary from one province to another.]

Widowed with 3 very young children, Marie Taphorin married Louis Charlan on the 15th of February 1762.

(Québec Register)

May 1st

Joseph Tousignan, a 12-year-old youngster, accidentally poisoned himself.

(Lotbinière Register)

July 6th

François Desfossés dit Sans-Crainte, one of Mr. Germain's soldiers in the *régiment de la Reine* [the Queen's Regiment], was killed in today's action where 150 servicemen were killed or drowned. He had married Thérèse Poulin.

(Register of the 'Procès-verbaux' [Official Statements] of the Archdiocese of Québec)

August 14th

The burial of Josué Gibrens, 35, an Irishman, married in Pennsylvania and captured and wounded in Carillon. He was buried in the Hôpital-Général of Montréal.

(L'Hôpital-Général de Montréal Register)

September 15th

The burial of Sieur François Régis Pinguet de Vaucour, *capitaine de la flûte du Roi* [Captain of the royal ship], *l'Outarde.*

(Québec Register)

September 26th

The burial of François Baillargeon, an 11 year old child who drowned on Mr. Maurin's ship after it broke up on the rocks near the chapel of the Ste-Vierge-à-l'Île-d'Orléans on the night of the 25th.

(St-Laurent-de-l'Île-d'Orléans Register)

The [numerous] problems encountered by the many Acadian families who were forced to leave their homes and settle in St-Charles parish on the Rivière-Boyer was the major reason for the unbelievably high total of 90 deaths in the parish during 1758.

(St-Charles Register)

In 1758, Jean Doucet, a native of Xaintes, contracted to serve on the Royal ship, the *Aigle*,which was going to Québec. After being shipwrecked in the straits of Bellisle, he arrived and wintered at the Rivière-Ouelle in November. The following Spring, he went up to Québec for the attack on that city.

(Register of the 'Procès-verbaux' [Official Statements] of the Archdiocese of Québec)

December 2nd

The burial of Dominique Videmand, a native of Brieu in Brittany [in France] and *canonnier* [gunner] on the ship the *Aigle*. He had died in St-Roch-des-Aulnets at the home of Pierre Morin.

(St-Roch-des-Aulnets Register)

1759

January 1st

We found the burial record of M. Nicolas Laurent, the *supérieur des missions Illinoises* [Superior of the Illinois missions] and *vicaire-général* [Vicar-General] for the Bishop of Québec[122].

(Cahokias Register)

February 19th

Trivio[123] and Trecesson[124], commandants of the two bataillons in the *régiment de Berry*, served as witnesses at the marriage of Pierre Sabathier, *tambour-major* [drum-major] in the same regiment, and Marthe Asselin.

(St-François-de-l'Île-d'Orléans Register)

April 4th

The burial of Louis Tousignan, 9, who was crushed to death while leading a wagon.

(Lotbinière Register)

April 23rd

We found the names of DeVillars-Lamontagne, *chambellan* [chamberlain] of His Majesty the King of Poland, and of the Duke of Lorraine.

(Montréal Register)

[The *chambellan* is the person charged with the direction and management of the household of a ruler or lord.]

Jean Launay dit Laguera, a native of the diocese of Xaintes, left for Canada before he was even 13 years old, but was taken prisoner and brought to England where he was ransomed for and sent back to Québec. Drafted into the *régiment de Berry*, in the *compagnie de Cadillac*, he took part in the *campagne de Carillon*.

122

Sent as a missionary in 1750, he worked alone until 1754. In the course of that year, a colleague arrived who was to be the last missionary sent by the Québec Seminary; M. François Forget-Duverger, who, in 1759, gave him his last rites and succeeded him as missionary at Ste-Anne and at Ste-Famille de Cahokias.

(Tanguay)

123

Slightly wounded on the 28th of April 1760 near Québec.

124

Killed in the battle of the 28th of April 1760.

May 14th

We buried the body of an unknown man – about 30 years of age – who had drowned near Ste-Croix. He carried a copy of the Good Book [Bible] on his person, a sign of his Catholicism.

(Ste-Croix Register)

May 19th

The *Île-d'Orléans* was evacuated[124] because of the war and the parishioners from the *paroisse* St-François were moved to the *paroisse* St-Augustin where they remained from May to October. Many children were baptized there and some of those who died were able to be buried there. The first entry in the Register after their return was dated the 25th of October 1759.

(St-François-de-l'Île-d'Orléans Register)

June 10th

Mr. de Saint-Gergue, Commandant of the *régiment de la Sarre*, was in Charlesbourg, where he made an entry in the Registers.

(Charlesbourg Register)

June 13th

Toupin, a resident at Cap-de-la-Madeleine, drowned and was buried at Lotbinière on that same day.

(Lotbinière Register)

Pierre Bonnet[125], 28, *boulanger* [baker] and native of Bordeaux [France], arrived at Québec on the ship *Le Marchand,* commanded by Captain Carson.

(Register of the 'Procès-verbaux' [Official Statements] of the Archdiocese of Québec, 1761)

June 24th

Antoine Bouchard, 77, one of the first *cultivateurs* [farmers] at Baie-St-Paul, died in a cabin in the forest, where he and other residents of his parish had taken refuge as the English approached.

(St-François-de-Xavier-de-la-Petite-Rivière Register)

June 25th

Théodose-Mathieu Denys deVitré, the son of Théodose and Marie-Joseph DesBergères, was born on the 8th of November 1724.

(Québec Register)

124

Garneau, Volume II, p. 315, 3rd Edition, said that the Isle was evacuated on the 24th of June.
125

Not to be confused with the Pierre Bonet who had arrived in 1750.

Garneau tells us that he had been in command of a French *frégate* when he was taken prisoner at Louisborg. *Traître* [traitor] to his nation, he served as *pilote à l'escadre anglaise* [pilot for the English fleet] which arrived near Île-d'Orléans on the 25th of June 1759. He was rewarded by being upgraded by one grade in the English service.

June 27th

The parishioners at Petite-Rivière, near Baie-St-Paul, had taken refuge in the woods to escape the enemy. In a small cabin, the wife of Jacques DeLavoye gave birth to a daughter named Marie-Geneviève-Marguerite-Angélique, who could not be baptized until the following 27th of September.

(Petite-Rivière Register)

July 1st

The burial of Jean Troye dit Lafranchise, the husband of Charlotte Richard, whose remains were found lying on the beach seven months after he had drowned. He was identified by his wife and by his brother, Claude Troye.

(Île-Dupas Register)

July 5th

During the siege of Québec, *curé* Eudo and all of the Ste-Famille parishioners hid in the Charlesbourg parish.

(Ste-Famille-de-l'Île-d'Orléans Register)

Joseph Bleau and his family were among the St-François-Xavier dite Petite-Rivière parishioners who took refuge in the woods during the war. His wife, Geneviève Gagnon, 63, died in one the shacks and was buried on the same day.

(Petite-Rivière Register)

July 16th

Jean Pouliot, 50, who lived in Ste-Foye, was killed by a bomb and buried in Québec.

(Québec Register)

Pierre Trudel, the husband of Françoise Massé, was killed by the English in the camp at Beauport. His widow married Charles Verret on the 24th of May 1762.

(Charlesbourg Register)

July 17th

The burial of Nicolas Marchand, *officier* and *milicien d'artellerie* [militia artilleryman] who had been killed by a cannon-ball.

(Québec Register)

July 23rd

From the St-Antoine-de-Tilly Register: "Buried in the new cemetery which has been consecrated on the land belonging to Claude Bergeron, in the house where we celebrate Mass, in the *deuxième concession*, where we had hidden because of the enemy."

(St-Antoine-de-Tilly Register)

[A *deuxième* (second) *concession* is a parcel of land granted right behind the more-desirable *première* (first) *concession* lands.]

July 27th

The burial of Joseph Fortier, 45, the husband of Élizabeth Noël, who had been killed by the enemy on the 26th.

(St-Michel Register)

August 19th

The Church of Deschambault was pillaged by the English.[127]

(Deschambault Register)

August 21st

Reverend Father Jacques-René, a *cordelier* [Franciscan Friar] and *aumônier* [chaplain] on the *frégate du Roi* [Royal frigate] *La Pomone*, had made an entry in the Grondines Register. He also made an entry on the 16th of February 1760 at Ste-Rose-de-l'Île-Jésus.

(Grondines Register)

No entries were made in the Registers between the 20th of August and the 7th of October in 1759. Marie-Louise, the daughter of Augustin Caron, died in September but was not buried in the cemetery until the 3rd of May 1760.

(St-Roch-des-Aulnets Register)

Jean-Baptiste Dubois, a native of Viala in the diocese of Auch, who had arrived on Sieur Cadet's fleet, was the *commmis aux vivres* [commissary clerk] at Lévis. Taken prisoner by the English, he was exchanged at the capture of Québec.

(Register of the 'Procès-Verbaux' [Official Statements] of the Archdiocese of Québec)

127

General Murray leading 1200 men went up the river to destroy the French flotilla at Trois-Rivières; but he was twice repulsed at Pointe-aux-Trembles by Colonel Bougainville, he disembarked at St- Croix which he destroyed by fire, and then threw himself against Deschambault where he plundered the camps of the French.

(Garneau, Volume II, p. 323, 3rd Edition)

Jean-Baptiste Leclerc, a resident at Lotbinière, was killed by the English and buried by Jean-Baptiste Houde. The specific date of his burial was not mentioned.

(Ste-Croix Register)

August 26th

The burial of René Portneuf, *curé* at St-Joachim, who was killed by the English on the 23rd of August while leading his parishioners in the defense against the English. His body was buried without a coffin, near the banister under the choir[128].

(Ste-Anne-de-Beaupré Register)

[People were rarely buried under the church. The privilege was reserved for priests who (ordinarily) had a place under the choir, and for seigneurs, under their seigneurial pews. Marcel Trudel noted that the custom eventually had to be limited because the graves were not dug very deep and 'pestilential odours' spread through the church.]

M. Rhéboule, commanding *la Carcassière* , made an entry in the Pointe-aux-Trembles of Québec Register.

(Pointe-aux-Trembles de Québec Register)

August 27th

The burial of the bodies of 7 residents of St-Joachim who, along with their parish priest, Father Portneuf, had been killed while fighting the English: Paré, Louis, 64 years of age; Gagnon, Jean, 69; Gagnon, Pierre, 61[129]; Languedoc, Charles, 48; Magnan, Michel, 30[130]; Fortin, Jean, 26; and Alaire, Louis, 20.

(Ste-Anne-de-Beaupré Register)

128

A detachment of 300 men, under the orders of Captain Montgomery, had been sent to St-Joachim where a few of the inhabitants were defending themselves and committing worse cruelties. The prisoners were massacred in cold-blood and in a most barbarous manner. M. de Portneuf, local priest, who had not wished to abandon his parishioners so that he could administer to their religious needs, was hit and cut with a sabre." (Garneau, Volume II, P. 318, 3rd Edition) "There were several of the enemy killed and wounded and a few prisoners taken, all of whom the barbarous Captain Montgomery, who commanded us, ordered to be butchered in a most inhuman and cruel manner." ('Colonel Malcolm Fraser's Lieutenant of the 78th, Manuscript Journal relating to the operations before Québec in 1759'.)

129

The husband of Étienne Cloutier.

130

The father of 6 children.

Marie-Anne Bélanger, the wife of Pierre Gingras, was assisted by her children while burying her son, François, in land which had not yet been consecrated due to the presence of the enemy.

(St-Antoine-de-Tilly Register)

August 30th

Pierre Gautron dit Larochelle, 64, was killed by the enemy.

(St-Michel Register)

September 1st

Due to the presence of the enemy, the inhabitants of St-Antoine had pulled back to the *troisième rang* [3rd range or row] of the parish.

[Marcel Trudel notes that the 3rd row represented a parcel of land somewhat far away from the most desirable riverbank land-grants.."...the occupation of the riverbanks was completed, and [then] a second row of seigneuries was begun behind the land-grants on the riverside." (*"Introduction to New France"*, Quintin Publications, 1997, p. 180). This second – and then a third – row of land grants was referred to as 2nd or 3rd *rang* or range.]

Baptisms during that period were performed in the home of Jean-Baptiste Coté.

(St-Antoine-de-Tilly Register)

M. Martel, a priest, at St-Laurent-de-l'Île-d'Orléans, along with the inhabitants of the area, had hidden in various parishes in Beauport and Charlesbourg during the months of August and September.

(St-Laurent-de-l'Île-d'Orléans Register)

September 8th

A note from M. Maisonbasse, the priest at St-Thomas:

"The English carried off the Registers for the period beginning the 21st of January to the 8th of September 1759 from their hiding places in the woods."

(St-Thomas Register)

Madeleine Houde, the wife of Joseph Bergeron, was buried by several of the members of the St-Antoine-de-Tilly parish since the enemy was still controlling the area. She had only been married since the 12th of February.

(St-Antoine-de-Tilly Register)

September 9th

During the siege of Québec, the inhabitants of the Baie de St-Paul remained hidden in the woods. After they returned to their homes, they buried several of the children who had died during the previous months in their cemetery.

(Baie-St-Paul Register)

September 13th

The burial of François Bilodeau, a resident of Ste-Famille parish in Charlesbourg.

(Charlesbourg Register)

September 14th

The name of Joseph Carmoy, *capitaine du navire* [Captain of the ship] *Élizabeth* from Bordeaux [in France] was found in the Batiscan Register.

(Batiscan Register)

Daniel Forbes, 22, a Scotsman who came to Québec in Colonel Fraser's regiment, was at the battle of the siege of Québec. Some time later, he moved to the lower area of the Rivière-du-Loup.

Montcalm's burial entry[131]:

"In the year 1759, on the 14th of September, was buried in the church of the Ursulines in Québec, the *Haut et Puissant* [High and Powerful] Seigneur Louis-Joseph, Marquis de Montcalm, *lieutenant-général des armées du Roi* [Lieutenant-General of the King's Armies], *commandeur de l'Ordre Royal et Militaire de St--Louis* [Commander of the Royal and Military Order of St-Louis], *commandant-en-chef des troupes-de-terre de l'Amérique Septentrional* [Commander-in-Chief of the ground troops in North America]; he died on the same day that he was wounded on after being fortified with the Sacraments which he had received with a great deal of devotion and religious fervor.

Present were Messrs. Resche, Cugnet and Collet, *chanoines*, M. de Ramezay, *commandant de la place* [Governor], and the entire corps of officers."

(SIGNED,)   Resche, *prêtre* and *chanoine*   [priest and canon].
              Collet, *chanoine*.

(Québec Register)

September 21st

The first marriage to be celebrated after the siege of Québec was the marriage of Jean-Pierre Massal, of the diocese of Beziers in the Province of Narbonnne, to Marie-Louise Pepin, the daughter of Louis-Michel Pepin and Marguerite Renault of the Charlesbourg parish.

(Québec Register)

131

Louis-Joseph Gozon, the Marquis de Montcalm, Baron of Galeriac and of the States of Gevandan.

September 22nd

The burial of 4 war victims who were killed by the English at St-Thomas on the 14th of September. They were: seigneur Jean-Baptiste Couillard, his son, Joseph Couillard, *ecclésiastique* [clergyman], René Damours de Courberon, the husband of Louise Couillard, and Paul Coté, the widower of Geneviève Langlois.

(St-Thomas Register)

October 2nd

The burial of Mathieu Farreau, a native of Bayonne. He was a member of the crew on the frigate *Le Maréchal de Sennetaire* [132], commanded by M. de Grand Rivière.

October 4th

The St-Joachim Registers did not show any entries from the 16th of January 1758 to the 4th of October 1759. That gap was caused by the disruption brought about by the fire which destroyed the church during the war.

(St-Joachim Register)

November 13th

The burial of Elie Desmarais, *chirurgien de la frégate* [surgeon on the frigate] *Le Marchand.*

(Trois-Rivières Register)

November 21st

We reburied 6 bodies in the St-Michel parish cemetery. Those six individuals were first buried in unconsecrated plots [due to the presence of the enemy] during the battle of Québec at some time between the 1st of July and the month of October.

(St-Michel Register)

[Any land on which Protestants might have fallen in battle was considered unconsecrated and so any Catholics who also fell on those lands were later either reburied in consecrated plots with the benefit of church services or had their graves blessed, again with the benefit of church services.]

132

Lost near Sault-de-la-Chaudière.

SAINTE ANNE DE-LA-POCATIÈRE CHURCH

November 23rd

At a service at Ste-Anne-de-la-Pocatière, the parish priest blessed the graves of the following 6 individuals who had never received the benefit of any church services at the time of their burials. They were: Ouellet, Joseph, 32; Ouellet, Geneviève, 16; Ouellet, Basile, 6; Mignier, Geneviève, 40; Pelletier, Marie, 12; Mignot, Véronique, 6 months.

December 11th

The bodies of several Canadians killed on the 2nd of September were not buried in the cemetery until the 11th and 12th of December, after the surrender of Québec.

The children born since September were not baptized until January 1760. There were also many deaths among the women.

(Lévis Register)

December 14th

The burial of Pierre Césard at St-Jean Deschaillons. Born in 1724, he came to Canada as a *timonier* [helmsman] on the frigate *Le Maréchal de Sennetaire*, commanded by M. de Grand Rivière which was lost near Sault-de-la-Chaudière. He was mortally wounded at the battle of the siege of Québec.

(St-Jean Deschaillons Register)

Pierre Césard had married Marguerite Bluteau, the widow of Philippe Poulin, in 1758. Her 3rd marriage was to François Provost on the 27th of August 1766.

(St-Joseph-de-la-Nouvelle Beauce Register)

December 20th

The burial – with appropriate religious services – of Pierre Poulin, the husband of Marie-Louise Boutillet, who had been killed by the English during the month of August.

His widow, Marie-Louise Boutillet, married Paul Bolduc at St-Joachim on the 9th of January 1764.

(St-Joachim Register)

Jean-Baptiste Caseau, a native of the parish of St-Pierre-l'Ange in the diocese of Avranches in Lower Normandy [in France], arrived in Québec when he was 18 years old.

(Register of the 'Procès-verbaux' [Official Statements] of the Archdiocese of Québec, 1767)

1760

February 4th

> Jean-Baptiste Jobert, *chirurgien* [surgeon] on the Royal highwayman, *La Marie*, married Charlotte L'Archévêque in Montréal. His father, Joseph Jobert, also a *chirurgien*, lived in St-Martin parish in the diocese of Langres.
>
> *(Montréal Register)*

March 28th

> Brother Justinian Constantin, Récollet, *missionnaire* since 1753 at the Nouvelle Beauce, died in his Mission and was buried on the following 2nd of April.
>
> *(Nouvelle-Beauce Register)*

April 28th

> Guillaume Sachet was struck by a cannon shell while standing near M. Morville.
>
> *(Register of the 'Procès-Verbaux' [Official Statements] of the Archdiocese of Québec)*
>
> His widow, Marie-Charlotte Métivier, married François Normand in Québec on the 23rd of January 1764.
>
> *(Québec Register)*

Many brave and generous military personnel were killed or wounded during the fighting on the 28th, the day before the battle of Québec. Our readers would certainly appreciate a list of those courageous individuals:

SOLDIER - REGIMENT	SOLDIER - NAME	INJURY NATURE	MORTAL?
deBourlamaque	Brigadier	Leg injuries from	Cannon shell
La Reine	Captain Montreuil	...	Mortal injuries
"	Ensign Dufay	Broken arm	...
"	Lieutenant Desnois	Minor	...
"	Lieutenant St- Martin	Minor	...
"	Lieutenant Degulier	...	Killed
La Sarre	Captain Palmarolle	...	Mortal injuries
"	Captain Duprat	...	Mortal injuries
"	Captain Forest	...	Mortal injuries

SOLDIER - REGIMENT	SOLDIER - NAME	INJURY NATURE	MORTAL?
"	1st Captain Duparquet	Leg injuries	...
"	1st Captain Beauclair	Arm injuries	...
"	1st Captain Meritem	Arm injuries	...
"	Lieutenant, chevalier of Savournin	...	Mortal chest injuries
"	Lieutenant Paonnet	...	Died wounded
"	Lieutenant Premillac	Broken leg	...
"	Lieutenant Lazure	Minor	...
"	Lieutenant Gravet	Minor	...
"	Lieutenant Lambanie	Minor	...
Languedoc	Lieutenant Senneterre	Minor	...
"	2nd Lieutenant Domange	...	Killed
"	Lieutenant Duleirac	Wounded	...
Royal-Roussillon	Captain Derouin	Leg injuries	...
"	Lieutenant Bonneville	Leg injuries	...
"	Lieutenant Léonard	Leg injuries	...
"	2nd Lieutenant Beausadel	...	Died wounded
"	Captain Destor	Minor	...
"	Captain Dufresnoy	Minor	...
"	Captain Lefebvre	Minor	...
"	Lieutenant Grand-Jean	Minor	...
Berry	Lieutenant Carery	...	Killed
"	Commandant Colonel Trecesson	...	Killed
"	Captain Duchesne	...	Mortal injuries
"	Lieutenant LaMalière	...	Mortal injuries
"	Adjutant Laplouze	Wounded	...

SOLDIER - REGIMENT	SOLDIER - NAME	INJURY NATURE	MORTAL?
"	Lieutenant Duguerms	Wounded	...
"	2nd Lieutenant Vaudemant	Arm injuries	...
"	2nd Lieutenant Pelissier	Arm injuries	...
"	2nd Lieutenant Laudenet	Wrist injury	...
"	Captain Legoin	Bad buttocks injury	...
"	Lieutenant Leclerc	Bad buttocks injury	...
"	Lieutenant Dallet	Arm injuries	...
"	Lieutenant Colonel Trivio	Minor	...
"	Captain Pressac	Minor	...
"	Captain Cambray	Minor	...
"	Captain Menard	Minor	...
"	Captain Bonchamp	Minor	...
Guyenne	Lieutenant Morambert	...	Mortal injuries
"	Captain Montaguet	Arm injuries	...
"	Captain Launay	Minor	...
"	Captain Dublot	Minor	...
"	Captain Chassignolle	Minor	...
"	Captain Bellot	Minor	...
"	2nd Captain Villemontès	...	Killed
"	Adjutant Valentin	...	Killed
Béarn	Captain Vassal	...	Mortal injuries
"	Lieutenant Salvignac	...	Mortal injuries
"	Lieutenant Totabel	...	Mortal injuries
"	Lieutenant Colonel Dalquier	Side injuries	...
"	Captain Monredon	Buttocks' injuries	...
"	Lieutenant Pinsen	...	Mortal injuries

SOLDIER - REGIMENT	SOLDIER - NAME	INJURY NATURE	MORTAL?
"	Lieutenant Fay	...	Mortal injuries
"	Lieutenant Jacob	...	Mortal Injuries
"	Adjutant Malartec	Minor	...
"	Captain Bernard	Minor	...
"	Captain Seguin	Minor	...
"	Lieutenant Raymond	Minor	...
"	Lieutenant Melay	Minor	...
"	Lieutenant Jourdain	Minor	...
"	Ensign Boucherville	Minor	...
"	Captain St-Martin	Minor	...
"	Captain Laronde	Minor	...
Béarn	Lieutenant Varennes	Minor	...
"	Lieutenant Corbière	Minor	...
Colonial	Captain Dubuisson	Shoulder injury	...
or	Captain Mezières	Leg injuries	...
Naval	Captain d'Hugues	Head injury	...
Detachment	2nd Lieutenant Daillebout	Leg injury	...
Troops	Ensign Hiché	Side injury	...
"	Ensign, *chevalier de la Corne*	Injured	...
"	Ensign Vassan	while	...
"	Ensign St-Luc	commanding	...
"	Captain Lorimier	Indians	...
"	Captain Lebourgne	"	...
"	Lieutenant Desnoyelles-Lanoy	"	...
"	Lieutenant Sabrevois	"	...
"	Ensign, *chevalier* Laperrière	"	...

SOLDIER - REGIMENT	SOLDIER - NAME	INJURY NATURE	MORTAL?
"	Ensign Herbin	"	...
Militia	Commandant Réaume	...	Killed
from	Lefebvre	...	Killed
the	Amelin	...	Mortal injuries
Montréal	Delisle	...	Mortal injuries
Batallion	Assistant Provost Marshal	...	Mortal injuries
"	Gaudet	Hand injury	...
"	Neveu	...	Dangerous injury
"	Julien of the Rivers	Minor	...
Militia	La Promenade	Minor	...
from	Decurry	Minor	...
the	Maugé	Minor	...
Montréal	Menard	Minor	...
Batallion	Heurtebise	Minor	...
"	Pierre Lefebvre	Minor	...
"	Augé	Minor	...
"	Chevalier	Minor	...

May 1st

The burial of Henri LeBellec at St-Antoine-de-Chambly. A native of Bourgelider in the diocese of Kimper, he drowned at Chambly.

(St-Antoine-de-Chambly Register)

May 22nd

The burial of Jean Larue, 48, who drowned after the *Atlante* Battle. He was married to Geneviève Huguet who later married Benjamin Deguise in November of 1763.

(Pointe-aux-Trembles de Québec Register)

June 1st

> The burial of M. DeLangis in Longueuil. He was an officer who had drowned after Easter near the Île-de-St-Paul.
>
> *(Longueuil Register)*

> Many people in Baie-St-Paul died from smallpox during the Fall season.
>
> *(Baie-St-Paul Register)*

> Many French soldiers from the *régiment du Royal Roussillon* were married in the Verchères parish after the [British] conquest.
>
> *(Verchères Register)*

MOVEMENT OF THE CATHOLIC POPULATION OF THE PROVINCE OF QUÉBEC 1751 TO 1760

	MARRIAGES	BIRTHS	DEATHS	OTHERS
1751	693	3067	1759	1308
1752	670	3305	1561	1744
1753	617	3408	1486	1922
1754	604	3414	1718	1696
1755	500	3497	2498	999
1756	595	3409	2348	1061
1757	802	3609	2486	1123
1758	567	3497	2957	540
1759	564	3319	2389	930
1760	821	3449	2563	886
TOTALS ➡	6433	33974	21765	12209
1608-1760	25464	138251	68858	69393

SEPTEMBER 1760
FRENCH TROOP EMBARKATION IN QUÉBEC

NAME OF SHIP	TROOPS	OFFICERS	SOLDIERS AND GUNNERS	SAILORS, SERVANTS, WOMEN & CHILDREN	DATE SHIP LEFT
Bristol Galley	Colonials	10	187	43	Sept. 3
CharlesTown	Colonials	10	178	22	Sept. 3
Yarmouth Packet	Colonials	8	80	19	Sept. 3
Grandville	Colonials	6	76	17	Sept. 3
Kingston	Colonials	10	126	46	Sept. 5
Élizabeth-Mary	Béarn	10	139	33	Sept. 6
Élizabeth	Béarn	10	92	25	Sept. 13
Élizabeth	Béarn & Languedoc	15 15	102 9	28 for both	Ships
Rebecca	Languedoc & Berry	7 3	54 30	20 for both	not
Lady-Mary	Languedoc	18	219	57	ready
Duke	Royal Roussillon & Berry	20 20	132 65	26 for both	to
Bro:howod	La Reine	19	172	38	leave
Mary-Jane	Guyenne & Berry	6 2	67 32	6 for both	on
Annac	Guyenne & Berry	10 10	113 33	...	Sept.
Young Isaac	Guyenne	5	67	9	13
Adventure	Marquis de Vaudreuil	7	30	total of 100	Sept. 18
Mary	Chevalier of Lévis	9	30	for both	...
Joanna	M. de Bourlamaque	...	15	...	...
James	l'Intendant	...	...	...	...

NAME OF SHIP	TROOPS	OFFICERS	SOLDIERS AND GUNNERS	SAILORS, SERVANTS, WOMEN & CHILDREN	DATE SHIP LEFT
Abigaïl	Languedoc	...	81	...	...
Jenny	La Sarre	...	200	...	...
Mulberry	La Sarre	...	76	...	...
...	Totals	230	2405	507	...

NOTE: The other ships intended as troop transports for the remaining troops had not yet been designated as such. Also, the *Kingston*, a frigate with 64 cannons, was due to land its troops in England where they were supposed to be placed aboard another transport. A Letter from the *chevalier* de Lévis (Rochelle, the 27th of November 1760)

October 31st

The baptism of Louis, the son of Gaspard Ferdinand and Cathérine Montmeillant.

Louis' mother had sought shelter at Ste-Anne-de-la-Pérade and his father had served with the English troops. There was some doubt as to the legitimacy of their marriage.

(Ste-Anne-de-la-Pérade Register)

November 11th

The marriage of Jean-Baptiste Rieutord, *chirurgien* [surgeon], to Pélagie-Victoire Perron at Baie-St-Paul in 1758. He had first arrived on *Le Nancy*. The Neilson and Hubert families are included among their descendants.

(Baie-St-Paul Register)

1761

March 8th

A case of *superfétation*. [A second conception during a pregnancy from an earlier conception.] Joseph Bédard and his wife, Marguerite Laberge, had their son baptized after his birth in Charlesbourg. He died on the following 21st of July. On the 2nd of August of that same year, a son, Joseph, was also born and baptized.

(Charlesbourg Register)

[There is some disagreement on the current definition of *superfétation*. "*Stedman's Medical Dictionary – 25th Edition, 1990*" specifies that the 2 fetuses of different ages are *not twins* and that the concept is an obsolete one whereas Joseph Segen's 1995 "*Current Med Talk, a Dictionary of Medical Terms, Slang and Jargon*" notes that the concept serves as a theoretical for the difference in times of delivery of *fraternal twins*.]

They also had a third child, Jacques, baptized on the 14th of August 1762.

April 27th

Many of the Beauport families were totally grief-stricken after today's distressing accident in which seven parishioners drowned while crossing the Rivière-St-Charles. They were: Joseph Vallée[132], 28; Marie Vallée, his sister, and daughter of Michel; Marie Vallée, the wife of Antoine Marcou; Jeanne Guillot, the wife of Lawrence; Ambroise Cantin; Antoine Niel and Nicolas Fortier.

(Québec Register)

May 25th

Louis Lernalle dit St-Louis, 26, married Marie-Louise Bouré in Charlesbourg. Born in Notre-Dame-de-Gray parish in the diocese of Bésançon, he served for 10 years in the *régiment Chaumont* which he deserted from in 1755 to go to the Îsle of Ré and from there to Canada in 1756. He was the *soldat canonnier* [gunnery soldier] in the colony.

(Register of the 'Procès-verbaux' [Official Statements] of the Archdiocese of Québec)

July 24th

A murder...Marie DeBlois, 16-year-old daughter of Jean-Baptiste DeBlois and Cathérine Gagné, was found with her throat cut near the woods, about one-quarter *lieue* [about .63 of a mile] from her father's home. The initial report was made by some English officers who were the first to investigate the site of the murder.

(St-François-de-l'Île-d'Orléans Register)

August 18th

The burial of Dominique Laguerre, *marinier* [a sailor], who steered the ship *Le Geneviève* and later drowned in the anchorage in front of the St-François-de-l'Île-d'Orleans parish.

(St-François-de-l'Île-d'Orléans Register)

NOTE: His widow, Madeleine Hévé, married Ambroise Rémillard on the 1st of May 1764 at St-Valier.

(St-Valier Register)

September 15th

The marriage of Nicolas Rué, 22, a native of Pouloy, diocese of Blois, and Marie-Françoise Gotreau. He had arrived in 1753 on the ship *Lafitteau*.

(Québec Register AND Register of the 'Procès-verbaux' [Official Statements] of the Archdiocese)

132

He was the husband of Suzanne Couture in 1759.　　　*(Genealogical Dictionary)*

November 15th

The *Auguste* was shipwrecked. The *chevalier de la Verendrye* and *lieutenant de Varennes* [Lieutenant in the Varennes unit] were among its victims.

(Marghy, Canadian Review, Volume IX, p. 383)

1762

March 19th

Double instance of *superfétation*. [A second conception during a pregnancy from an earlier conception.] The baptism and birth of François, son of Gabriel Benoit and Marie-Renée DuBeau dit Potvin. They had also had a son, Michel, on the preceding 5th of February.

[There is disagreement on the current definition ot *superfétation*. *"Stedman's Medical Dictionary – 25th Edition, 1990"* specifies "that the 2 fetuses of different ages are *not twins*" and that "the concept is an obsolete one" whereas Joseph Segen's 1995 *"Current Med Talk, a Dictionary of Medical Terms, Slang and Jargon"* notes that the concept serves "as a theoretical explanation for the difference in times of delivery of *fraternal twins*".]

On the 15th of March 1756, they had another son, Alexis, and on the 10th of August of that same year, a daughter, Marguerite.

(Baie-Febvre Register)

April 11th

The Baie-St-Paul Registers noted that Jean-Baptiste LeCollen had been taken to England as a prisoner-of-war.

(Baie-St-Paul Register)

June 9th

Joseph Lereau, the husband of Geneviève Falardeau and *cultivateur* [farmer] from Charlesbourg, was killed by thieves.

(Charlesbourg Register)

Philip Amplement was born in 1741 in Cailleperik (spelling?), Upper Germany. He had come to Chibouctouche in 1754 with his parents. He enlisted in the English regiment *"Selse parment Bland"* two years later and took part in the siege of Québec in 1759. In 1762, he went on leave and renounced his Protestantism while in the presence of Jesuit Father LeFranc.

(Register of the 'Procès-verbaux' [Official Statements] of the Archdiocese of Québec, 1766)

⇨⇨⇨ [Of all of the information in Father Tanguay's book, this mysterious regimental name was certainly one of the most difficult bits of information to research. Local historian, Arthur Delorey, had determined that there was no such regiment as *"Selse parment Bland"*. Canadian historian, Marcel Trudel, agreed and felt that the good Father had perhaps misread his source document when writing the regimental name and that the answer would be found in the *Régistre des procès-verbaux d'abjuration* for 1766 or in the *Register of the 'Procès-verbaux' (Official Statements) of the Archdiocese of Québec, 1766.* Since the fairly extensive abjuration records maintained by the Mormons in Utah failed to shed any new light on this question, the answer does undoubtedly lie in the latter of the two above-referenced documents.

What we do know is that a regiment called the 9th English Regiment of Foot was formed in 1685 and served under various colonels' names until it was designated as the 9th in 1751. In May of 1776, it arrived in Québec and served in operations at Lake Champlain in 1777 as part of General Burgoyne's Army interned at Saratoga. A Major General Thomas Lord Saye and *Sele* was affiliated with it as a Colonel from 1783 to the War's end. The *Sele* portion of his name closely resembles the *"Selse"* in the *"Selse parment Bland"* above but the significance of this possibly Hessian or other Germanic regimental name has still not been determined. In addition, the years don't seem to match.]

September 13th

The general confusion and other problems brought about by the siege of Québec were the reasons for a number of late baptismal entries. Several of the records were not even entered in the Registers until after 1761 and we found one – that of Charles Laberge – which was not entered until the 13th of September 1762.

(l'Ange-Gardien Register)

December 2nd

The marriage (in Québec) of Jacques Crémazy, born in 1735 in Artigat parish in the diocese of Rieux, and Geneviève Chupin dit Lajoie, the widow of Pierre Monier[133].

1763

January 17th

His Excellency the Governor of Montréal, Thomas Gage, authorized the marriage of Joseph Riewes and Charlotte Gaudry.

(Montréal Register)

[The King of France was sincerely convinced that he represented God on earth for the common good and thus he did his best to reign as a 'good father of the family'. This paternalism was exercised in many areas. For instance, the King and his representatives, the Governor and the Intendant, had the power to approve or prevent marriages especially if they felt that the new husband was not good material for himself also being or becoming a 'good father of the family'.]

133

He is the ancestor of the Canadian poet, Octave Crémazie.

January 22ᵈ

The marriage of Pierre Paisan, *chirurgien* [surgeon] and native of Trun in the diocese of Seez, and Marie-Cathérine Desjadons.

(Lévis Register)

Born in 1725, he left France in 1758 on the frigate *La Fidèle* commanded by M. de Sallaberry. Since 1741, he had served in the German army, and in 1743, in the armies of Flanders and Italy; in 1748, he was affiliated with the Hôpital in Lisle, from which he went over to the *régiment Guyenne* in 1751; finally, in 1756, he joined the navy and, in 1758, landed at Louisbourg where he was taken as a prisoner-of-war and brought to Halifax. He ended up by being transported to Québec in 1760.

(Register of the 'Procès-verbaux' [Official Statements] of the Archdiocese of Québec)

May 16ᵗʰ

The marriage of Paul-Joseph Farineau, a native of the parish of St-Germain in the village of Mont, in Hainault, and Marie-Angélique Demeule.

(Québec Register)

In the *Registre des Procès-verbaux*, he was referred to as *'Divertissant'*, a native of St-Sulpice in Paris, and *sergent* under M. Penneleau in the *Berry* regiment.

(Register of the 'Procès-verbaux' [Official Statements] of the Archdiocese of Québec)

June 4ᵗʰ

Several Englishmen were massacred by the Sauteux Indians at Fort Michillimakinac. Father Dujaunay left for Détroit by canoe a few days later and was back at the Makinac station by the 30ᵗʰ of the month.

(Mackinac Register)

July 5ᵗʰ

Pierre Laville, 26, who had arrived in Canada in 1751 as a *mousse* [ship's boy] on the ship *La Reine des Anges*, married Madeleine Mateau.

(St-Joseph-de-la-Nouvelle Beauce Register)

July 6ᵗʰ

The burial of de Belhumeur, a soldier in the *compagnie Baschalis* of the *régiment de la Reine*, who was killed near the *chûte de Carillon* [Carillon Falls] while returning from a prospecting trip.

Denis Saillant, a soldier in the *compagnie Dalmas* in the same *régiment*, paid him his last honors.

(Register of the 'Procès-verbaux' [Official Statements] of the Archdiocese of Québec)

Pierre Lagüe[135], a French *navigateur*, lived in Île-aux-Coudres after having married Madeleine Tremblay in 1756 and rased 5 children. In the Fall of 1762, he took charge of an English ship as its pilot and was brought to Europe, never to return to Canada.

October 24th

The burial of Joseph Gauvreau, the husband of Marie-Joseph Tessier, after he drowned at the Bout-de-l'Île in Montréal.

(Bout-de-l'Île de Montréal Register)

1764

February

"When referring to the first battle fought on the *plaines d'Abraham* and to

BATTLE OF THE PLAINS OF ABRAHAM

the surrender of Québec on the 13th of September 1759, our historians estimated the number of Canadian and French combatants both killed and wounded at 1000, which included 250 soldiers who were taken prisoner.

(Garneau, Volume II, p. 337, 3rd Ed.)

135

The name has changed to Lagueux. All of the Lagueux families from Lévis consider him as one of their ancestors.

(Tanguay)

What was the fate of those 250 men ? History tells us very little about how they were treated however we were fortunate enough to uncover one original and unedited document which gives us quite a bit of information on that topic. It is the *témoignage de liberté* [proof of freedom] of Alexis Dumontier given to the widow of Alexis Gagné dit Belavance so that she could remarry.

[The *témoignage* was testimony, usually in writing, to prove someone's marital (or other) status.]

Here is the statement, dated February 23rd:

Témoignage de liberté to allow Alexis Gagné dit Belavance's widow to remarry[135].

"I, Alexis Dumontier, living at the Pointe-à-Lacaille (St-Thomas), swear to the following to the best of my knowledge and belief:

1. That after having been taken prisoner at Québec on the 13th of September 1759, along with many other Canadians, we were placed on a troop transport ship, all together on some days and then later divided up to be placed on other ships.

2. That all of the Canadian prisoners had their papers checked two or three times before arriving in England, and that after the said inspections they were all loaded on war ships and brought to Plymouth.

3. That having arrived in Plymouth, we were all made to disembark and to march off to jail where we stayed for 4 months, and after the said 4 months we were brought to Dieppe, a port in France.

4. Having arrived in Dieppe with all of the prisoners, M. Lacombière-Lacorne instructed me to make a list of all of the Canadian prisoners, which I did very carefully, without omitting a single one.

5. That Alexis Gagné dit Belavance, one of my relatives who lived in the St-Pierre, Rivière-du-Sud Parish, did not appear among the prisoners, nor in the inspections which were carried out in Canada, before embarking on the ships to go to Plymouth, nor upon arriving in Plymouth, nor at Dieppe, when M. Lacombière-Lacorne had had the list made of all of the Canadian prisoners, which is one proof that he died in combat, which I believe to be the case."

"In testimony whereof, I have signed on the 23rd of February, 1764."

"Alexis Dumontier."

135

"The original copy is in the hands of the author."

(Tanguay)

NOTE: Alexis Gagné had married Cathérine Boucher on the 25th of November 1743 in Berthier.

July 6th

The burial of Reverend Father Gonnau, a Jesuit, who had drowned while returning to his Mission in Bécancourt. About 2½ months later, his body washed ashore on our beach, in our grasslands. People from as far away as 10 *lieues* [about 25 miles] had hastened to his funeral to express their sentiments which clearly showed the depth of the loss. His body was laid to rest in the *sanctuaire,* on the side of the Gospel, near the stairway.

(Deschambault Register)

[People were rarely buried under the church. The privilege was reserved for priests who (ordinarily) had a place under the choir, and for seigneurs, under their seigneurial pews. Marcel Trudel noted that the custom eventually had to be limited because the graves were not dug very deep and 'pestilential odours' spread through the church.]

November 28th

Jean Lepage, a 48-year-old *meunier* [miller] from the Île-Perrot, and Étienne Crevier, the 18-year-old son of Jean-Baptiste Crevier, died from an accident. Their bodies were found in the seigneurie of Beauharnois and were buried on the 30th of November 1764 at Ste-Anne-du-Bout-de-l'Isle.

(Ste-Anne-du-Bout-de-l'Île-de-Montréal Register)

1765

February 20th

François Provost, a native of St-Servé in the diocese of St-Malo, married Madeleine Landais, the widow of François Brisson in Rimouski. Provost, AKA *'Lafleur',* first became a soldier in the *régiment* du *Languedoc.* In 1766, he returned to France, leaving his wife, Madeleine, with the clear impression that he had had a wife there and that she, Jacqueline Moussard, was still alive. As a result, the *officialité* [court] of Québec invalidated his second marriage on the 15th of January 1771 and recorded that annulment in the Registers of the *Rivière-Ouelle* on that date.

[I used AKA (Also Known As) here since the translation could have been either surnamed OR nicknamed *Lafleur* which really have different meanings in the English language. It is, therefore, better shown as an AKA name.]

February 28th

The exhumation and transfer of the ashes of the late Simon Anger, one of the first priests at Lotbinière. His body was originally buried in the old church[136] on the 9th of December 1733 but was now deposited in the sanctuary of the new church[137].

(Lotbinière Register)

[People were rarely buried under the church. The privilege was reserved for priests who (ordinarily) had a place under the choir, and for seigneurs, under their seigneurial pews. Marcel Trudel noted that the custom eventually had to be limited because the graves were not dug very deep and 'pestilential odours' spread through the church.]

March 24th

The first person to be buried in the St-Henry-de-Lauzon cemetery was Françoise Pasquier, the 90-year-old widow of Paul Boulé.

(St-Henry Register)

May 15th

The burial of Michel Grondin, the son of Louis Grondin and Marie-Anne Mignier-Lagacé, who had drowned at St-Jean Deschaillons.

(St-Jean Deschaillons Register)

May 25th

The marriage of Pierre Fontaine to Marie-Madeleine Lavergne which was celebrated on the 23rd of October 1752, was today declared invalid *propter faeminae impotentiam* [due to female impotence].

(St-Pierre, Rivière-du-Sud Register)

July 2nd

The blessing of Mr. la Gorgendière's small *'Chapelle de la Visitation'*, which was located near the seigneurial manor.

(Deschambault Register)

136

The old church was located at the exact site of the seigneurie's flour mill.

137

We could still see some of the ruins of the new church at the Bernier Foundry.

Smallpox ravaged the Kamouraska vicinity now as well as in 1767 and 1771.

(Kamouraska Register)

September 7th

Simon 8ab8lak the mighty chief of the Algonquins was from Lac-des-Deux-Montagnes. He died from smallpox and was buried at the *cimetière du Lac.*

(Lac-des-Deux-Montagnes Register)

[For more information regarding problems encountered when spelling or pronouncing Indian names, please see my comments after the entry of October 27th 1747.]

November 5th

We exhumed the bodies from the old cemetery of Lotbinière and transported and reburied them in the new one.

(Lotbinière Register)

1766

February 4th

A plot of land on Kamouraska is called *'Bon Courage'.* ['Keep Your Chin Up !']

(Kamouraska Register)

June 13th

The burial of Pierre Chicouagne, 50, at Ste-Anne du Nord. A *cultivateur*[farmer] in Verchères, he drowned on the 6th of January and was [also] found today at Ste-Anne-du-Nord.

(Ste-Anne Register)

July 6th

The burial of Jean-Baptiste Sauvé's 3-year-old child after he had drowned in a well. Jean-Baptiste had been a *cultivateur*[farmer] at Ste-Anne-du-Bout-de-l'Île.

(Ste-Anne-du-Bout-de-l'Île Register)

September 1st

The marriage of Pierre Métayer, a native of Neufbourg, to Marie Fournier at Ste-Foye. AKA *'la Giberne'*, Pierre had come to Louisborg as a soldier at 16-years-of-age. In 1759, he was taken prisoner by the English and brought to New England where he joined the English forces laying siege on Québec. After the surrender of Canada, he left the service and settled in Ste-Foye. He had been a soldier in the *Royal-Américain* regiment.

(Register of the 'Procès-verbaux' [Official Statements] of the Archdiocese of Québec)
[I again used AKA (Also Known As) here. Again, the translation could have been either 'surnamed' or 'nicknamed' *la Giberne* but since there is an obvious distinction between the two in English, it is better shown simply as an AKA name.]

Étienne Couseau arrived in Canada in 1752 on *Les Ficheurs* and fought in several campaigns during the war right up to the surrender of Canada.
(Register of the 'Procès-verbaux' [Official Statements] of the Archdiocese of Québec, 1766)

October 15th

Pierre Cailla, 72, *capitaine de milice* [Captain, leader of parish militia], *chantre* and *marguiller*, was buried in the church Choir on Île-Dupas after he had drowned.
(Île-Dupas Register)

[a) The *captaine de milice* represented both the Governor and the Intendant to the settlers.

b) A *chantre* was a singer or chorister.

c) A *marguiller* or churchwarden was responsible for the secular affairs of the parish.]

October 27th

Michel Robichau and Marguerite Landry, Acadians, renewed their marital vows in the presence of Father Ménage. The wording in the entry in the Register reads:

"The said Michel Robichau and Marguerite Landry showed us a document on which it was noted that after having been taken as prisoners by the English and run out of their country, and because they were being instructed in the ways and doctrine of the English clergymen, they had married in New England in the presence of their assembled family members and Acadians elders, in hopes of renewing their vows if they should ever fall into the hands of French priests once they had finished their prison terms."
(Deschambault Register)

November 12th

The marriage of André Leblanc, 35, a native of St-Nizier in the City of Lyon [in France], to Marie-Joseph Baugis. He had been taken prisoner at Fort Duquesne by the English In 1755[139] in the *détachement* [detail] commanded by Jumonville, and [later] became a *cuisinier* [cook] in the Boston home of Governor Sharley. He was under the command of Colonel Mckay in Halifax by 1758 and followed him on his military expeditions against Montréal, to Martinique, to Havana and then to London.
(Register of the 'Procès-verbaux' [Official Statements] of the Archdiocese of Québec)

Tite Robichau and Marie Landry also renewed their marital vows for the same reason as Michel Robichau.   SEE: October 27th entry above.

139

At first, a cook at Intendant Bigot's for 2 years and then at the Marquis de Péan's home.

November 20th

Charles Babin and Marguerite Robichau renewed their vows for the same reasons.

(Deschambault Register)

1767

January 30th

Reverend Father Ambroise Rouillard, a Récollet, buried the body of Toussaint Cartier, the Hermit of St-Barnabé Island[140] in the church at Rimouski.

(Rimouski Register)

From the 1767 Burial Register:

"On the 30th of January 1767, in this St-Germain of Rimouski parish, a man named Toussaint Cartier, approximately 60 years of age, died, a resident of the said parish, after having received the sacramants of Penance, Holy Eucharist and Extreme Unction. His body was buried with the usual funeral services in the parish church, on the last day of January.

In testimony whereof I have signed on the above day and year.

(SIGNED,)   Father Ambroise."

THE HERMIT OF SAINT-BARNABÉ

"Tradition, in agreement with the written word, tells us that in the year 1728, a young man, approximately 21 years of age, arrived at St-Germain de Rimouski parish, then a simple mission; he had wandered along the route, through the forest which led from Ristigouche to Métis near Lac Matapédiac; no one had ever known and no one would ever know where he came from. Who was he? Did he have a fixed plan when he walked here?

These questions, which we asked him in a thousand different ways, he simply left unanswered, and curiosity, as lively as it was, was finally overcome by the silence maintained until death by the one who was the object of all of that curiosity.

140

The "Chronique de Rimouski" tells us the legend of this Hermit. Also, see the Genealogical Dictionary's article on 'Cartier, Toussaint'.

The new guest, who – at the moment – was staying at the hospitable home of seigneur Lepage, revealed nothing but his name: Toussaint Cartier. He was, moreover, a man with perfect manners, one who seemed to have suffered, which was shown by a constant gloominess, and although uneducated, he had considerable knowledge especially of those things which constitute a Christian.

He had only been with the good people of Rimouski for several hours when he stopped cold while walking with his host along the water's edge, and stared for quite some time toward St-Barnabé Island. All of a sudden he seemed to break out of his deep state of mind and exclaimed to his host: "Sur cet ilot sauvage, ferai mon hérmitage!" ["On that small secluded island, I will make my home.!"]

Those words uttered with great conviction could not help but make an impression on the person whom he was addressing and they were and still are accurately retained in the traditional tales told by the Lepages, the then proprietors of the seigneurie de Rimouski and of l'Île-St-Barnabé.

This young Toussaint Cartier, whose maturity of soul and spirit was far ahead of his years did not have to bargain for long for permission to carry out his plan. It was given more quickly than one could have believed possible.

At that very moment, Father Ambroise Rouillard, Récollet and missionary, and a very humble man who often signed his name simply as 'Brother Ambroise' , happened to be on his mission at Rimouski: this saintly man, was – as usual – among the good Christians and since he was a wise man, he was consulted by M. Lepage and Toussaint Cartier. The good Father detected such a strong faith and such a strong will in this young man that he immediately, and with divine inspiration, approved of the project which had been laid before him, and on that same day, a contract was drawn up and approved between the seigneur de St-Barnabé and the young man who was henceforth known as the Hermit of St-Barnabé."

That interesting document having been filed at a later date as a certified true copy in the archives of M. Deschenaux, a notary, still exists, and I was able to obtain a certified copy of it in 1790, and here is the quotation:

A verified copy of a deed from a beneficial owner of a piece of land on the Île-de-St-Barnabé made as a private agreement on the 15th of November 1728, by M. Lepage from St-Barnabé, with Toussaint Cartier.

"P.L. Descheneaux"

Here now is the document itself:

"Before the Reverend Father Ambroise Rouillard, Récollet, a missionary, performing the functions of priest at the St-Germain parish and the below-named witnesses, were present in person, M. Lepage from St-Barnabé, seigneur of the said property, which of his own free will and purpose, did give, cede, leave and abandon to a man called Toussaint Cartier, a plot on the said Île-de-Saint-Barnabé and as much land as he could clear, and this only during his lifetime, without the said Toussaint Cartier being able to sell nor combine it, considering that he had requested it of the said M. LePage under those conditions and that after the death of the said Toussaint Cartier the said plot of land along with the land which he would have cleared would revert to the said M. LePage or to his heirs, and for cause, considering that the said Cartier had explained his plans with the said M. LePage that he did *not* wish to marry and that he merely wanted to live alone in a [secluded] area in order that he might find his salvation, and that he did not claim nor intend to lay claim to any rights to the said property except for the duration of his lifetime, and in case the said Toussaint Cartier wished to make use of and take advantage of the house as his own child might, the said M. LePage obligates himself to allow him to do it as he would do for his children but only for his care and existence, and, on the contrary, if the said Toussaint Cartier wishes to do more than that, he will do as he is able to and will use all that he can harvest for his own welfare on his said property while being the master without, however, being able to prevent the said Sieur – the donor in fact of the said island – from doing what he felt was appropriate regarding taking all that he shall need of his hay, fish, or grazing-ground for his animals which he shall remain the master to do as he wishes without the said Toussaint Cartier being able to prevent him or his; yielding only to the said Cartier the location which he himself can occupy and the ground which he himself shall be able to clear and work for his subsistence alone, and in case the said Toussaint Cartier grows old [and unable to take care of himself] having taken care of the house, I, LePage, obligate myself and my heirs to feed and to maintain him in my home, looking upon him from that time on as a member of my family, at which time the said property shall revert to me or to my heirs, without the said Toussaint Cartier or others being able to maintain that anything had been accorded him alone except that which might have been accorded him during his lifetime, after informing me that he wanted nothing after his death."

Prepared in the presence of the Reverend Fathers Ambroise Rouillard, de Charles Souslevent and de Basile Gagnier, witnesses who have signed with us, the said Toussaint Cartier having declared that he did not know how to read nor write of this, following the Ordinance at St-Germain, on this, the 15th day of November 1728.

(SIGNED,)   Father Ambroise,   M. LePage of St-Barnabé,
                   Toussaint (his mark) Cartier,   Charles Souslevent.

Comes then the certification, as follows:

"Verified and certified as original and copy, word for word and letter for letter by the notaries in the Province of Québec, residing in Québec, the undersigned, from the original on paper, presented to us and at once given back.

Prepared and verified in Québec, 1790, on the 30th day of August, after noon.
(SIGNED,)   Jh. Planté, L. Descheneaux."

"Here is a contract which is worthy of being known about and preserved, a contract made *to help to find one's salvation !*"

"The contract was honored by the contracting parties for almost 40 years, with that moral rectitude and trustworthiness which so characterized the times and men of good faith."

"Toussaint Cartier immediately set to work setting up his secluded retreat: during all of the time that he needed to prepare to subsist on the crops which he was growing, M. LePage fed and took care of him and he took LePage's interests at heart, all as if he were the man of the household; then, when his newly farmed land was ready to provide for his needs, he retired to the small island from which he was never to leave except to take part in mission activities. He spent his time working, meditating and praying, while living off the food from his small garden. He had built himself a very small cottage in which he lived alone, along with a small shed for his cow and several chickens.

In 1759, the entire area but especially the remote parishes on both sides of the river below Québec began to suffer from the English invasion when the fleet going up the St-Lawrence with a huge force – especially when compared to the small number of people scattered along the banks of the river – spread devastation and terror. The Île-de-St-Barnabé was one of the first places that they touched upon. The residents of Rimouski were incapable of mounting the least resistance and had led their families into the woods while the men watched the movements of the ships. Only the Hermit did not change his style of living, becoming equally unmoved by fear and by curiosity. Launches landed their military squads but after several trips to the Island, they believed it to be deserted and since they were at some distance from the mainland, they reboarded their ships without having discovered the Hermit's dwelling which was undoubtedly under God's protection.

He had lived in that humbled state for 39 years spreading his holiness when, on the morning of the 29th of January 1767, Charles LePage, a 14-year-old boy, and the son of Pierre LePage, the donor in the contract which I've just reproduced, noticed that no

-222-

smoke was coming out of the chimney of the Hermit's cottage. Having informed his father, he was ordered to immediately saddle a horse and to go to see why the old Hermit did not have a fire going on this very cold day.

The young LePage left with a friend and traveling by carriage on the icy bridge to the Island, they soon covered the distance which separated them from the Hermit's home. There was only one room in the cottage and in the middle they found the saintly man stretched out, unconscious, on the floor. A small dog, the holy man's only companion, was lying down on his master's chest licking his face and happily jumping around at the arrival of his 2 young friends.

Toussaint Cartier, wrapped tightly in blankets, was brought to the home of M. LePage, where he regained consciousness shortly after being brought to the heated home and after having received some warm and loving care. In the meantime, once he was able to speak, he said that he felt that his hour had arrived and so wished to speak to Father Ambroise.

The good Father who almost 40 years before had witnessed the contract with M. LePage and who was still then a very young man, the good Father Ambroise, laden with the years and with good deeds, was at that moment performing his duties in Rimouski, as if by permission of divine Providence: he assisted his friend, gave him the sacraments of the Holy Church and was there on the 30th of January 1767 for the last breath of the Hermit of St-Barnabé. The following day, the 31st of January, he buried the devoted recluse in the chapel which served also as Rimouski's parish church, and wrote the record of his burial which we read earlier in the Register."

The background of this Hermit remains a mystery. No one has ever known where he came from, why he had separated himself from the rest of the people, nor even if the name which he had given us was in fact his real name. However that may be, the solitude in which he had hoped to be buried was not as complete as he had wished it to be. The word of his secluded existence had spread as far away as Québec and the English themselves had paid attention to the matter. Lady Montague speaks of it in a book published in London in 1769. The book's romantic theme and the reasons for his having done what he did do not detract from his worth; on the contrary, we see by the manner in which the author speaks of him that he held with the general opinion. There is a moral lesson in this adventurous story spoken out of the mouth of Cartier and it can be addressed to those who live according to the needs of the moment.

Here, moreover, are the passages from the work in question:

'Barnabé Island, 13 October 1766'

"I today made a somewhat peculiar visit. It was to a hermit who has lived alone for 40 years on this island. I came here with some very strong prejudices against him; I have no opinion of those who flee society; of those who seek a state apart from all others which is the most contrary to our very nature. If I were a tyrant and wished to inflict the most cruel form of punishment that human nature could stand, I would deny criminals the good things of our society as well as the sight of their counterparts.

I'm absolutely certain that I could not survive for one year alone; I'm miserable enough with the degree of solitude that we are compelled to live with on board a ship; no words could explain the joy that I felt when I came to America when I first saw something which resembled men's homes; the first man, the first house, even the first smoke from an Indian's campfire as the smoke wafted through the trees, gave me a joy beyond mere words.

However, let's return to my hermit: his appearance disarmed my repugnance; he was an old man, tall, with a beard and white hair, giving the impression of someone who has seen better days, yet showing on his face the signs of utter and deep-seated kindness. He greeted me with the utmost hospitality, offered me from all of his fruits, and brought me some fresh milk as well as some spring-water from a source close to his home.

After having spoken to him for some time, I expressed my wonder and amazement at what proofs of goodness and humanity which any one man could have shown me while able to remain happy despite living apart from his fellow man : I spoke very slowly on this subject and he listened to me very attentively."

"You seem," he said, "to be the type of person to feel pity for the misfortunes of others. My story is short and simple. I loved the loveliest of women and was loved in return. The greed of our parents who looked to profit [from any union] excluded a union based on our happiness. My Louise whom they threatened with an immediate marriage to a man whom she detested proposed that we flee the tyranny of our parents. She had an uncle living in Québec whom she loved. The forests of Canada, she would tell me, could give us the refuge which our cruel homes denied us. After a secret marriage, we left. Our trip had till now been a very happy one; I disembarked on the opposite shore to get something to refresh my Louise; upon my return and still feeling happy to be able to help and to please the object of my love and tenderness, a storm came up which forced me to seek refuge in the area. The storm worsened and I watched its progress with an inexplicable anxiety and a concern beyond words; the ship was in sight but could no longer withstand the fury of the storm – the sailors threw themselves into a launch; they kindly assisted my Louise on board and began heading in my general direction; my eyes were fixed on hers and my arms were longing to receive her; I offered up my most fervent prayers to the heavens when [all of a sudden] an immense wave rolled right over the launch. I heard a loud cry – I thought that I might even have heard my Louise's cries. The wave moved on......the sailors did as much as they could......a second wave......and everyone disappeared.

That dreadful scene is always on my mind. I fell, inanimate on the shore; when I came to, the first thing which I saw was Louise's cold body outstretched at my feet. The heavens granted me the gloomy consolation of my being able to say my final goodbyes and to bury her. In that grave lay all of my happiness. I knelt near her and made a vow to the heavens to wait here for the time when I would be reunited with all that was dear to me. Every morning, I visit the grave of my beloved and I beg the Heavens to hasten the hour of my death. I sense that we will not be separated for a long while now, I will soon go to her never to leave her again."

"He paused and believing himself to be alone, advanced quickly towards a small chapel which he had built on the shore near his Louise's burial place; I followed him for a few steps and saw him throw himself onto his knees.....and respecting his grief, I returned to the house.

Though I could not entirely agree with him, I do not only forgive him but I admire his worldly renunciation. Compassion is perhaps the only thing which can soothe the wounds caused by an unfortunate love. The heart in any such instances can only be touched by truly great remedies."

"I'm back; Mme. D. and her friends are unwilling to visit the Hermit. I sensed nothing but good in his conversation. He seemed appreciative of the fact that I sympathized with him for all of his suffering and we separated from one another with a great deal of regret. I offered him a gift but he wanted nothing."

"Ed. Rivers."

MONEY

From the date of the discovery of Canada until the Reign of Louis XIV, the means of exchange in the new colony was accomplished with a great deal of difficulty and it was necessary to resort to several resources to be able to pay for the military, the craftsmen, etc. The [exported] products of such a new nation did not suffice to balance to the value of the imports and so every year the balance of commerce in the colony showed a deficit.

It was only a matter of time before the money brought into the colony simply disappeared.

In order to deal with these difficulties, Louis XIV ordered that cod, corn, furs, etc. be used as legal tender; but since the economy was so unpredictable and not particularly strong, we eventually had to resort to money made from playing cards, appropriately cut up and with a value marked on the reverse along with the signature of the Intendant. During the period, counterfeiting was barely possible because of the small number of people who could even write.

Nevertheless, in 1667, a *faux monnayeur* [counterfeiter] was hanged in Québec, but it was the only such case mentioned for that period.

Later, the Intendant resorted to promissory notes.

This system of unlimited issuing of notes caused a great depression as well as a great loss of confidence in the notes.

A new importation of money was therefore undertaken but one which could be somewhat costly, that is, a note worth 5 *livres* [about $1.00] in France would have a value of 10 *livres* [about $2.00] in Canada, and a 1 *livre* piece [about 20¢] would be worth 2 [about 40¢].

> [No *livre* pieces of any denomination were ever issued in New France. The denomination was used strictly for accounting purposes.]

All of these methods having failed and the need for money being felt more and more, Louis XIV decreed the following Ordinance, dated the 19th of February 1670:

"Louis, by the Grace of God, King of France and of Navarre; to all those whom these letters shall reach, Greetings.

> The General Directors of the West Indies Company having pointed out to us that for the facilitation of commerce on the islands, mainland America, and other locations which we have accorded them, and for the convenience of our subjects who dwell in them, it was necessary to pay them with common monies, so that the crafts people and the daily workers who have not as of yet been paid for their work except with sugar and tobacco which they were then obliged to send to France to exchange for their full value, as well as with commodities necessary for their subsistence, which they could not gain any assistance from except for one year to the next, [simply because it could take that long to send the commodities back to France and to wait for their exchange-value to be returned] whereas the strangers who live in the neighboring islands have received the use of various

monies which they [are able to] use in their businesses, which attracts the majority of the craftsman and journeymen to the said islands causing our subjects to have this working against them because they lack the workers needed to cultivate the sugars and tobacco and to do other essential works, and as our primary aim is to establish religion in these said islands and on mainland America, and could not have the desired effect unless our subjects were not called upon and hired for commerce and for the means to maintain it; we have resolved to have up to 100,000 *livres* [about $20,000.00] worth of new kinds of money fabricated out of silver and copper in the money of our good city of Paris, with the same *poids* [weight], *titre* [denomination], *remède* [remedy], and *valeur* [worth] as those which are currently in use in our Kingdom, and to bring back into use:(1) our right of *seigneuriage*[141]; (2) our right of *foiblage*[142]; (3) our right of *escharsetés*[143], all 3 as *remèdes*[144] [remedies] under this Ordinance to improve the health of the existing system [and] in exchange for the advances which the said Company shall have made of materials, experimental and start-up losses suffered during the minting process itself, in addition to any costs incurred for the shipping of the various species to the said colonies.

For those reasons and other considerations, and acting on the advice of our Council and [based on] our undisputed knowledge, full power and royal authority, we have said and ordained, do say and do ordain, do wish and are pleased by these letters signed by our hand, that different species be processed in the mint of the said city of Paris, until the sum of 100,000 *livres* [about $20,000.00] has been reached, to be used currently in the islands and on mainland America and

---

[141]

The Right of *Seigneuriage* for the fabricating of money belongs to the Prince. It isn't always the same and changes according to the wishes of the Prince or the needs of the State. It is partly for the payment of this right that we began to use alloys, i.e. other metals mixed with gold and silver, for the fabrication of money. This right under King Louis XIII and even under King Louis XIV (until 1679), was set at 6 *livres* [about $1.20] per gold mark, and 10 *sols* [about .10¢] per silver mark.

[142]

Foiblage is our right to slightly reduce the weight of the various metals used in the coining process.

[143]

Escharsetés is our right to reduce the purity of the various metals used in the coining process.

[144]

Remède...the permission accorded the *maitres des monnaies* [e.g. money makers] to make different species of money at slightly less weight than legally called for by the various edicts or order. So, a *louis d'or* which should weigh 22 carats, only weighed 21¾, which is ¼ of *remède* [e.g. medicine] granted the 'money-maker'; and the *louis d'argent* which should have weighed 11 *deniers*, only weighed 10 *deniers* and 22 rains of silver, which is 2 *deniers* of *remèdes* [*medicine*] likewise accorded the 'money-maker'.

in other locations in the concession of the said East Indies Company, namely: 30,000 *livres* [about $6000.00] in 15 *sol* pieces, and 50,000 *livres* [about $10,000.00] in 5 *sol* pieces of the same *poids* [weight], *titre* [denomination], *remède* [remedy] and *valeur* [worth] as those which are currently in use in our Kingdom, and for 20,000 *livres* [about $4000.00] in *doubles* made of pure rosette-copper [reddish-brown] of the same dimensions and remedy as those which are also currently in use in our Kingdom as 2 *denier* pieces, all of the species shall be made in a mint and on a machine for striking money and stamped, namely: the 15 and 5 *sol* pieces as well as our 15 and 5 *sol* pieces, with these words on one side: 'Ludovicus Decimus Quartus Franciae et Navarrae Rex' [Louis XIV, King of the French and Navarres (citizens of a former kingdom on the French-Spanish border)], and on the reverse, 'Gloriam Regni Tui Dicent'. [They shall speak of the glory of Thy kingdom.] and the said doubles made of copper, on one side with a crowned 'L' with the same words, 'Ludovicus Decimus Quartus Franciae et Navarrae Rex', on the reverse with the words *'Double de l'Amerique Française* [*Double* from French America] and the same legend; and to that end the dies, squares and matrices necessary for these to be made at once by a general engraver subject to reasonable salaries, to have the said species circulating in the said nations at the previously ordained price and sent by the said Company and received by the said residents, in the market-place without their possibly being transported elsewhere nor that our other subjects be able to receive them or allow them to circulate in France, at the risk of confiscating the said species and of an exemplary punishment [to serve as a warning or deterrent]. And in consideration of the advance which those of the said Company shall make of the materials and startup and experimental costs, and the costs of shipping of the said species to the said nations, we have brought into use again and will bring into use again by these presents, Our right of *seigneuriage, foiblage* and *escharsetés* as remedies specified by the Ordinance.

We here instruct our beloved and faithful counselors, the parties responsible for our monies, that they read, publish and register according to their *forme* [shape] and *teneur* [content], and deliver the said species to the General Directors of the said East Indies Company, up to the amount of the said sum of 100,000 *livres* [about $20,000.00] only, and, after the said work is done, destroy the said dies, squares and matrices which shall have been used for this job, notwithstanding all else to the contrary, no matter which obstacles and hindrances might be and if either [obstacle or hindrance] happens, we reserve ourselves and our Conseil the right to know, and for that purpose forbid our courts and judges, and shall give credit for copies of the originals here present, carefully checked by one of our beloved faithful counselor's secretaries, *car tel est notre plaisir* [for that is our wish]."

"Given at St-Germain en Laye on the 19th of February 1670, in the 27th year of our reign,

(SIGNED,)   LOUIS, By the King, Colbert."

"Sealed with yellow wax under double tail."

The official pieces which circulated under the French rule were then the 15 *sols* piece, the 5 *sols* piece, the *double denier* and the *sou.*

The tokens of the West Indies Company from 1751 to 1758 were the following:

1751   [this token shows an Indian in lillies]   "Sub omni sidere crescent."
["They grow under every constellation."
        ... referring to the fact that the AmerIndians were numerous and seemed to be everywhere.]

1752   [this token shows Mercury flying]   "Utrique facit commercia mundo."
["He established commerce with both worlds."
        ... referring to King Louis XV's policies.]

1753   [this token shows the Eastern and Western hemispheres]   "Satis unus utrique."
["One is sufficient for both."
        ... referring to the shrinking size of the world.]

1754   [this token shows beavers building a dam]   "Non inferiora metallis."
["Not inferior to metals."
        ... referring to beavers' teeth (their fur was highly sought after.)]

1755   [this token shows an Argonaut vessel]   "Nonvillius aureo."
["Not less valuable than gold."
        ... referring to those preciously sought-after beaver pelts.]

1756   [this token shows bees and hives] "Sedem non animum mutant."
["They change their seat but not their minds."
        ... political references.]

1757   [this token shows Neptune and a warrior] "Parat ultima terra triumpho."
["The remotest lands prepare him triumphs."
        ... referring to the potential value of explorations abroad.]

1758   [this token shows a flight of eagles at sea] "Eadem trans aequora virtus."
["The same valor beyond the seas."
        ... referring to the strength needed to succeed abroad.]

[Note that these tokens or *jetons* merely <u>resembled</u> coins and were in fact used as 'counters' for calculation purposes by the various merchants. A box with the required number of compartments was provided to the various merchants (for purposes of calculating and accounting) and when twelve *jetons* had been accumulated in the *denier* slot, they were removed and put into the *sol* compartment (until 1794, 12 *deniers* equaled 1 *sol*) and when twenty *sols* had been accumulated, they were removed and put into the *livre* compartment (until 1794, 20 sols equaled 1 *livre*), and so on.]

The following statement made by Louis XV on the 5th of July 1717, revoked a pending Ordinance:

> "As the nation's money which has been introduced in Canada is of no use to the colony, and the 2 kinds of money which we can use cause some confusion in the market-place, we have rescinded and will rescind, in Canada, the said money of the nation, and as a result we wish – and it pleases us – to make all *stipulations de contrats* [contract stipulations], *baux à ferme* [land leases], *redevances* [rental contracts], and other ordinarily-transacted business matters, to begin with the registration of those which presently exist with the *Conseil Supérieur* of Québec, on value based on the money of France; about which value it shall be made mention of in the acts or on the banknotes, after the amount which the Retailer shall be responsible for, and that the different species of money of France shall have the same value in the colony of Canada as in our Kingdom."

LOUIS. For the King, by the Duke of Orléans, Régent, here present
(SIGNED,)   Phelypeaux.
"And sealed with the Great Seal with Yellow Wax."

This statement of the King, in the form of *lettres patentes* [licensed letters] formally transcribed, was recorded at the Clerk's Office of the *Conseil Supérieur* of Québec, after the close of the day; heard along with the claimant M^{tre} Paul Denys de St-Simon, Consellier, acting *procureur-général du Roi* [Attorney General for the King], by me, the *Conseiller Secrétaire du Roi* [King's Counselor-Secretary], *greffier en chef* [chief clerk] of the said Conseil, undersigned: in Québec, on the 11th of October 1717.

(SIGNED,)   DeMonseignat

1767

June 5th

On his visit to Kamouraska, Mgr. Jean-Olivier Briand ordered that <u>two</u> sets of Registers be maintained on the vital statistics of people.

(Kamouraska Register)

July 12th

During his pastoral visit to Point Lévis, Mgr. Briand made a notation in the parish Register to bring attention to the loss of several pages from the Registers. He wrote:

"There are several pages missing from the Registers for the years 1759 and 1760. They were lost during the siege, in the absence of the priest."

(Lévis Register)

August 9th

The children of a large number of Acadian families who had not been baptized were brought to church by their families so that they might receive the sacrament of rebirth.

(Ste-Anne-de-Yamachiche Register)

August 17th

In the Ste-Anne-de-la-Pérade parish Register, we read the following document:

"Joseph-François Perrault, *chanoine* [canon] of the Cathederal, *vicaire-général* [Vicar-General] for Mgr. Briand, the most Illustrious and Reverend bishop in Québec.

[*Canons* were priests who were not allowed to teach or become parish priests. Their essential function was to pray together and, in a few cases, when they lived in a presbytery, to serve as missionaries.]

To all those to whom this pertains, Greetings.

As in 1761, based on some adequate and virtually undisputed evidence, it would certainly have appeared that the man named Joseph Vallé, a resident of the rapids and seigneurie of Ste-Anne, might have died from his wounds after having been left at the site of M. de Montcalm's battlefield, during the siege of Québec, and as a result, a *certificat de liberté* [affidavit to prove that he was dead] would have been delivered to Angélique Tessier, his wife, who would have been married shortly thereafter, without any obstacles and in good faith, to a man named Joseph Douville, in the said parish and seigneurie of Ste-Anne, but that today it being obvious from the déposition of a man named Languedoc, an arrival from France and living in Machiche, [that deposition] delivered by Mr. Chefdeville, the curé of the said parish, on the 1st of August 1767, that the said Joseph Vallé had been seen alive in Larochelle on several occasions over a four-year period by the said Languedoc, among other times on the night before his departure – on the jour de la Quasimodo – that the said Joseph Vallé had asked him if he could climb aboard the same ship as he was on to return to join his wife in Canada, Languedoc adding that he presumed that the said Joseph Vallé would have gone with another group once he had learned from M. Levreau, a recent arrival in LaRochelle from Canada, that his wife had been married during his absence; seeing that it is still obvious according to a letter from the said Charles Vallé, only brother of the said Joseph Vallé, and who had not been in this Province since 1758, [that letter] written to his father and mother on the 12th of July 1766 from Michillimakinac where he had regularly traveled since he had entered Upper Canada, that the above-named Languedoc had not mistaken one for the other and had not been mistaken about the name nor the person of the said Joseph Vallé who is the real husband of the said Angélique Tessier, and whom he declared having seen alive in his deposition."

-231-

[In the Roman Catholic Church, Quasimodo refers to the first Sunday after Easter, or Low Sunday. It is so called because the Introit – the first part of the Mass – on that day begins with the words '*quasi modo geniti infantes*' ('as newborn babes...').]

"Considering the fact that the said deposition and the said letter now rest in our hands and are affixed to the minutes of the present hearing, we have placed and do place with the procès-verbal [minutes] of 1761, the proofs of the death of the said Joseph Vallé which now had no legal value, as well as the *certificat de liberté* [evidence of freedom] which, as a result, had been expedited; we declare, moreover, that the marriage of the said Angélique Tessier and the said Joseph Douville, although celebrated in good faith, was in no way contracted, and so the record shall be crossed off. As a result, permission is granted to the above-named Joseph Douville to marry another unimpeded woman when it is right for him to do so. It is forbidden for the said Angélique Tessier and the said Joseph Douville to live together and to call or view themselves as husband and wife, and that, under threat of penalty, during that state and conduct, of being deprived of the sacraments and of a *sépulture ecclésiastique* [religious burial]."
>[Being denied the sacraments and a religious burial also implied being denied entry into the Kingdom of Heaven, a VERY strong deterrent to the faithful.]

"We order M. Guay, curé of the parish and seigneurie of Ste-Anne, to advise them of this, to speak to them of the implications and to give them copies of the minutes properly reviewed.

Our Order shall be included in the marriage Registers of the said parish at the crossed-off-record of the alleged marriage of the above-named individuals, to have recourse to and to serve for whatever reason."

"Given in Québec, under our signature, with the seal of the Diocese, on the 17th of August 1767."   "PERRAULT, Chanoine [Canon], Vicar-General,
By Mr. the Grand-Vicar, Hubert, priest and Secretary to Mgr. the Bishop."

September 1st
>Rose Gaudet, an Acadian, disclosed that her husband, Jean-Pierre Emond, also an Acadian, had been taken captive by the English and brought to Philadelphia; that she herself had hidden with several family-members at St-Valier in 1755; that desiring to marry Louis Boutin, she produced a *certificat* from the Reverend Father Louis, *missionnaire* at Bécancour, according to which Olivier Thibodeau, recently arrived from New England, swore to having a letter which made note of her husband's death; moreover, a man called Tempdoux, an Acadian, returning from Philadelphia, and *porteur des hardes* [bearer of her husband's old clothing] of the said Jean-Pierre Emond, spoke of his having seen him buried.
(Register of the 'Procès-Verbaux' [Official Statements] of the Archdiocese of Québec, 1767)

As a result, she married Louis Boutin at St-Valier on the 15th of October.

(St-Valier Register)

[Strangers who had just arrived in the Colony had to have a *certificat de liberté* to certify that they were not already married and therefore free to marry.]

October 14th

Ste-Anne-du-Nord parish had been *privée de son curé* [without a priest] since October of 1761. Parish baptisms, marriages and burials had therefore been conducted at Château Richer and at St-Joachim until October of 1767. As a matter of fact, since the departure of their curé in October 1761, the parish had, until October of 1767, been ministered to by neighboring priests, MM. Duburon, a Récollet, and the *curé* [priest] at the Ange-Gardien parish, as well as by Marcou, a *curé* from St-Joachim, and the parish had only celebrated two solemn feasts, one on the third Easter and on the other on the Feast of their patron, St-Anne. The dead were buried in neighboring parishes except for those who died during springtime and who could not be transported due to poor roads. The parish had brought the problem upon itself because of the disrespectful manner in which the old parishioners had treated their priest and also because they themselves had asked the Bishop to remove him. The problem began when the parish priest refused to accept a parishioner as a godfather because he had not performed his Easter obligations. This had set off a lively dispute – right in the Church – and had been the cause of some of the trouble.

(Ste-Anne-de-Beaupré Register)

December 13th

The baptism of Gabriel, the son of Louis Michel and Rose de Repentigny. On the 4th of January of that same year, Rose had had *trois jumeaux* [3 ' twins'] baptized. Those [obviously triplets] had only survived for about 15 days.

(Ste-Anne-du-Bout-de-l'Île of Montréal Register)

[The French word for twins is bessons (m.) or bessonnes (f.); jumeaux (m.) or jumelles (f.). Triplets are now referred to as triplés (m.) or triplées (f.).]

December 20th

The baptism at Trois Pistoles of Jean-Baptiste, the son of Jean St-Laurent and of Marie LePetit, by Father Ambroise Rouillard, missionnaire.

(Trois-Pistoles Register)

This baptism was the last one performed by this priest. He drowned in July of 1768 near Cap-à-l'Original on his way from Trois Pistoles to Rimouski where he was going to assist with someone's religious needs. Father Ambroise had been the close friend of the Hermit, Toussaint Cartier.

(Tanguay)

1768

March 27th

Clement Choret, *maître huissier* [bailiff or process server] in Québec, was mortally wounded after being shot by M. Belarbre, *marchand* [merchant] in Islet. He died and was buried in Kamouraska.

(Kamouraska Register)

June 3rd

The burial of Amable Guérin , 32, who drowned and was found in Sorel. He was the son of Jean-Baptiste Guérin and Cathérine Boudreau from LaPrairie.

(Sorel Register)

Jacques-Louis Benoit, the husband of Marie-Joseph Soumande, drowned near the Îles-de- Varennes.

(Varennes Register)

Pierre Chapoulon dit Beausoleil, a native of St-Maurice parish in Limoges [France], and *soldat de la marine* [marine], had arrived in Canada in 1760 in Mr. DesLigneries Company on the ship *l'Outarde* commanded by Captain Pinguet.

(Register of the 'Procès-verbaux' [Official Statements] of the Archdiocese of Québec)

August 3rd

The burial of Mathieu Favreau, 24, who had drowned at Sorel.

(Sorel Register)

The marriage of Jean-Baptiste Dalciat, Sieur de la Fayolle, a 26-year-old native of the Bastude de Seron, diocese of Correserant ? [Tanguay's question mark], in the Province of Foix [in France] , to Marie-Louise Chauveau, the widow of Pierre Bellet. When he was 16, he had served in two campaigns in the service of the Baron de Sintnac after which he had gone to London with Mr. Jaquin, a Québec merchant, and from there to Québec.

(Register of the 'Procès-verbaux' [Official Statements] of the Archdiocese of Québec, 1768)

September 28th

Raymond Mesnard married Geneviève DelaRoche in Montréal. She had been the widow, by first marriage, of Pierre Gallet and, by second marriage, of Paul-Maurice-Jean Navarre, *chirurgien major* [head-surgeon] on the ship *Le Favory*, one of *King Très-Chrétien's* frigates. Navarre perished in 1757[144] when his ship was wrecked off the coast of Terreneuve. His widow moved to Montréal after recovering some of his belongings from the wreck.

[*King Très Chrétien* here was actually King Louis XVI who reigned from 1715 to 1774. This title was one bestowed by the early Popes on the kings of France.]

Paul Navarre's parents were Jacques Navarre and Marie Mouseux from Monbourguet in the diocese of Tarbes in Armagnac.

(Montréal Register)

François Guichard, a native of St-Sauveur, on Île-Dieu, in Poitou [France], had married Madeleine Tardif in 1756. In 1759, he was taken prisoner on Sieur Fortier's ship after having gone fishing at the poste St-Modeste. He was imprisoned in England and died shortly thereafter.

(Register of the 'Procès-verbaux' [Official Statements] of the Archdiocese of Québec, 1768)

November 6th

The marriage of François Rousseau dit Bonnet, 32, a native of St-Vivien in the diocese of LaRochelle, to Marie-Claire Langlois at St-Thomas de Montmagny. He had arrived in Québec in 1752 as a *mousse* [deck-boy] on Captain Vincelot's ship. He deserted and went to live in the home of François Gosselin, *syndic* in the new church at St-Thomas.

(Register of the 'Procès-verbaux' [Official Statements] of the Archdiocese of Québec)
[A *syndic* could have been an officer representing a government or community or an elected official for some community groups. Collectively, syndics were a body of officers or a council. In a church setting - as above - a *syndic* served as a trustee.]

November 14th

The burial of Jacques Ladéroute who had been killed by the Indians back in January.

(Kaskakia Register)

144

See the 1757 entries.

1769

March 18th

Michel Boucher, 24, died *en route* to Lac-Témiscouata, and was buried at St-Louis in Kamouraska.

(Kamouraska Register)

June 27th

The marriage of Jean-Baptiste Donohue and Cathérine Noreau. He was born in 1734, in Mitchelstone, in the diocese of Cloane, Province of Munster, in Ireland. He traveled to Bordeaux [France] in 1754 and arrived in Québec in 1759 on the ship *La Toison d'Or*. He then set up a shop at the foot of Côte-de-la-Montagne.

(Register of the 'Procès-verbaux' [Official Statements] of the Archdiocese of Québec)

September 4th

Valentin Poirot, from the diocese of Toul, in Lorraine, married Cathérine Policain, the widow of Pierre Labrie, in Lévis. Born in 1734, he came to Canada in 1756, as a *soldat de la marine* [marine] in Mr. de Beaujeu's company. He first fought in the Carillon campaign and later was part of M. de Gaspés company in the garrison at Niagara when it was taken by the English. He was then brought to New York and to Georgia. He returned to Montréal in 1765.

(Idem)

September 18th

The second marriage of Jean-François Thomas, a native of St-Martin at Pont-à-Mousson parish, in the diocese of Metz, in Lorraine, to Marie-Françoise Jacques, the widow of Laurent Poirier.

(St-Joseph of Nouvelle Beauce Register)

Thomas had been a soldier in France but had deserted in 1757 to come in *Les Ficheurs*. He was drafted into the *troupes de la marine* [marines under the Naval Department] until after the capture of Québec. In 1761, he married Marie-Charlotte Audon and worked as a *chaudronnier* [tinsmith].

(Register of the 'Procès-verbaux' [Official Statements] of the Archdiocese of Québec)

Charles Gautier, a native of Angoulême [in France], and *sergent* [sergeant] in Mr. Remon's company until 1760, had returned to Rochefort where he married Marie-Joseph L'Hermite. In 1763, he moved to Martinique but lost his wife in 1766. He returned to Québec with his daughter in 1768 and set himself up as a *coutelier* [cutler] on rue Couillard.

(Idem)

[A *coutelier* or cutler is one who manufactures, repairs or sells cutlery.]

October 3rd

The body of Brother Justinian (Louis-Alexandre-Constantin) was transported and reburied in St-Joseph church in Nouvelle-Beauce. He was first buried on the 28th of March 1760 in the chapel which served as parish church on M. de la Gorgendière's property.

(Register of St-Joseph in Nouvelle Beauce)

1770

Jean Germain, born in 1739 in Montferrant, diocese of Clermont, in Auvergne [France], left from LaRochelle in 1757 and arrived in Canada. He was then drafted into the *Berry* regiment, taken prisoner at Île-aux-Noix, and brought to New York where he was held for 4½ years. Once freed, he returned to Québec and worked as *portier* [door-keeper] at the Québec Seminary.

(Register of the 'Procès-verbaux' [Official Statements] of the Archdiocese of Québec, 1770)

August 21st

We blessed *'Marie-Olivier'*, the bell belonging to the St-Joachim parish.

(St-Joachim Register)

[The last of the eight bell-blessings recorded in this book. Roman Catholics have a great deal of faith in the value of having things blessed. They themselves receive special blessings at the time of their baptisms and marriages and illnesses and deaths and ask for blessings for their throats...and their prayer beads...and their fishing boats...and their gifts... etc. etc. . And so it is not surprising that during a period when the Church was so important in the colonists' everyday lives, a time when they were too poor to be able to afford individual timepieces, that they had to rely on church or other public bells to keep track of the time of day. Bells signaled the start and close of religious ceremonies and of workdays. They tolled to warn of emergencies or to advise of deaths or of happier events. They summoned citizens to assembly or to prayer or to arms or to fight fires. They indicated when it was time to sleep ... and to awaken. They rang to let merchants know when they could open up their shops... and when they had to close them. The colonists would surely have insisted upon blessing the very bells which guided their daily activities since they were absolutely essential to the life of the community.]

October 23rd

Guillaume Pellerin from the Avranches diocese in France came to Gaspé on M. Gouenard's ship when he was only 15. Brother Bonaventure gave him this referral:

"In Québec, on the 23rd of October 1770, I, the undersigned, certify that the man named Guillaume Pellerin, from the Val-St-Père-sous-Avranches parish in the Archdiocese of Avranches , came to the Baie des Chaleurs, as a *trente-six mois*, at a young age and, six months after his arrival, moved in with me at

Miramichy for 17 years. I saw and knew several others whom he came from France with, who assured me that he was a free man, and I can assure you that he is free to marry.

[s.]   Brother Bonaventure."

[A *trente-six-mois* or thirty-six monther is a nickname for a young and undoubtedly inexperienced tradesman from France who would normally contract out his services for a period of 3 years (thirty-six months) after being assured of passage and board at the expense of the person who had recruited him. His 3 years of experience in New France was oftentimes considered equal to 6 years of experience in his trade and qualified him as a Master at his trade. He could then return to France and open up his own shop. His travel time to New France was often also part of his 36-month term and so this was a somewhat popular apprenticeship program. Unfortunately for the colony, however, many of the new 'Masters' preferred to return to France after they had served their apprenticeship-periods, rather than to subject themselves to the colony's many hardships. This was but one of the problems encountered when trying to build up the number of colonists.]

Pellerin settled at St-Valier and at St-Pierre du Sud.

(Register of the 'Procès-verbaux' [Official Statements] of the Archdiocese of Québec)

MOVEMENT OF THE CATHOLIC POPULATION OF THE PROVINCE OF QUÉBEC 1761 TO 1770

	MARRIAGES	BIRTHS	DEATHS	OTHERS
1761	1007	3580	2147	1433
1762	799	4045	1922	2123
1763	847	4399	1773	2626
1764	871	4507	1902	2605
1765	808	4591	3169	1422
1766	759	4889	2117	2772
1767	806	4926	2161	2765
1768	727	5023	2224	2799
1769	593	4908	2912	1996
1770	699	4738	2336	1402
TOTALS ➡	7916	45606	23663	21943
1608-1770	33380	183857	92521	91336

[Tanguay's 'DEATHS' detail adds up to 22,663 yet his 'TOTAL' is 23,663.]

1771

January 15th

The marriage of François Provost and Madeleine Landais, widow of François Brisson, was celebrated on the 20th of February 1765 at Rimouski[145] but was today declared invalid at the Rivière-Ouelle.

(Rivière-Ouelle Register)

[After investigating Madeleine's claim that François had a living wife (Jacqueline Moussard) the marriage was declared invalid.]

The son of *chevalier* Huard d'Ormicour was born in Québec and traveled for 8 years in Marie-Galante, one of the *Antilles Françaises.* When he returned to Québec in 1773, he had a *certificat de liberté* from the Reverend Father Alphonse Bélaire de Chevrier, a Carmelite friar from that island.

(Register of the 'Procès-verbaux' [Official Statements] of the Archdiocese of Québec)

[A *certificat de liberté* is a document attesting to somebody's status – marital or otherwise. It was usually written under oath and in the presence of witnesses and usually signed by an official.]

July 3rd

The body of one of the early priests, M. LeBlond, was removed from the old chapel, and transported and buried under the sanctuary in the new Baie St-Paul church.

(Baie-St-Paul Register)

1773

In 1734, Étienne Guillemin from St-Paterne, Issoudun, in Berry [France], was a soldier in the *régiment de Noailles.* He came to Canada in 1750 where he remained in the military but in the *régiment de la Reine* right up to the time of the capture of Montréal. He then established himself as a *maître d'école* [school teacher] in Beauport.

(Register of the 'Procès-verbaux' [Official Statements] of the Archdiocese of Québec)

Philibert Vautier, born in 1727, in Blais, Bugeat, in the diocese of Annecy, arrived in Québec in 1757, as a soldier in Berry's First batallion, in the Cadillac Company. Taken prisoner at the battle of Carillon, he was brought to New York where he stayed until 1768. He then settled in Beauport.

(Idem)

145

See the 20th of February entry in the 1765 Rimouski Register.

June 12th

Pierre Bélanger drowned in Nicolet.

(Nicolet Register)

August 15th

"The consecration of a chapel dedicated to Saint Michael the Archangel. The chapel had been built by the residents of the parish on Madeleine Poulin's property which was occupied by her nephew, Louis Racine. M. Perrault, *vicaire-général*, had given his permission to build it there. The wife of Charles Normand, who lived near the crossing from the *Petite-Rivière-St-Charles* to Québec, donated a painting of Saint Michael the Archangel which I then placed in the Chapel. The official *syndics* [trustees] were Louis Racine and Étienne Morel."

(SIGNED,)   P. R. Hubert, curé

(Ste-Anne de Beaupré Register)

1774

January 30th

Marguerite Tibaudeau, 20, daughter of the *meunier* [miller] at the Écureuils parish, was crushed to death between the pavement and the mill-wheel.

(Écureuils Register)

March 24th

A case of *superfétation.* [A second conception during a pregnancy from an earlier conception.] The baptism of Augustin, the son of Augustin Blais and Angélique Mercier, who was born the night before. Another son, Jean-Baptiste, was baptized on the following 4th of May right after he was born. Both of these baptisms took place in the Berthier-Bellechasse parish.

(Berthier Register)

[There is some disagreement on the current definition ot *superfétation.* " *Stedman's Medical Dictionary – 25th Edition, 1990* " specifies that the 2 fetuses of different ages are *not twins* and that the concept is an obsolete one whereas Joseph Segen's 1995 *"Current Med Talk, a Dictionary of Medical Terms, Slang and Jargon"* notes that the concept serves as a theoretical explanation for the difference in times of delivery of *fraternal twins.*]

Could a *laïque* [a lay person] be invested with the power to dispense with the announcement of the banns or with the impediments by relationship or by blood which automatically nullify a marriage, and yet receive the expression of consent of the two parties contracting marriage? We must distinguish between impediments which are due to natural law, or to divine law, or those which are purely ecclesiastical. We find an answer to that question in the following article:

> "In 1774, Louis Robichaud, 71, the husband of Jeanne Bourgeois, and an Acadian refuged in Québec, happened to be in Salem, New England. This respectable old-timer had received extraordinary powers to dispense with the publication of the banns and the impediments to marriage, etc., for the Catholics who could not possibly appeal to the ministry of a priest [who might have been as far away as] in New England".

Here was Robichaud's format for a marriage certificate:

"Salem,....................1774.

'By virtue of the powers accorded me, Louis Robichaud, by M. Charles-François Bailly, *prêtre, vicaire-général* of the diocese of Québec, and presently settled in Halifax as a *missionnaire* for the Indians and the French, to receive the *consentment mutuel* [mutual consent] of catholic individuals in this Province who might wish to join together; or to grant a dispensation to those who might wish to marry – to this or that extent – as much by *affinité* [mutual attraction] as by *consanguinité* [close blood relationship], to those who will need it, I admit to having received the mutual consent of marriage of ....
and .... of the 3rd to 4th degree of blood relationship............. ...., the said parties have promised and do promise to receive the nuptial blessing from a priest approved by the holy Apostolic and Roman Catholic Church as soon as they are first able to locate such a priest.

The said act made in the presence of ....'

1775

July 8th
Mgr. Jean-Olivier Briand's pastoral visit to Kamouraska.

(Kamouraska Register)

July 19th

The following individuals died in a shipwreck at Baie-St-Paul: Benjamin Dufour, 18; Félicité Gagnon, 21, and Pascal Gagnon, his son, 5 years of age.

(Baie-St-Paul Register)

December 31st

Louis Valeran, 26, the son of Jacques Valeran and Cathérine Gorget, was killed today when the enemy launched its attack.

(Québec Register)

1776

November 2nd

The bodies of the parishioners who had been buried in the old cemetery in the first parish settlement, were today transported to the new cemetery.

(Baie-St-Paul Register)

1777

Pierre-Joseph Céloron from Blainville, *Chevalier de l'Ordre de St-Louis*, and *major du Détroit*, had married Demoiselle Cathérine Eury from Laperelle in Montréal in 1743.

After her husband died, she entered the Grey Nuns Convent in Montréal in 1777 as Sister Cathérine Eury. She died on the 2nd of November 1797.

Her father, François Eury, Sieur de Laperelle, had been *major* of Île-Royale.
[At the end of the 17th century, when the King of France no longer allowed Canadians to become nobles, only one important honor remained, *l'Ordre-Royal-et-Militaire-de-Saint-Louis*. That military order was divided into 8 Grand-Croix, 24 commanders and an unlimited number of *chevaliers* and was the only military order in which New France had the honor of taking part. To obtain the decoration, one had to be an officer in the regular forces which immediately eliminated the entire parish militia system and other ranks. Also, one could only serve the King of France in order to qualify.

The first person to receive the decoration in Canada was Callières, the Governor of Montréal, who received it in 1694, and the first Canadian chevalier was Pierre le Moyne d'Iberville who attained that distinction in 1699. From 1693-1760, *only about 145 men* were so decorated in Canada whereas France decorated 12,180 of its citizens from 1814-1830 alone. After the Conquest, only about a dozen of these *Chevaliers-de-Saint-Louis* remained in Canada and about 6 of those eventually took an oath of alliegance to the King of England, thereby severing their alliegance to Canada and France.

The glory and prestige of the decoration still remains in Canada because of its rarity whereas comparatively little value remains to the holders of the French decoration.]

1778

November 19th

The baptism of Charles-Michel, the son of Ignace de Sallaberry and Cathérine-Françoise Hertel of Rouville. He is also known as the *'Héros de Châteauguay'*.

(Beauport Register)

[Due to the military and tactical skills of Lieutenant-Colonel Charles de Sallaberry during the War of 1812, a decisive battle against an American army invading Lower Canada – the Battle of Châteauguay – was won on the 26th of October 1813. He was recognized accordingly.]

1779

June 4th

Joseph Brazeau, the husband of Françoise Didier and a native of Montréal, was killed by Indians near the *Rivière-Kaskakia*.

(Kaskakia Register)

June 8th

The burial of Charles Robin, 33, the husband of Marie-Anne Roy and a native of Canada, on one of the Îles of the Mississippi. He had been killed by Indians at the mouth of the *Rivière-Kaskakia*.

(Kaskakia Register)

1780

April 20th

Joseph Lafleur was buried by all of his fellow-travelers at Île-aux-Boeufs. He and Jean deNoyon had been killed by the Indians on the 1st of April at Belle-Rivière while guiding a narrow barge and a canoe.

(Kaskakia Register)

June 22nd

The burial of Joseph Vincent, a *matelot* [sailor] on the *Amazone* commanded by Captain Henry. The ship was at anchorage in Québec.

August 4th

Pélagie Filion, the wife of Albert Ouimet, drowned while unsuccessfully trying to save their daughter Pélagie, a 12 year older, from drowning. The family was from Terrebonne.

(Terrebonne Register)

MOVEMENT OF THE CATHOLIC POPULATION OF THE PROVINCE OF QUÉBEC 1771 TO 1780

	MARRIAGES	BIRTHS	DEATHS	OTHERS
1771	814	5175	2284	2891
1772	874	5279	2794	2485
1773	930	5401	3145	2256
1774	951	5619	2529	3090
1775	948	5841	2600	3241
1776	722	5590	3981	1609
1777	857	5570	4307	1263
1778	953	5920	2894	3026
1779	1010	5881	2733	3148
1780	931	6180	2895	3285
TOTALS ➡	8990	56456	30162	26294
1608-1780	42370	240313	122683	117630

1781

July 17th

The blessing of the first stone for the Nicolet church. The old church dated back to 1734 and the new one was blessed on the 23rd of June 1784 by M. Saint-Onge, *vicaire-général.*

(Nicolet Register)

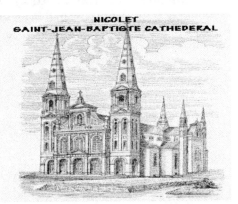

[This practice of blessing the first stone used in the construction of a new church was comparable to today's practice of blessing the cornerstone for new buildings.]

December 6th

Captain George deShoell, Commandant of the Hesse regiment, renounced his religion and was baptized in the church at the Rivière-Ouelle.

(Rivière-Ouelle Register)

1782

June 20th

The burial of Marie-Anne Monarque, 60, the wife of Michel Quevillon, in Terrebonne. She had been killed the night before in an electrical storm.

(Terrebonne Register)

1783

June 18th

The burial in Repentigny of Marie-Joseph Leprohon, 28, the wife of Joseph LeBellec. She had drowned in the *Rivière-de-l'Assomption.*

(Repentigny Register)

September 15th

At the request of the *Dames Ursulines* and by order of M. Gravé, *vicaire-général* of the diocese, several bodies buried in an enclosure within their Monastery were exhumed and reburied in Ste-Anne's Chapel Cemetery near the Cathedral.

(Québec Register)

1784

June 8th

The marriage of Jean-Baptiste Oneille and Thérèse Aide-Créquy was celebrated in Québec by the Reverend Father Félix Berry, the Récollets' *commissaire provincial.*

(Québec Register)

NOTE: The name of Jean-Baptiste Oneille, *sacristain* [sexton] of the Cathedral for almost 60 years, has become legendary in Québec. It would be interesting to compile all of his good words and clever retorts kept alive to this day in the minds of his fellow-citizens.

Although the general opinion is that he was born in Ireland, official documents point to his *père originaire* [fatherland] as being in the diocese of Dijon on the *Côte-d'Or* [Gold Coast] of Burgundy in France]. He married Marie-Joseph Chandonné in Québec in 1753 and had a son, Jean-Baptiste, baptized in 1756. This Jean-Baptiste became a respectable old-timer who died in Québec in 1836.

(Tanguay)

June 23rd

The burial of Louis-Joseph Bertrand, 28, who drowned at St-Augustin.

(St-Augustin Register)

THE YEAR OF THE GREAT BLACKOUT

"On the 15th of October, at about 3:15 in the afternoon, it became exceptionally overcast, so much so that the air over the countryside became a brilliant yellow; then there were some gusts of wind and rain which continued for a good portion of the night, with lots of thunder followed by lightning, something especially surprising since there had been a deep freeze on the night before.

On the next day, Sunday, the morning air was very calm with a thick fog which lasted until 10:00 at which time a wind from the East began to break it up. About half-an-hour later, it became so dark that we could not read without a candle; this was followed by a violent wind and then thunder and lightning after which everything seemed to clear up a bit; but from noon to 3:00 it became so dark [again] that the priests were forced to interrupt their masses until the church candles were lit; it was as dark then as it would ordinarily have been at midnight *whenever there is no moon*. It should be noted that each period of darkness was both followed and preceded by rain, lightning and thunder. We noted that there were two currents of air running in opposite directions in the atmosphere: the upper current was pushing a stretch of luminous clouds towards the northeast, and the other moved some thick, dark clouds towards the southwest at a swift pace and the rains which fell seemed as black as ink.
We attributed this freakish event to the smoke from a fire in some sulfur mines in some of our neighboring areas which had thickened the air and chased its thickened clouds towards our part of the country. The darkness was seen as far away as Niagara, if not further."

(Recollections of Nicolas-Gaspard Boisseau, Notary, p. 31)

November
    Pierre Drapeau[147], a 66 year old man, disappeared from his home in Québec. His body was not recovered until the 20th of April 1785, on the downward slope of the *Anse-des- Mères*.

(Québec Register)

147

Born in 1718 in Beaumont, the son of Pierre Drapeau and Marie-Anne Lacroix, he had married Dorothy Hens (Hains) in 1742.

(Genealogical Dictionary)

1785

November 21st

In Québec, we celebrated the marriage of Charles-Antoine Godfroy, Sieur de Tonnancour, seigneur de Tonnancour, Godfroy, Yamaska, Roctaillade, Labadie, Gatineau, etc., and Lieutenant in the *corps des Chasseurs au service de sa Majesté* [her Majesty's Hunting Corps], to Reine Frémont, the daughter of Louis Frémont and Cathérine Boucher from Boucherville.

(Québec Register)

1788

February 23rd

When reading through the Québec Registers we discovered that an artist specializing in portraits and landscapes lived in Québec. He was Louis-Chrétien Deheer.

(Québec Register)

[Tanguay had made a footnoted appeal to his readers: "Could we locate – somewhere – paintings with his (Deheer's) signature?" Whether or not anything came of the appeal is somewhat difficult to ascertain especially since the period that he was living in was a period when this form of Canadian art was almost non-existent except perhaps for topographic works – maps – and possibly also because relatively little is still known of the history of Canadian Art from that period. We do know of a Récollet priest, Claude François (or Frère Luc), who distinguished himself during 1670-71 as a painter of some 30 works of art on the inside of some churches but he had only lived in Canada for that 1-year period. We also know that Abbé J. Aide Créquy, who died in 1780, was probably Canada's first native-born painter.]

May 5th

David Line was listed as *coroner* in the Québec Register.

(Québec Register)

1789

August 26th

Charles-Joseph, the son of Baron Frederick de Schuffalyki and Rose Vigneau, was baptized in Boucherville.

(Boucherville Register)

MOVEMENT OF THE CATHOLIC POPULATION
OF THE PROVINCE OF QUÉBEC 1781 TO 1790

	MARRIAGES	BIRTHS	DEATHS	OTHERS
1781	969	6309	2847	3412
1782	973	6363	2727	3636
1783	1116	6551	2920	3031
1784	936	6437	5824	613
1785	1122	6974	3034	3940
1786	1186	6827	3675	3152
1787	1366	7206	3270	3936
1788	1214	7726	3628	3898
1789	911	7303	3480	3823
1790	1137	6825	4212	2613
TOTALS ➡	10,930	68,321	35,617	32,704
1608-1790	53,300	308,634	158,300	150,334

[a) Tanguay's 'BIRTHS' detail adds up to 68,521 yet his 'TOTAL' is shown as 68,321.
b) Tanguay's 'OTHERS' detail adds up to 32,054 yet his 'TOTAL' is 32,704.]

1791

January 3rd

The burial of Pierre Archibald Loffard who was born in 1724 in Peking, China. He had been married to Louise Landry.

(Québec Register)

1792

April 10th

Mgr. Bailly de Messein, Bishop of Capse and *coadjuteur* [assistant to the Bishop] to Mgr. Hubert, baptized Edouard-Alphonse, the son of Ignace de Sallaberry and Cathérine-Françoise Hertel, and brother of the *'Héros de Châteauguay'*, in Beauport. His Royal Highness Prince Edward insisted on being the godfather. [SEE: November 19, 1778 note.]

(Beauport Register)

1793

March 12th

Louis Clermont and Pierre Lacoste from Montréal were both murdered by the Indians on the *Rivière-Cumberland* and buried today at the Kaskakia mission.

(Kaskakia Register)

THE STATE OF THE CHURCH IN CANADA AFTER THE TREATY OF 1763

The 1758 ordination of Father Jean-Baptiste Pétrimoulx was the last conferred under the French regime. Almost 8 years went by before any young Levite [early name for a clergyman] was ordained into the priesthood in Canada. Several young Canadians had traveled to France and once ordained had returned to devote their lives to the Canadian missions.

The Bishop of Québec, who was not seated until 1766, sadly watched as his huge diocese was reduced to a very small number of religious. Even now, almost two thirds of his clergy were from abroad. The Jesuit and Récollet Orders were suppressed [and could not help]. The Diocese by itself could furnish but a very few subjects to replace those who were lost, and the spiritual needs were being felt more and more after the misfortunes of the war. The only other option was to call upon the priests from France to help the Diocese. For 30 years we made unbelievable efforts to do just that without being able to overcome the English[147] government's unshakeable resistance.

It took nothing less than the French Revolution to remove the obstacle for it showed what was thought of the French *ecclésiastiques* [clergymen]; how attached they were to the old ways of doing things, and therefore enemies of change. So, in 1793 – and since – all French priests with a passport signed by one of the *secrétaires du Roi*, were received in Québec with the least amount of difficulty.

That is how Canada enriched itself with the spoils of the Church of France and had the double advantage of giving asylum to the unfortunate, and of obtaining some of the subjects who had been afflicted by that persecution for itself. More than 30 French priests were thusly brought over to assist the Canadian missionaries.

147

In 1783, a request from the Catholics of the Province of Québec was presented to the Court of London, earnestly asking that the bishop of Québec be allowed to bring over some ecclesiastical candidates from Europe.

The following documents show us of the steps taken by Mgr. Briand, the Bishop of Québec, for that purpose:

To the Honorable William Smith, Chief-Justice, in Québec:

"Sir, I have the honor of transmitting to you, and through you to His Excellency and to the *Conseil*, my ideas regarding the means of facilitating access and establishing a system for dealing with the French emigrants in Canada. The humanitarian conduct and spirit of generosity which the British government holds towards them is one of the very strong forces enabling them to gain the favour of all tenderhearted souls. As close as I am to the majority of these illustrious exiles, by means of a common faith and a common priesthood, I feel especially obligated to help them in any way that I am in a position to do so, and I note, Sir, with much relief, that your personal inclinations are no less favorable to them. It is in our working together along with the efforts of our open-minded and generous government, that these victims of the old ways of doing things can hope to finally find calm and peace, after the violent battles which have so disastrously scattered them about."

"I have the honor,   Jean-François,
Bishop of Québec."

Québec, on the 16th of April 1793.

"The opinion of the Bishop of Québec on the means of providing for the maintenance and the settlement of the *ecclésiastiques* and the *nobles* whom the French Revolution forced to leave their country, and who seem to wish to be refuged in this nation, humbly submissive to His Excellency the *Lieutenant-Gouverneur* of the Province of Lower Canada and to His Majesty's *Conseil*.

His Excellency, and the *Conseil*, can be persuaded that at all times and under all circumstances, the Bishop of Québec, justly compassionate to the tragic condition of the French emigrants, will do all that he can, and will use all of his influence to reduce the misery of those who will take refuge in this nation after their expatriation.

If all that was involved was to provide for the needs of a hundred or so French religious, he would not hesitate to take it upon himself to place them, within a year, in different parts of the Diocese, where there would have the double-advantage of living with the people and finding themselves helpful to those same people by the simple exercise of their religious duties. It is likewise possible to presume that a small number of emigrant families would find, from the generosity of the residents of the land, and from their own efforts, prompt and sufficient resources.

But since it is probable that a much greater number of *ecclésiastiques* and French families would reach Québec during the first few months of the next sailing season, it becomes absolutely essential for the Province to take more extensive measures, as much to welcome them without overburdening ourselves as to then set them up in a concrete and lasting living environment.

> [As to the short sailing season...due to the climate in Canada, travel from France was seldom attempted for at least six months out of the year since the 'Great River of Hochelaga', the St-Lawrence River, was rough, uncharted and would even freeze up. Satirical works such as Rabelais' *"Quart Livre"* – viewed by thousands in Europe – also did not help the early Europeans' perceptions of the weather..." the cold in Canada was so intense that words froze on the lips of the sailors and remained suspended in mid-air...when the spring sunshine came, the words thawed, and then sailors returning to the same spot might hear, from the captain's bridge, words which had been uttered the previous winter." (Douville & Casanova, *"Daily Life in Early Canada"*, 1968, p. 39).]

As to the first of these two objectives, it is important to spread these emigrants about in different parts of the Province, as soon as they arrive; the most populous city of the Province not being able to feed – even for 8 days – 3000 or 4000 strangers without running the risk of starving itself. So here is a method of spreading them about promptly which would probably not be without success.

The Bishop could, in calling for the assistance of his diocesan priests for the French emigrants by *lettre circulaire* [a letter circulated among the various parishes and read to all church-goers], immediately ask them to inform him just how many that their respective parishes could accommodate either by putting them up in their own homes, or in those of the seigneurs, or in a common home which would be rented for that purpose, or finally in private homes. There would be few parishes which would not be able to accommodate 10 or so, others could accept 20, others 40, and others perhaps more according to their facilities and the good will as much of the seigneurs and the priests as of the *tenanciers* [property managers] and the parishioners. We could also, either by taking a collection or by a contribution from each parish, buy them the more essential furnishings.

Each of the two cities of Québec and Montréal, can, in the same manner, and with a like contribution, shelter 100 or 200 refugees; and Trois-Rivières, 50, especially with the facilities offered by several almost-deserted communities.

It would appear more appropriate that the 3 hospitals in these 3 cities be reserved as *retraite aux malades* [hospitals for the sick] and there could not help but be a large number after a long and possibly unhealthy journey.

Other than the collections and contributions which we would hasten to raise throughout the countryside so that we might be in a better position to help the French emigrants who would be sent to the various areas, it seems altogether necessary to immediately create, in each of the 2 principal cities of the Province, an office or committee which would be expected to prepare the routes for the reception of these exiles, to receive them, to divide them into groups, and to facilitate their being brought to the various parishes, where they will be expected; and for that purpose to immediately begin a program to raise funds for such a contribution and to urge the generosity of the citizens of these two cities for these emigrants. The Bishop of Québec, while economizing with those modest revenues, now offers 50 guineas of his own, as his contribution towards this program.

Assuming that the suggested measures listed above have the success which we are hoping for, the French emigrants could then rest from the rigors of their trip for several weeks; after which we would consider taking added measures to settle them more permanently in the countryside, the last thing that the British Minister seems to be worrying about, and regarding which it would perhaps be wise to await further direction.

Here, however, is what we can propose in the meantime:

In order to put into action His Majesty's charitable plan to receive and establish the large resource of French emigrants especially those who would be connected to the cultivation of the land, and in His spirit of generosity and nobleness, he could, without a doubt, furnish them with food supplies for 2 or 3 years along with agricultural implements. Armed with this help, they could then clear various lands – the land owned either by the Crown or privately owned by the seigneuries and closer to the river. These, from their perspective, would add to the benefits which the emigrants would have received from the government, or would at least put them in a position to be better able to benefit from them. The departments or committees proposed above, could, by virtue of an *acte de la Législation* or *lettres-patentes* [legislative act or documents granting some right or privilege], be authorized to prepare options for that purpose along with the private seigneurs of the Province, and could even contract with them in the name of the emigrants for more advantageous terms[148].

The Bishop of Québec might realistically envision a *communauté d'ecclésiastiques émigrés* [community of ecclesiastical-emigrants] in possession of the Jesuits' property in Canada, if His Majesty has not otherwise disposed of those properties, and assign them the tasks which had at other times kept the

---

[148]

The seigneuries of Beauharnais, Beaupré, Rivière-du-Loup, at the foot of the river, of Île-Verte, Trois-Pistoles, Bic, and Rimouski, could become ideal sites for the emigrants because of their shipping or maritime locations.

religious busy, as much with respect to certain Indian missions as to the Province's public education which the Québec clergy could serve as the center for.

The *ecclésiastiques-émigrés* might be able to make use of the following resources which the diocese of Québec is prepared to make available for that purpose:

1. The Montréal Seminary has a pressing need for subjects.

2. New parishes have to be established.

3. Some older parishes need new – or additional – priests.

4. Other parishes are simply too populated for only one priest and also need assistants.

The Bishop will attempt with all of his power to increase those resources, limited only by the resources themselves and by the financial state of the various vicars and missions. At least, he will do nothing to discourage the subjects in the Province, and will take whatever time is needed to get to know a little about any new subjects before giving them missions of their own."

1794

May 6th
The marriage of Augustin Scavoie and Marie-Anne Coupeau from St-Marin, in Québec. His Royal Highness Prince Albert had Augustin, a native of Thionville in Lorraine, as his *maître de musique* [music teacher].

(Québec Register)

1795

March 28th
Michel Champou, 35, a *cultivateur* [farmer] in Nicolet parish, was crushed by a falling tree.

(Nicolet Register)

1796

THE DESTRUCTION BY FIRE OF THE RÉCOLLETS' CHURCH

September 11th
Reading from the Sermon book of Notre-Dame de Québec for the 17th Sunday after Pentecost:

> "In the ruins of the Récollet Fathers' Church we found the remains of a number of early religious as well as the ashes of some of the early Governors of the region[149] which had been buried there. We placed all of these precious remains in a coffin to be brought to and buried in the Cathedral. This transfer will take place immediately after today's High Mass and you are all invited to assist in the process[150]."

[Although originally an agricultural festival on which the people were expected to show gratitude to God for an early harvest, Pentecost later – at the time of Jesus Christ – began to have a less agricultural significance both to Christians and to Jews. For Christians, Pentecostal Sunday – the 7th Sunday (50 days) after Easter – memorizes the descent of the Holy Spirit on the Apostles empowering them to witness to Jesus Christ. For Jews, it is a celebration in observance of the giving of the Torah, the Jewish body of divine instructions, teachings and law, by Moses on Mount Sinai.]

Three of the early *gouverneurs* were buried in the Récollets' Church:
1. The Count Louis de Baude de Frontenac, *chevalier, comte de Palluau,* died on the 28th of November 1698 and buried on the following 1st of December;
    [He had served as Governor from 1672-82 when he was recalled to France.]
2. Philippe de Rigault, *chevalier, seigneur de Vaudreuil,* husband of Louise-Élizabeth de Joybert, buried on the 13th of October 1725;
    [He had served as Governor from 1703-25.]
3. The Marquis de la Jonquière, born around 1686 in the Château de la Jonquière, in Languedoc [France], *Gouverneur* in 1749, and died on the 17th of May 1752.

149

M. Auguste de Saffray, *chevalier, seigneur de Mezy, gouverneur* of New France from 1663 to 1665, died in Québec on 5 May 1665, but was not buried in the Récollets church. Rather, he was buried in the Paupers' cemetery of the Hôtel-Dieu (Québec's Hospital for the sick) as he had wished according to the terms of his will and testament. His funeral ceremony was solemnly celebrated by Mgr. the Bishop of Petrée.

150

The announcement made by the priest from Québec, M. Joseph-Octave Plessis.

[Although appointed Governor by the King in 1746, he did not arrive until 1749 and only served in that capacity from 1749-52. In the interim, Intendant Bégon's brother-in-law, Roland-Michel Barrin de la Galissionière served as Governor.]

[At the end of the 17th century, when the King of France no longer allowed Canadians to become nobles, only one important honor remained, *l'Ordre-Royal-et-Militaire-de-Saint-Louis*. That military order was divided into 8 Grand-Croix, 24 commanders and an unlimited number of *chevaliers* and was the only military order in which New France had the honor of taking part. To obtain the decoration, one had to be an officer in the regular forces which immediately eliminated the entire parish militia system and other ranks. Also, one could only serve the King of France in order to qualify.]

In an entry dated the 5th of December 1702 in the Notre-Dame de Québec Registers, we found a record of the burial of Marie-Anne LeNeuf de la Poterie, the widow of René Robineau, Sieur de la Poterie and an officer in the *régiment Turenne*, also *chevalier* of *St-Michel, seigneur de Bécancour* and *baron de Portneuf.*

M. DeFRONTENAC'S HEART

From the statements of Major Lafleur and M. de Gaspé, who was an eye-witness to the destruction by fire of the Récollet Church, the lead coffins which had been setting on iron slabs in the Church vaults were partly melted ! A small lead box which contained M. de Frontenac's heart was on his coffin.

According to Frère Louis, one of the last Récollets to be secularized [converted from a religious to a lay or secular person] after the burning of the Monastery on the 6th of September 1796, tradition recalls that M. de Frontenac's heart was enclosed in a lead box after he died and was sent to his wife, the Countess. She did not wish to accept it and returned it to Canada, saying "that she did not want the heart of a dead man which, when he was alive, had never belonged to her !!"

The bones of the *anciens gouverneurs* [early governors], at first transferred from the ruins of the Récollet Church to the Notre-Dame-de-Pitié chapel in the Cathedral in Québec were, several years later, placed in the vaults of the Ste-Anne's chapel, in the Lower Choir, on the side of the gospel, where they, as well as M. de Frontenac's heart, are still located.

The tradition preserved by Frère Louis and continued by M. de Gaspé in his "*Anciens Canadiens*", was well recorded in a letter written some time after the death of Governor de Frontenac, a letter which even identified the Récollet priest who was given the responsibility of bringing M. de Frontenac s heart to France.

We read in the above-mentioned letter:

"The Reverend Father Joseph[152], a Récollet, *Canadien, supérieur du couvent Récollet* [Superior of the Récollets' Monastery] in Québec, was charged with the responsibility of bringing the Count de Frontenac s heart to France. This good priest is a man of extraordinarily sterling qualities whose exemplary devotion could only serve as a model for someone who wishes to become even more virtuous. The priests in that Monastery are the trustees of these remains in the magnificent church which the Governor had, at his expense, built for them."

1797

February 7th

The burial of Robert Lane, 48, the *exécuteur des hautes-oeuvres* [public executioner].

(Québec Register)

June 30th

The burial of Jacques Perrault, Joseph Derome and Pierre Voyer, the son of Charles Voyer. All three of them drowned at Sault-de-la-Chaudière.

(Québec Register)

July 19th

The baptism of Marie-Angélique, 20, the daughter of Sagotenta, an Englishman, and Kaentian. She had been kidnapped from the Lac-des-Deux-Montagnes Indians by a man named Antoine Lebrun.

(Lac-des-Deux-Montagnes Register)

152

The Reverend Father Joseph was the son of Pierre Deny, Sieur de la Ronde, and of Cathérine LeNeuf de la Poterie. He had been appointed Superior of the Récollets' Monastery in 1697.

1798

June 14th

The burial of Nicolas Vénier who was born in Venice, Italy, in 1722. He was married in 1742 in Venice but his wife died in 1756. In order to establish himself in Canada, he left from Genoa on the privateer *La Belle Française* in 1761 and later married Jeanne Sédilot. His AKA name was *'Nicole'*.
(Register of the 'Procès-verbaux' [Official Statements] of the Archdiocese of Québec)

[AKA (Also Known As) was used here since the translation could have been either surname or nickname *'Nicole'* and since there is a clear distinction between the two in the English language. It is better shown simply as an AKA name.]

MOVEMENT OF THE CATHOLIC POPULATION OF THE PROVINCE OF QUÉBEC 1791 TO 1800

	MARRIAGES	BIRTHS	DEATHS	OTHERS
1791	1365	7946	4671	3275
1792	1449	8306	3961	4345
1793	1372	8127	4016	4111
1794	1679	8514	3837	4677
1795	1544	9146	4303	4843
1796	1388	9018	4308	4710
1797	1531	9224	4859	4365
1798	1559	9617	4400	5217
1799	1459	9776	4329	5447
1800	1666	10,080	4701	5379
TOTALS ➡	15,012	89,754	43,385	46,369
1608-1800	68,312	398,388	201,685	196,703

Although " _Travers les Registres_" closes out at the end of the 18th century, it might be useful to furnish you with the tables showing the changes in population[152] until 1880.

The tables show that after the surrender of Québec the cumulative number of marriages rose to 22,117; of births, to 150,275; and of deaths, to 74,700; leaving a surplus of 75,575 souls and giving us a grand total of 247,092[153] birth/marriage/death entries in the Registres. The years from 1763 to 1800 give us an additional 40,000 marriages; 248,000 births; 127,000 deaths, leaving a surplus of 121,000 births over deaths which increases the number of birth/marriage/death entries included in the various Registers to 650,000 as of 1800.

The number of parishes which regularly maintained their Registers regarding the status of the population as of the date of Canada's surrender to England was 115. From that date to the end of the 18th century, the number increased by another 26.

Here are the first parishes whose _Registres_ are such a precious source of information to us:

CANADIAN PARISHES WHICH REGULARLY MAINTAINED REGISTERS ON ITS MEMBERS DURING THE FRENCH REGIME

[List shown as in '_A Travers les Registres_'.]

#	PARISH	YEAR
1	Québec	1621
2	Trois-Rivières	1635
3	Sillery	1636
4	Montréal	1642
5	Sainte-Anne-de-Beaupré	1657
6	Château-Richer	1661
7	Sainte-Famille, (Île-d'Orléans)	1669
8	Boucherville	1668
9	l'Ange-Gardien	1666
10	Laprairie	1670

152

See pages 181, 182, 183, 184 and 185.
153

We meet up again with all of these records although further analyzed in the "_Dictionnaire Généalogique des Familles Canadiennes_" which also includes the data for the Gulf of Saint Lawrence as well as for the Western Territories.

#	PARISH	YEAR
11	Sorel	1670
12	Beauport	1673
13	Pointe-aux-Trembles, (Montréal)	1674
14	Lorette	1676
15	Lachine	1676
16	Lévis	1679
17	Saint-Thomas	1679
18	Cap-Saint-Ignace	1679
19	Islet	1679
20	Saint-Pierre, (Île-d'Orléans)	1679
21	Saint-Laurent, (Île-d'Orléans)	1679
22	Saint-François, (Île-d'Orléans)	1679
23	Charlesbourg	1679
24	Pointe-aux-Trembles, (Québec)	1679
25	Cap-Santé	1679
26	Champlain	1679
27	Repentigny	1679
28	Saint-Jean, (Île-d'Orléans)	1679
29	Grondines	1680
30	Contrecoeur	1680
31	Baie-Saint-Paul	1681
32	Saint-Ours	1681
33	Batiscan	1682
34	Lachenaye	1683
35	Rivière-Ouelle	1685
36	Saint-Joachim	1687
37	Cap-de-la-Madeleine	1687

#	PARISH	YEAR
38	Rivière-des-Prairies	1688
39	Saint-Augustin	1691
40	Beaumont	1692
41	Lotbinière	1692
42	Saint-Michel-de-la-Durantaye	1693
43	Sainte-Anne-de-la-Pérade	1693
44	Varennes	1693
45	Saint-Nicolas	1694
46	Notre-Dame-de-Foi	1699
47	Rimouski	1701
48	Verchères	1702
49	Saint-Antoine-de-Tilly	1702
50	Saint-François, (Île-Jésus)	1702
51	Sainte-Anne-du-Bout-de-l'Île	1703
52	Île-Dupas	1704
53	Saint-Sulpice	1706
54	Chambly	1706
55	Pointe-Claire	1713
56	Deschambaux	1713
57	Saint-Valier	1713
58	Trois-Pistoles	1713
59	Rivière-du-Loup, Trois-Rivières	1714
60	Longueuil	1715
61	Sainte-Anne-de-la-Pocatière	1715
62	Île-Verte	1715
63	Saint-François-du-Lac	1715
64	Saint-Antoine, (Baie-du-Febvre)	1715

#	PARISH	YEAR
65	Saint-Antoine-de-la-Valtrie	1716
66	Sainte-Croix	1716
67	Bécancour	1716
68	Nicolet	1716
69	Saint-Laurent, (Montréal)	1720
70	Lac-des-Deux-Montagnes	1721
71	Longue-Pointe	1724
72	l'Assomption	1724
73	Hôpital-Général of Montréal	1725
74	Kamouraska	1727
75	Saint-Michel-d'Yamaska	1727
76	Berthier, (Montréal)	1727
77	Terrebonne	1727
78	Saint-François-du-Sud	1727
79	Notre-Dame-des-Anges, Hôpital-Général, Québec	1728
80	Sainte-Geneviève-de-Batiscan	1728
81	Berthier-Bellechasse	1728
82	Yamachiche	1728
83	Éboulements	1732
84	Saint-François-Xavier-Petite Rivière	1734
85	Saint-Roche-des-Aulnets	1735
86	Saint-Pierre-les-Becquets	1735
87	Saint-Roch	1735
88	Sault-Saint-Louis	1735
89	Lanoraie	1735
90	Châteauguay	1736
91	Sault-au-Récollet	1736

#	PARISH	YEAR
92	Saint-Joseph, (Nouvelle-Beauce)	1738
93	Saint-Mathias	1736
94	Saint-Denis-de-Chambly	1741
95	Saint-Antoine	1741
96	Saint-Charles	1741
97	Hôtel-Dieu of Québec	1741
98	Saint-Jean-Deschaillons	1741
99	Écureuils	1742
100	Pointe-du-Lac	1742
101	Saint-Maurice	1743
102	Saint-Vincent-de-Paul	1744
103	Sainte-Marie, (Nouvelle-Beauce)	1745
104	Sainte-Rose, (Île-Jésus)	1745
105	Saint-Joseph-de-Chambly	1746
106	Saint-Pierre-du-Sud	1748
107	Saint-Charles, (Rivière-Boyer)	1749
108	Île-aux-Coudres	1750
109	Saint-Joseph-de-Soulanges	1752
110	Saint-Constant	1752
111	Saint-Philippe	1757
112	Sainte-Geneviève, (Île-de-Montréal)	1758
113	Carleton	1760
114	Saint-Henri-de-Mascouche	1761
115	Saint-Régis	1762

CANADIAN PARISHES
ESTABLISHED UNDER THE ENGLISH GOVERNMENT
FROM 1763 TO 1800

NUMBER	PARISH NAMES	YEARS
1	St-Jean-Port-Joli	1769
2	St-Eustache	1767
3	St-Cuthbert (Maskinongé)	1770
4	Beloeil	1772
5	Vaudreuil	1773
6	Maskinongé	1773
7	Malbaie	1774
8	St-Jacques-de-l'Achigan	1774
9	St-Martin (Île-Jésus)	1775
10	St-Hyacinthe	1777
11	St-Henri-de-Lauzon	1780
12	St-Gervais	1780
13	St-François (Nouvelle-Beauce)	1780
14	Bonaventure	1780
15	Gentilly	1784
16	Blairfindie	1784
17	The Île-Perrot	1786
18	St-Paul-de-la-Valtrie	1786
19	St-Roch-de-l'Achigan	1787
20	Ste-Anne-des-Plaines	1788
21	Ste-Thérèse-de-Blainville	1789
22	St-André-de-Kamouraska	1791
23	St-Marc-de-Chambly	1794
24	St-Jean-Baptiste-de Rouville	1797
25	St-Hilaire-de-Rouville	1799
26	St-Benoit	1799

As expected, the growth in the Canadian population continued and was due to her excellent organizational plan which was none other than the original plan set up by the Canadian clergy, the only body of the state which had not 'abandoned its post' after the defeat. This truly remarkable fact was greatly acknowledged by one of Canada's distinguished historians whose impartiality cannot be suspect. We speak of M. Françis Parkman, who, at the end of his "*The Old Regime in Canada*" made the following statement: "The English conquest shattered the whole apparatus of civil administration at a blow, but it left her untouched. Governors, superintendents, councils and commandants, all were gone; the principal seigniors fled the colony; and a people who had never learned to control themselves or help themselves were suddenly left to their own devices. Confusion – if not anarchy – would have followed but for the parish priests, who in a character of double paternity, half spiritual and half temporal, became more than ever the guardians of order throughout Canada."

("*The Old Regime in Canada*", by F. Parkman, p. 400; Boston: Little, Brown & Co., 1874.)

MOVEMENT OF THE CATHOLIC POPULATION OF THE PROVINCE OF QUÉBEC 1801 TO 1810

	MARRIAGES	BIRTHS	DEATHS	OTHERS
1801	1778	10226	5442	4784
1802	1886	10970	5834	5136
1803	1929	10830	6826	4004
1804	1864	11473	5957	5516
1805	1690	11448	5006	6442
1806	1746	11578	5188	6390
1807	1887	11835	5223	6612
1808	2092	11975	5157	6818
1809	2080	12183	6240	5943
1810	2139	12555	8269	4286
TOTALS ➡	19091	115073	59142	55931
1608-1810	87403	513461	260827	252634

MOVEMENT OF THE CATHOLIC POPULATION OF THE PROVINCE OF QUÉBEC 1811 TO 1830

	MARRIAGES	BIRTHS	DEATHS	OTHERS
1811	2346	12802	6040	6762
1812	2593	13308	5629	7679
1813	2029	13386	7922	5464
1814	2453	13543	7645	5898
1815	2778	14482	7021	7461
1816	2376	14807	6117	8690
1817	2407	14653	7026	7267
1818	2646	15938	6684	9254
1819	2796	16371	7731	8640
1820	2806	16816	9981	6835
TOTALS	25230	14610	71796	74310
1608-1820	112633	65956	332623	326944
1821	2959	17442	9181	8261
1822	2831	17852	8887	8965
1823	2877	18342	8347	9995
1824	3128	18769	7921	10848
1825	3362	19366	10443	8923
1826	3582	20090	10775	9315
1827	3529	20752	9748	11004
1828	3142	20736	9566	11170
1829	3190	20896	9114	11782
1830	3844	21930	10957	10973
TOTALS	32444	19617	94939	101236
1608-1830	145077	85574	427562	428180

[Tanguay's 'OTHERS' detail for 1608-1820 adds up to 73,950 but his 'TOTAL' is 74,310.]

MOVEMENT OF THE CATHOLIC POPULATION
OF THE PROVINCE OF QUÉBEC 1831 TO 1850

	MARRIAGES	BIRTHS	DEATHS	OTHERS
1831	4331	23693	11614	12079
1832	4341	24243	19868	4375
1833	4491	24766	10638	14128
1834	3911	24384	15028	9356
1835	4308	25509	9392	16117
1836	3861	25589	11094	14495
1837	3250	24230	13431	10799
1838	3583	24899	11574	13325
1839	4038	24707	11056	13651
1840	4758	26162	11795	14367
TOTALS ➡	40872	248182	125490	122692
1608-1840	185949	110392	553052	550872
1841	4937	27955	13478	14477
1842	5,007	28,498	13,826	14,672
1843	5,155	30,627	13,310	17,317
1844	5,324	30,705	12,240	18,465
1845	5,360	32,169	12,918	19,251
1846	5,921	32,530	16,413	16,117
1847	5,593	33,984	16,836	17,148
1848	5,156	33,693	13,548	20,145
1849	5,126	33,232	16,633	16,599
1850	5,240	34,527	13,371	21,156
TOTALS	52,819	317,920	142,573	175,347
1608-1850	238,768	1,421,84	695,625	726,219

MOVEMENT OF THE CATHOLIC POPULATION
OF THE PROVINCE OF QUÉBEC 1851 to 1870

	MARRIAGES	BIRTHS	DEATHS	OTHERS
1851	5453	34066	14165	19901
1852	5649	35599	14288	21311
1853	6302	36483	14646	21837
1854	6440	36818	19470	17348
1855	6319	37169	17637	19532
1856	6133	38519	16194	22325
1857	6055	38323	16335	21988
1858	6392	39602	16594	23008
1859	6147	41189	17148	24041
1860	6462	41976	16591	25385
TOTALS ➡	61352	379744	163068	216676
1608 to 1860	300120	1801588	858693	942895
1861	6927	42856	17366	25490
1862	7317	44737	19408	25329
1863	7026	45545	19643	25902
1864	7202	44884	22154	22730
1865	7481	44504	22190	22314
1866	6827	42813	20448	22365
1867	6792	43757	21897	21860
1868	6971	43783	21347	22436
1869	7532	43920	20221	23699
1870	7810	43760	21276	22484
TOTALS ➡L	71885	440559	205950	234609
1608 to 1870	372005	2242147	1064643	1177504

MOVEMENT OF THE CATHOLIC POPULATION OF THE PROVINCE OF QUÉBEC 1871 TO 1880

	MARRIAGES	BIRTHS	DEATHS	OTHERS
1871	8322	44730	20934	23796
1872	9045	46216	26298	20418
1873	9122	47848	24371	23477
1874	8924	49712	28878	20834
1875	8229	52085	29682	22403
1876	7866	52568	27626	24942
1877	7477	51722	28745	22977
1878	8201	52915	27215	25700
1879	8128	51648	25082	26566
1880	8360	51889	27230	24659
TOTALS	83674	501833	266061	235772
1608 to 1880	455679	2743980	1330704	1413276

La Fin

RECOMMENDED READING
AND
REFERENCE LIST

Paul J. Achteimeier, *"Harper's Bible Dictionary"*, Harper and Row, Publishers, 1985

Fleurette Asselin & Jean-Marie Tanguay, *"Transcriptions d'actes notariés, Notaire Guillaume Audouard – 1657-1661"*, Club de Généalogie de Longueuil, Inc., Vol III

B. A. Balcom, *"The Cod Fishery of Isle Royale, 1713-58"*, Canadian Government Publ, 1984

Hilaire Belloc, *"Richelieu – A Study"*, J.B. Lippincott Company, 1929

H. P. Biggar, *"The Early Trading Companies of New France"*, Toronto University Library, 1901

Hugh Brody, *"Maps & Dreams"*, Pantheon Books, 1982

Canon Law Society of America, *"The Code of the Canon Law"*, Paulist Press, 1985

Canon Law Society of Great Britain and Ireland, *"The Code of the Canon Law"*, William B. Eerdmans Publishing Company, 1983

"Catechism of the Catholic Church", Libreria Editrice Vaticana, 1994

Rémi Chénier, *"Québec – A French Colonial Town in America, 1660-1690"*, Canada Communication Group Piublishing, 1991

Emma Lewis Coleman, *"New England Captives Between 1677 and 1760 During the French and Indian Wars"*, Southworth Press, Portland, 1925

F. L. Cross, *"The Oxford Dictionary of the Christian Church"*, Oxford University Press, 1957

Louise Dechêne, *"Habitants & Merchants in Seventeenth Century Montréal"*, McGill-Queens University Press, 1992

J. Deladande, *"Conseil Souverain de la Nouvelle France"*, Québec, Louis-A. Proulx, 1927

RECOMMENDED READING
AND
REFERENCE LIST

Normand J. Demers, *"Revolution in Québec"*, Peter E. Randall, Publisher, 1995

John Demos, *"The Unredeemed Captive"*, Alfred A. Knopf, 1994

Yvon Desloges, *"Tenants Town"*, Canada Communication Group Publ., 1991

"Dictionary of Canadian Biography", University of Toronto Press & Les Presses de l'Université Laval, 1969, Volumes I & II

Arthur G. Doughty & Adam Shortt, *"Canada and Its Provinces"*, Glasgow, Brook & Company, 1914, Vol II

James Douglas, *"Old France in the New World – Québec in the Seventeenth Century"*, The Burrows Brothers Company, Cleveland and London, 1905

Raymond Douville & Jacques Casanova, Translated by Carola Congreve, *"Daily Early Life in Canada"*, The Macmillan Company, 1964

Raymond Douville & Jacques D. Casanova, *"Des Indiens du Canada a l'Époque de la Colonisation Française"*, Hachette Librairie, 1967

Raymond Douville & Jacques Casanova, *"Le Canada de Champlain à Montcalm"*, Hachette Librairie, 1964

Claude Drouin, *"Dictionnaire National des Canadiens Français – Partie Généalogique – 1608-1760"*, Institut Généalogique Drouin, Volumes I and II

R. P. Duchaussois, *"Aux Glaces Polaires - Indiens et Esquimaux"*, Noviciat des Oblats, Canada P.Q., 1921

W. J. Eccles, *"Canada Under Louis XIV – 1663-1701"*, Canadian Centenary Series, McClelland and Stewart Limited, 1964

RECOMMENDED READING
AND
REFERENCE LIST

Tout en Un - "*Encyclopédie des Connaissances Humaines*", Librairie Hachette

Guy Frégault, "*La Civilisation de la Nouvelle France*", Éditions Pascal, 1944

Ernesrt Gagnon, "*Louis Jolliet*", Librairie Beauchemin, Ltd., Montréal, 1913

Andrew Gallup, "*Memoir of a French & Indian War Soldier*", Heritage Books, 1993

Glanze, Anderson & Anderson, "*Mosby Medical Encyclopedia*", Plume Book, 1992

Allan Greer, "*The Patriots and the People*", University of Toronto Press, 1996

Pauline Gregg, "*King Charles I*", University of California Press, 1981

Richard Colebrook Harris, "*The Seigneurial System in Early Canada – A Geographical Study*", McGill-Queens University Press, 1984

Pierre-Maurice Hébert, "*Les Acadiens du Québec*", Éditions de l'Écho, 1994

R. H. Hubbard, "*An Anthology of Canadian Art*", Oxford University Press, 1960

René Jetté, "*Dictionnaire Généalogique des Familles du Québec*", Presses de l'Université de Montréal, 1983

Eric Jonasson, "*The Canadian Genealogical Handbook*", Wheatfield, 1978, Second Edition

'*Jugements et Déliberations du Conseil Souverain de la Nouvelle France*', A. Coté et Compagnie, Volumes I-IV, Québec, 1885-1888

'*Jugements et Déliberations du Conseil Supérieur de la Nouvelle France*', A. Coté et Compagnie, Volumes V & VI, Québec, 1889-1890

RECOMMENDED READING
AND
REFERENCE LIST

Edna Kenton, "*The Jesuit Relations and Allied Documents*", Quintin Publications, 1997

D. G. G. Kerr, "*Historical Atlas of Canada*", Thomas Nelson & Sons (Canada), 1954

André Lachance, "*Crimes et Criminels en Nouvelle France*", Boréal Express, 1984

André Lachance, "*La Vie Urbaine en Nouvelle France*", Boréal Express, 1987

Thomas J. Laforest, "*Our French-Canadian Ancestors*", LISI Press, 1983

Gustave Lanctot, "*L'Administration de la Nouvelle France*", Éditions du Jour, 1971

Gustave Lanctot, "*A History of Canada*", Clarke, Irwin & Company, Volumes I, II & III, 1963, 1964, 1965

Denise Lemieux, "*Les Petits Innnocents - L'Enfance en Nouvelle France*", Institut Québécois de Recherche sur la Culture, 1985

Germain Lemieux, "*La Vie Paysanne - 1860-1900*", Les Éditions Prise de Parole & Les Éditions FM, 1982

Marc Lescarbot, "*The History of New France*", Champlain Society, Toronto, Vol II, 1911

Michel Lessard & Huguette Marquis, "*Encyclopédie de la Maison Québécoise*", Éditions de l'Homme, 1949

Beth Light and Alison Prentice, "*Pioneer and Gentlewomen of British North America*", New Hogtown Press, Toronto, 1980

John D. Light and Henry Unglik, "*A Frontier Fur Trade Blacksmith Shop*" – 1796-1812, Canada Communication Group Publishing, 1987

D. Peter MacLeod, "*The Canadian Iroquois and the Seven Years War*", Dundurn Press, 1996

RECOMMENDED READING
AND
REFERENCE LIST

Roger Magnuson, *"Education in New France"*, McGill-Queen's University, 1992

Gratham McInnes, *"Canadian Art"*, MacMillan Company of Canada, 1950

Nancy Mitford, *"The Sun King"*, Harper & Row Publishers, 1966

Horace Miner, *"St. Denis, a French-Canadian Parish"*, Univ. of Chicago Press, 1939

Dale Miquelon, *"Dugard of Rouën. French Trade to Canada and the West Indies, 1729-1770"*, McGill-Queen's University Press, 1978

Estelle Mitchell, S.G.M., *"Marguerite d'Youville , Foundress of the Grey Nuns"*, Palm Publishers of Montréal, 1965

Cameron Nish, *"Les Bourgeois Gentilshommes de la Nouvelle-France – 1729-1748"*, Éditions FIDES, 1968

Cameron Nish, *"The French Régime"*, Prentice-Hall of Canada, 1965

Nos racines - l'histoire vivante des Québécois, Ch. 1-144, Les Éditions T.L.M., Inc., 1979-1983

Francis Parkman, *"France and England in North America"*, New York: F. Ungar, V. I, II, 1963

Howard H. Peckham, *"Captured by Indians"*, Rutgers University Press, 1954

Gilles Proulx, *"Between France and New France – Life Aboard the Tall Sailing Ships"*, Dundurn Press Limited, 1984

Albert Quesnel, *"Requête de Pierre Pichet pour Légitimer les Enfants de Cathérine Durand à Québec, en 1673"* AND *"Procès de Jacques Bertault, Gilette Baune et Isabelle Bertault pour l'Assassinat de Julien de La Touche à Québec, en 1672"*, Éditions Quesnel de Fomblanche, 1978

RECOMMENDED READING
AND
REFERENCE LIST

Pierre-Georges Roy, '*Bulletins des Recherches Historiques*', Volumes 1-54, Lévis & Québec, 1895-1948

Pierre-Georges Roy, "*Les Mots Qui Restent*", Éditions Garneau, 1940

Pierre-Georges Roy, "*Les Petites Choses de Notre Histoire*", Librairie Garneau, 1923

La Curne de Sainte-Palaye, "*Dictionnaire Historique de l'Ancien Langage Français*", H. Champion, Librairie, 1877

Joseph C. Segen, "*Current Med Talk – Dictionary of Medical Terms, Slang & Jargon*", Appleton & Lange, 1995

Robert Lionel Séguin, "*La Vie Libertine en Nouvelle France au Dix-Septième Siècle*", Leméac, Volumes I & II, 1972

George G.G. Stanley, "*New France – The Last Phase – 1744-1760*", Canadian Centenary Series, McClelland and Stewart Limited, 1968

George F. G. Stanley, "*The Birth of Western Canada, A History of the Riel Rebellions*", Longmans, Green and Company, 1936

Thomas Lathrop Stedman, "*Stedman's Medical Dictionary*" , Williams & Wilkins, 1990

Raymond Phineas Stearns, "*Pageant of Europe*", United States Armed Forces Institute, 1947

Norah Story, "*The Oxford Companion to Canadian History and Literature*", Oxford University Press,1967

Reverend Cyprien Tanguay, "*Dictionnaire Généalogique des Familles Canadiennes*", Eusèbe Senécal, Imprimeur, Éditions Élysée, 1975, Introduction and 7 Volume reference

Marcel Trudel, "*Introduction to New France*", Quintin Publications, 1997

RECOMMENDED READING
AND
REFERENCE LIST

Marcel Trudel, "*Les Vaines Tentatives – 1524-1603*", Éditions Fides, Ottawa, 1963

Marcel Trudel, "*Histoire de la Nouvelle France – Le Comptoir – 1604-1627*", Éditions Fides, Ottawa, 1966

Walter Ullmann, "*Canon) Law and Politics in the Middle Ages*", Cornell University Press, 1975

Jack Verney, "*The Good Regiment*", McGill-Queens University Press, 1991

H.H. Walsh, "*The Church in the French Era-from Colonization to the British Conquest*" (1763), The Ryerson Press, Volume I, 1966

Eugène Weber, "*The Western Tradition – From the Ancient World to Louis XIV*", D. C. Heath and Company, 1965

Webster's New Universal Unabridged Dictionary", Deluxe Second Edition, Dorset & Baber, 1979.

The author of this translation is a 58-year old native of Woonsocket, Rhode Island, with a Degree in French from the University of Massachusetts at Amherst with which he was associated as an administrator for 30 years, and an avid interest and pride in his family, rich heritage, and background.

LIST OF ILLUSTRATIONS

GENEALOGICAL INDEX

iii

v

x

xvi

xxx

SUPPLEMENTARY INDEX